STAR-LORD GAMORA ROCKET RACCOON GROOT DRAX VENOM CAPTAIN MARVEL

GUARDIANS OF THE GALAXY

THROUGH THE LOOKING GLASS

WRITER: **BRIAN MICHAEL BENDIS**

ANNUAL #1

ARTIST: **FRANK CHO** COLOR ARTIST: **JASON KEITH**

LETTERER: **VC'S CLAYTON COWLES** COVER ART: **FRANK CHO & JASON KEITH**

ISSUES #24-27

ARTIST: **VALERIO SCHITI** COLOR ARTIST: **JASON KEITH**

LETTERER: **VC'S CORY PETIT** COVER ART: **VALERIO SCHITI & JASON KEITH**

ASSISTANT EDITOR: **XANDER JAROWEY** EDITORS: **MIKE MARTS & NICK LOWE**

COLLECTION EDITOR: **JENNIFER GRÜNWALD** ASSOCIATE EDITOR: **SARAH BRUNSTAD**
ASSOCIATE MANAGING EDITOR: **ALEX STARBUCK** EDITOR, SPECIAL PROJECTS: **MARK D. BEAZLEY**
VP, PRODUCTION & SPECIAL PROJECTS: **JEFF YOUNGQUIST** SVP PRINT, SALES & MARKETING: **DAVID GABRIEL**

EDITOR IN CHIEF: **AXEL ALONSO** CHIEF CREATIVE OFFICER: **JOE QUESADA**
PUBLISHER: **DAN BUCKLEY** EXECUTIVE PRODUCER: **ALAN FINE**

GUARDIANS OF THE GALAXY VOL. 5: THROUGH THE LOOKING GLASS. Contains material originally published in magazine form as GUARDIANS OF THE GALAXY #24-27 and ANNUAL #1. First printing 2016. ISBN# 978-0-7851-9738-6. Published by MARVEL WORLDWIDE, INC., a subsidiary of MARVEL ENTERTAINMENT, LLC. OFFICE OF PUBLICATION: 135 West 50th Street, New York, NY 10020. Copyright © 2016 MARVEL No similarity between any of the names, characters, persons, and/or institutions in this magazine with those of any living or dead person or institution is intended, and any such similarity which may exist is purely coincidental. **Printed in the U.S.A.** ALAN FINE, President, Marvel Entertainment; DAN BUCKLEY, President, TV, Publishing & Brand Management; JOE QUESADA, Chief Creative Officer; TOM BREVOORT, SVP of Publishing; DAVID BOGART, SVP of Business Affairs & Operations, Publishing & Partnership; C.B. CEBULSKI, VP of Brand Management & Development, Asia; DAVID GABRIEL, SVP of Sales & Marketing, Publishing; JEFF YOUNGQUIST, VP of Production & Special Projects; DAN CARR, Executive Director of Publishing Technology; ALEX MORALES, Director of Publishing Operations; SUSAN CRESPI, Production Manager; STAN LEE, Chairman Emeritus. For information regarding advertising in Marvel Comics or on Marvel.com, please contact Vit DeBellis, Integrated Sales Manager, at vdebellis@marvel.com. For Marvel subscription inquiries, please call 888-511-5480. **Manufactured between 2/3/2016 and 3/7/2016 by R.R. DONNELLEY, INC., SALEM, VA, USA.**

10 9 8 7 6 5 4 3 2 1

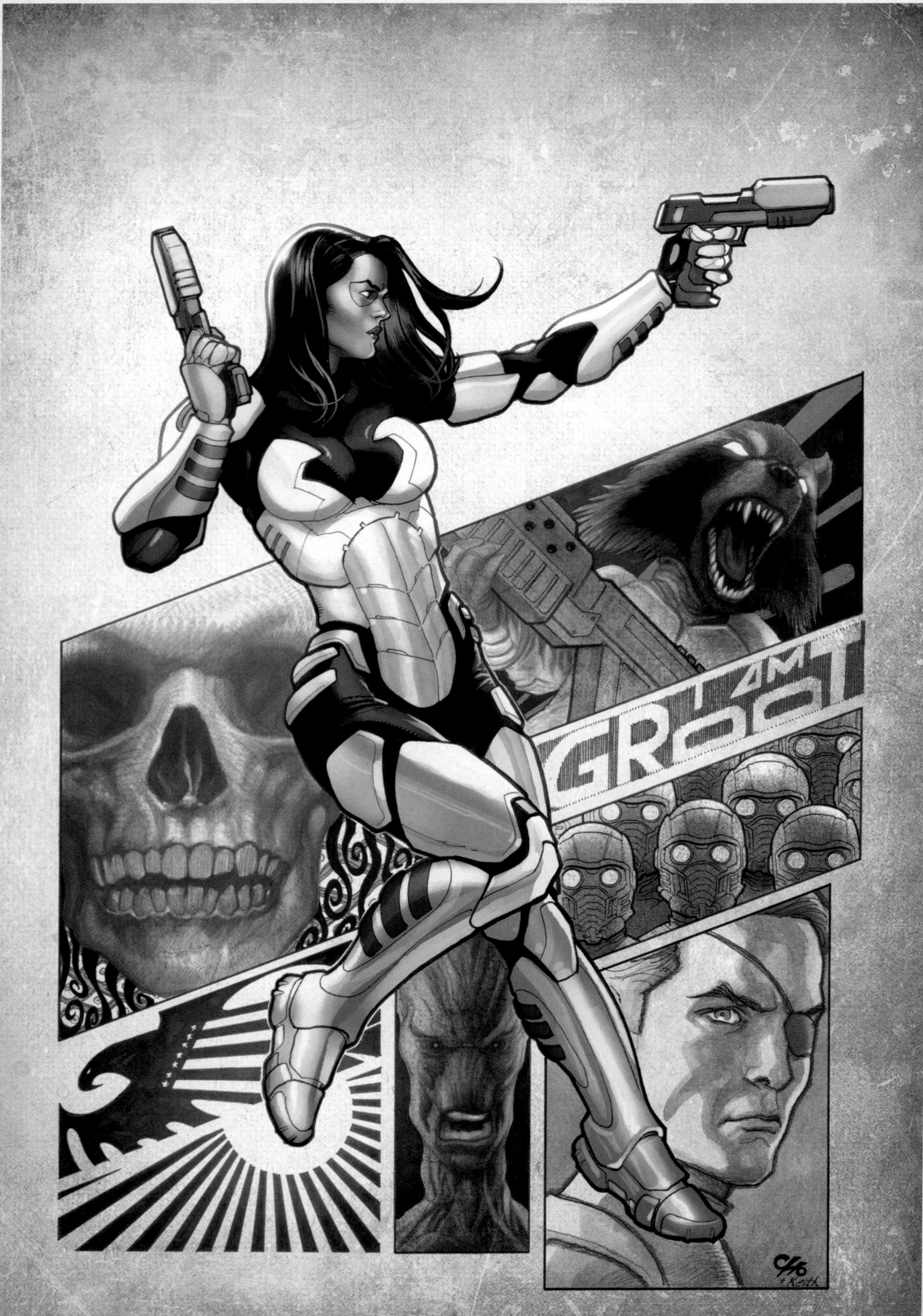
I AM GROOT

ANNUAL 1

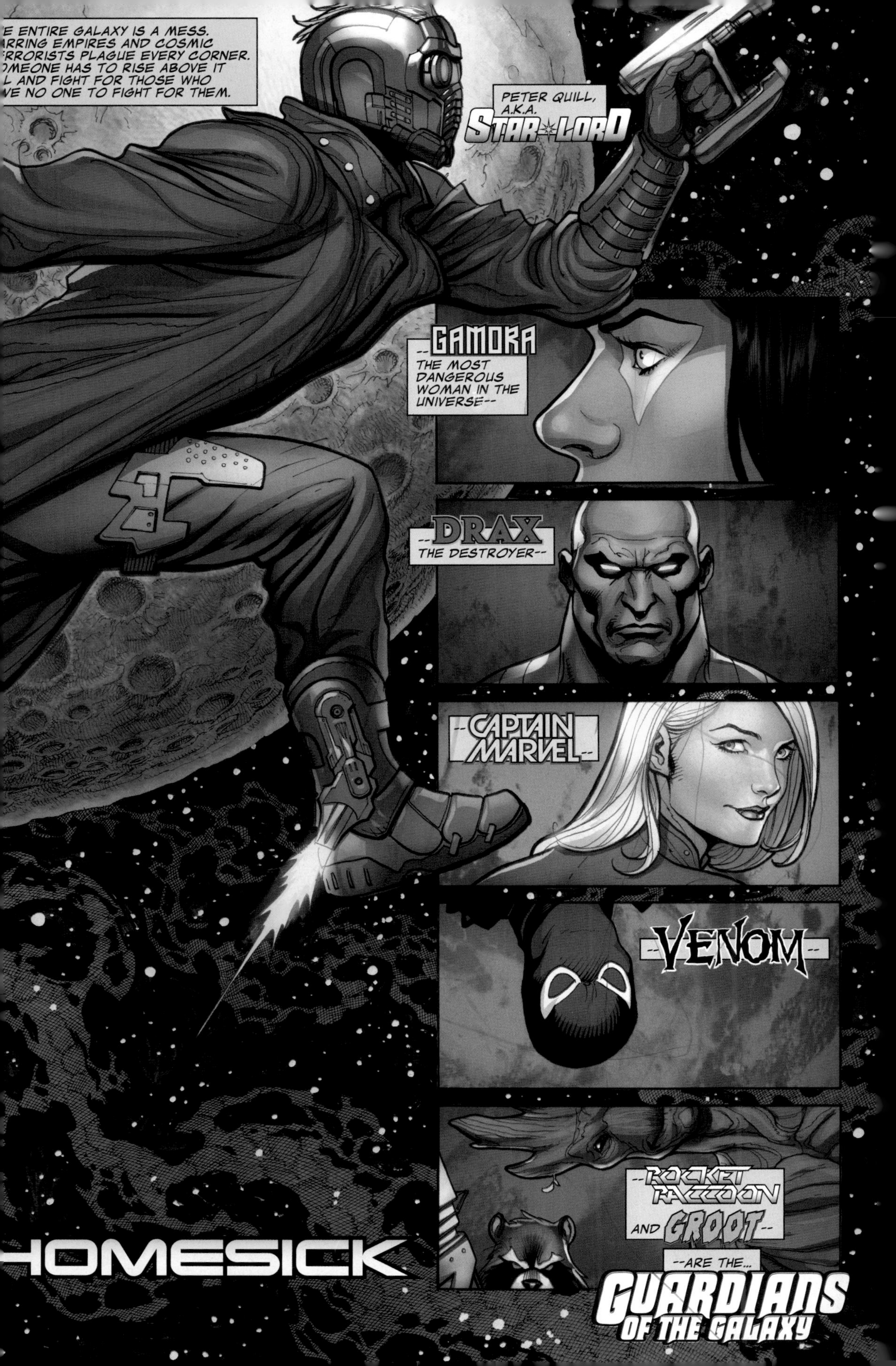
E ENTIRE GALAXY IS A MESS. ARRING EMPIRES AND COSMIC ERRORISTS PLAGUE EVERY CORNER. OMEONE HAS TO RISE ABOVE IT L AND FIGHT FOR THOSE WHO VE NO ONE TO FIGHT FOR THEM.
PETER QUILL, A.K.A. STAR-LORD
--GAMORA
THE MOST DANGEROUS WOMAN IN THE UNIVERSE--
--DRAX THE DESTROYER--
--CAPTAIN MARVEL--
--VENOM--
--ROCKET RACCOON AND GROOT--
--ARE THE...
GUARDIANS OF THE GALAXY
HOMESICK

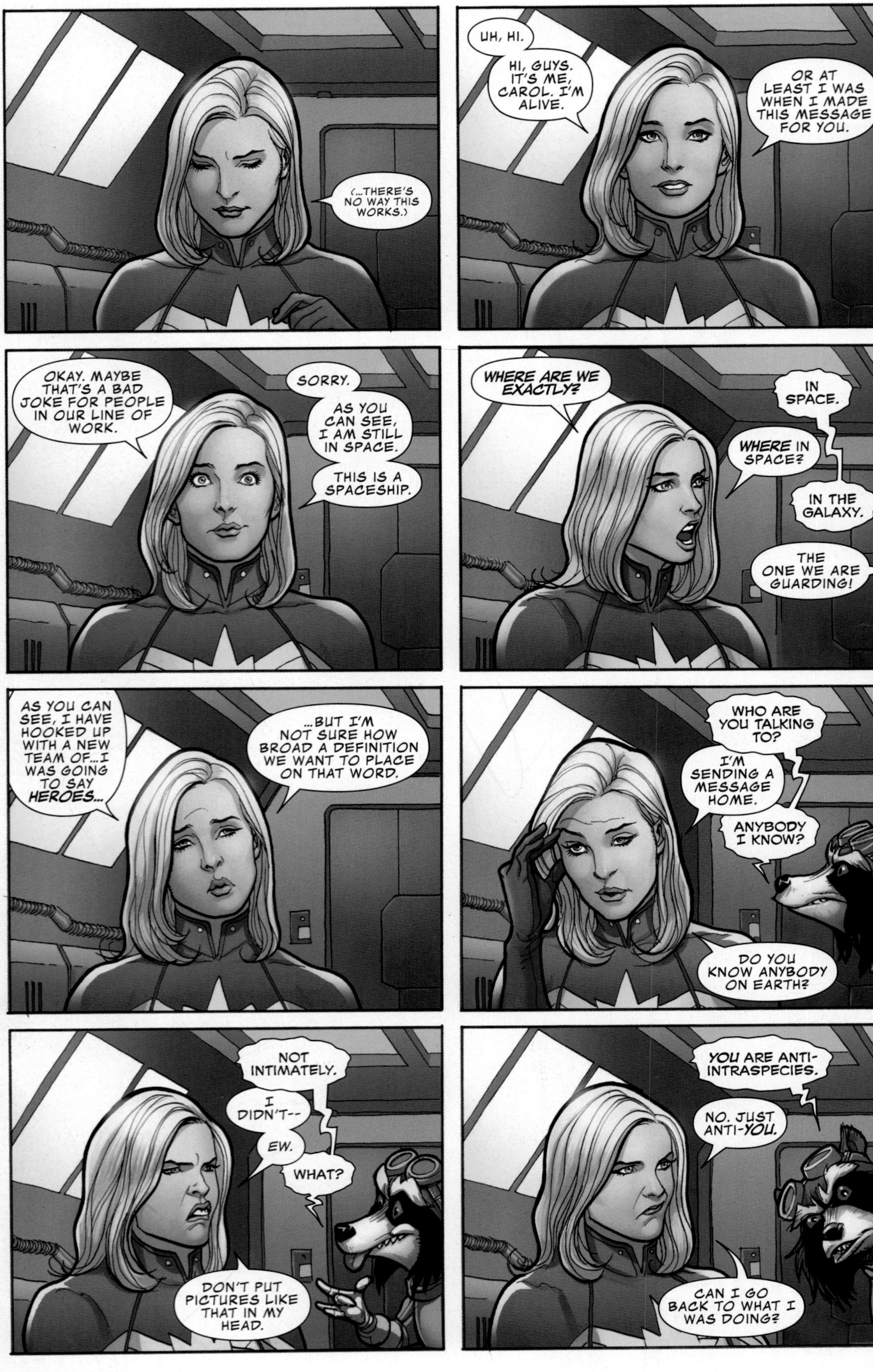
(...THERE'S NO WAY THIS WORKS.)
UH, HI.
HI, GUYS. IT'S ME, CAROL. I'M ALIVE.
OR AT LEAST I WAS WHEN I MADE THIS MESSAGE FOR YOU.
OKAY. MAYBE THAT'S A BAD JOKE FOR PEOPLE IN OUR LINE OF WORK.
SORRY.
AS YOU CAN SEE, I AM STILL IN SPACE.
THIS IS A SPACESHIP.
WHERE ARE WE EXACTLY?
IN SPACE.
WHERE IN SPACE?
IN THE GALAXY.
THE ONE WE ARE GUARDING!
AS YOU CAN SEE, I HAVE HOOKED UP WITH A NEW TEAM OF...I WAS GOING TO SAY HEROES...
...BUT I'M NOT SURE HOW BROAD A DEFINITION WE WANT TO PLACE ON THAT WORD.
WHO ARE YOU TALKING TO?
I'M SENDING A MESSAGE HOME.
ANYBODY I KNOW?
DO YOU KNOW ANYBODY ON EARTH?
NOT INTIMATELY.
I DIDN'T--
EW.
WHAT?
DON'T PUT PICTURES LIKE THAT IN MY HEAD.
YOU ARE ANTI-INTRASPECIES.
NO. JUST ANTI-YOU.
CAN I GO BACK TO WHAT I WAS DOING?

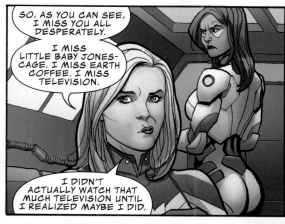

SO, AS YOU CAN SEE, I MISS YOU ALL DESPERATELY.

I MISS LITTLE BABY JONES-CAGE. I MISS EARTH COFFEE. I MISS TELEVISION.

I DIDN'T ACTUALLY WATCH THAT MUCH TELEVISION UNTIL I REALIZED MAYBE I DID.

I'M NOT SURE WHEN I DID, BUT I MUST HAVE BECAUSE I'M REALLY MISSING IT.

OR MAYBE I'M MISSING THE IDEA THAT I COULD WATCH IT.

ANYWAY, I JUST WANTED TO TELL YOU THAT THINGS OUT HERE ARE INTERESTING.

I DON'T KNOW IF YOU KNOW THIS, BUT--

CAN I HELP YOU?

I AM GROOT.

YES.

HE IS GROOT.

ANYWAY, I WAS GOING TO CATCH YOU UP ON ALL MY STUFF, BUT...THAT'S PRETTY MUCH--

HOLY @#$@#$@!

ALL STATIONS!

IS SOMETHING WRONG?

YOU'RE GOING TO WANT TO SEE THIS!

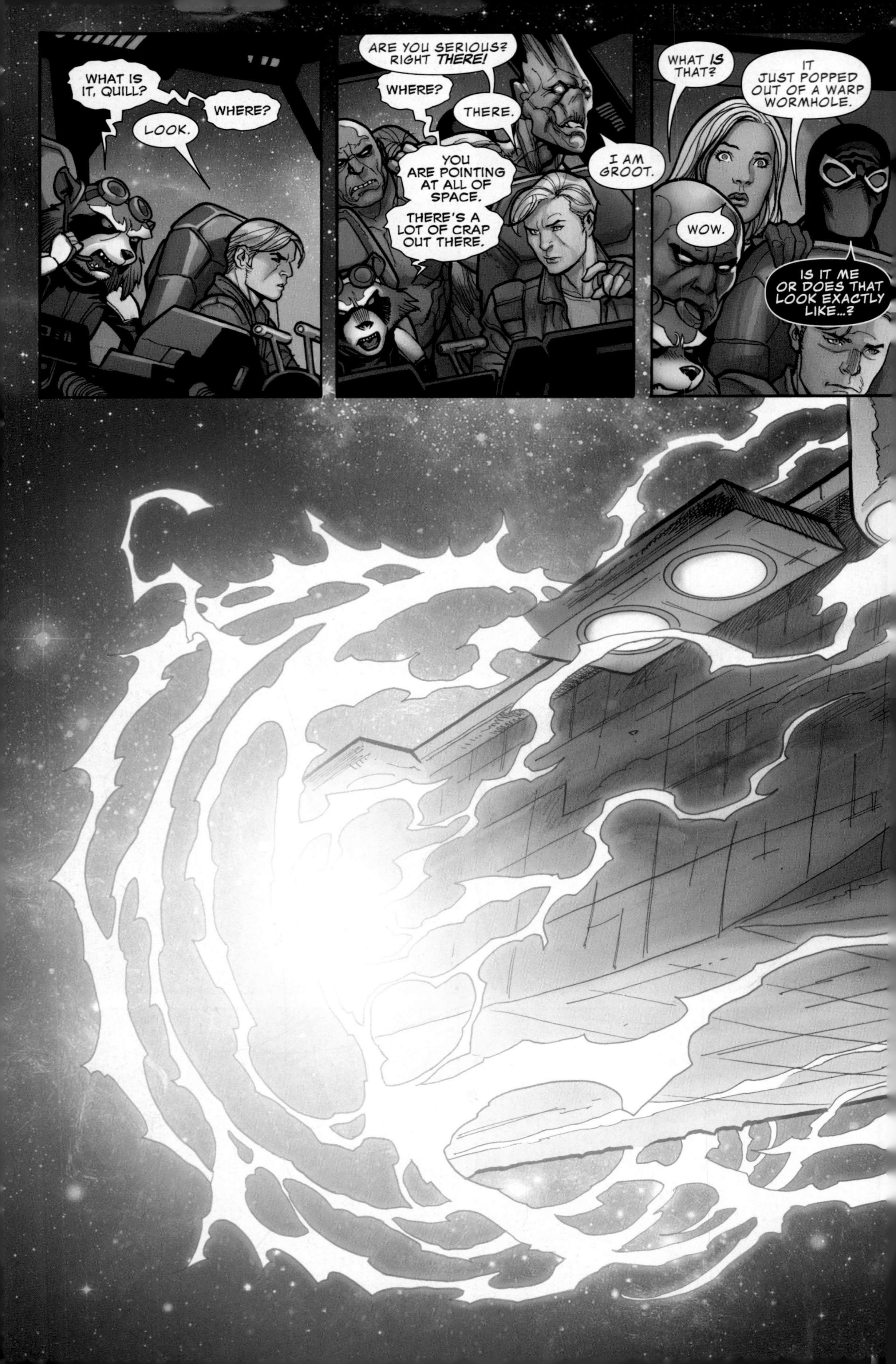
WHAT IS IT, QUILL?
WHERE?
LOOK.
ARE YOU SERIOUS? RIGHT THERE!
WHERE?
THERE.
YOU ARE POINTING AT ALL OF SPACE.
THERE'S A LOT OF CRAP OUT THERE.
I AM GROOT.
WHAT IS THAT?
IT JUST POPPED OUT OF A WARP WORMHOLE.
WOW.
IS IT ME OR DOES THAT LOOK EXACTLY LIKE...?

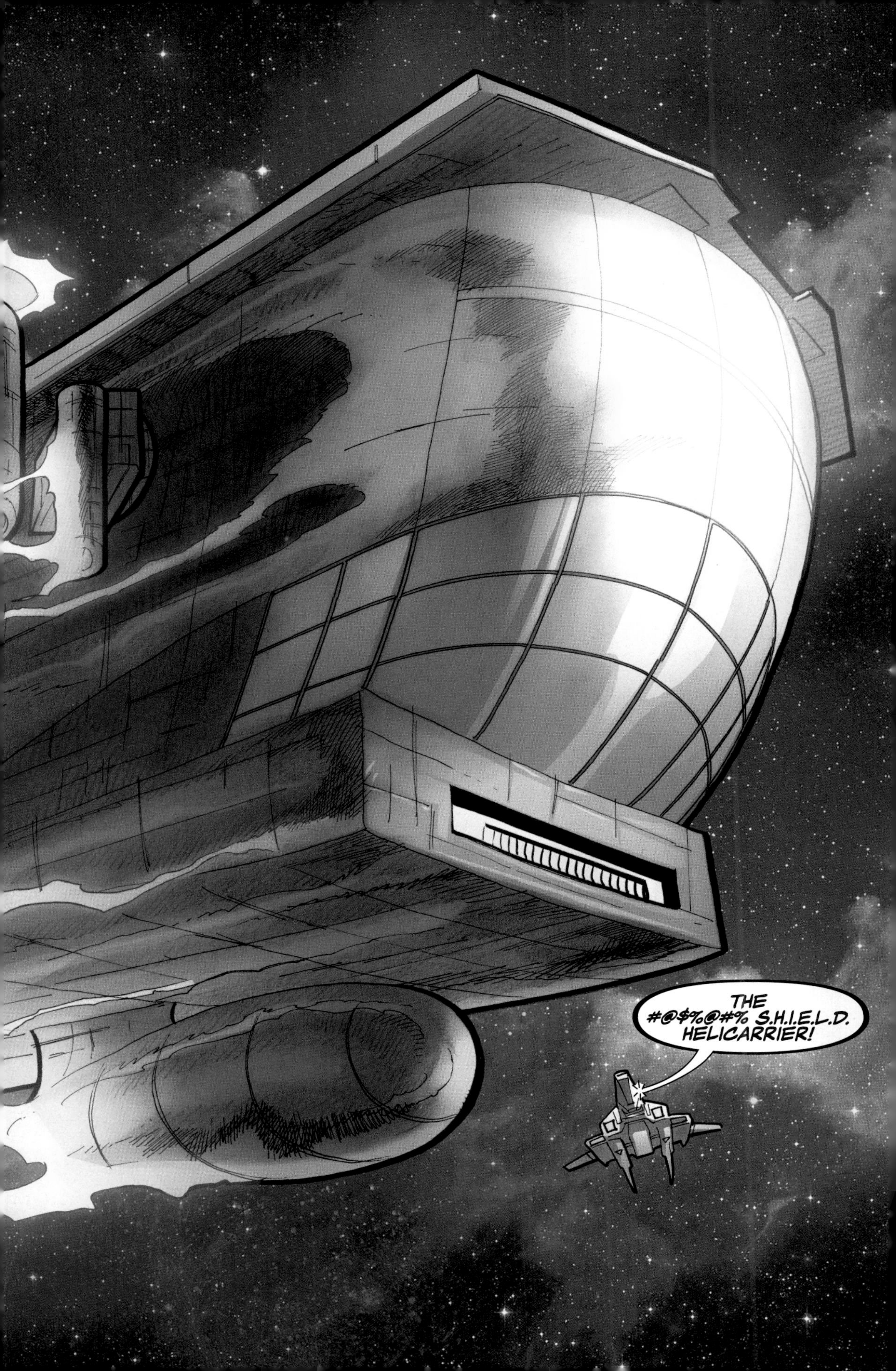
THE #@$%@#% S.H.I.E.L.D. HELICARRIER!

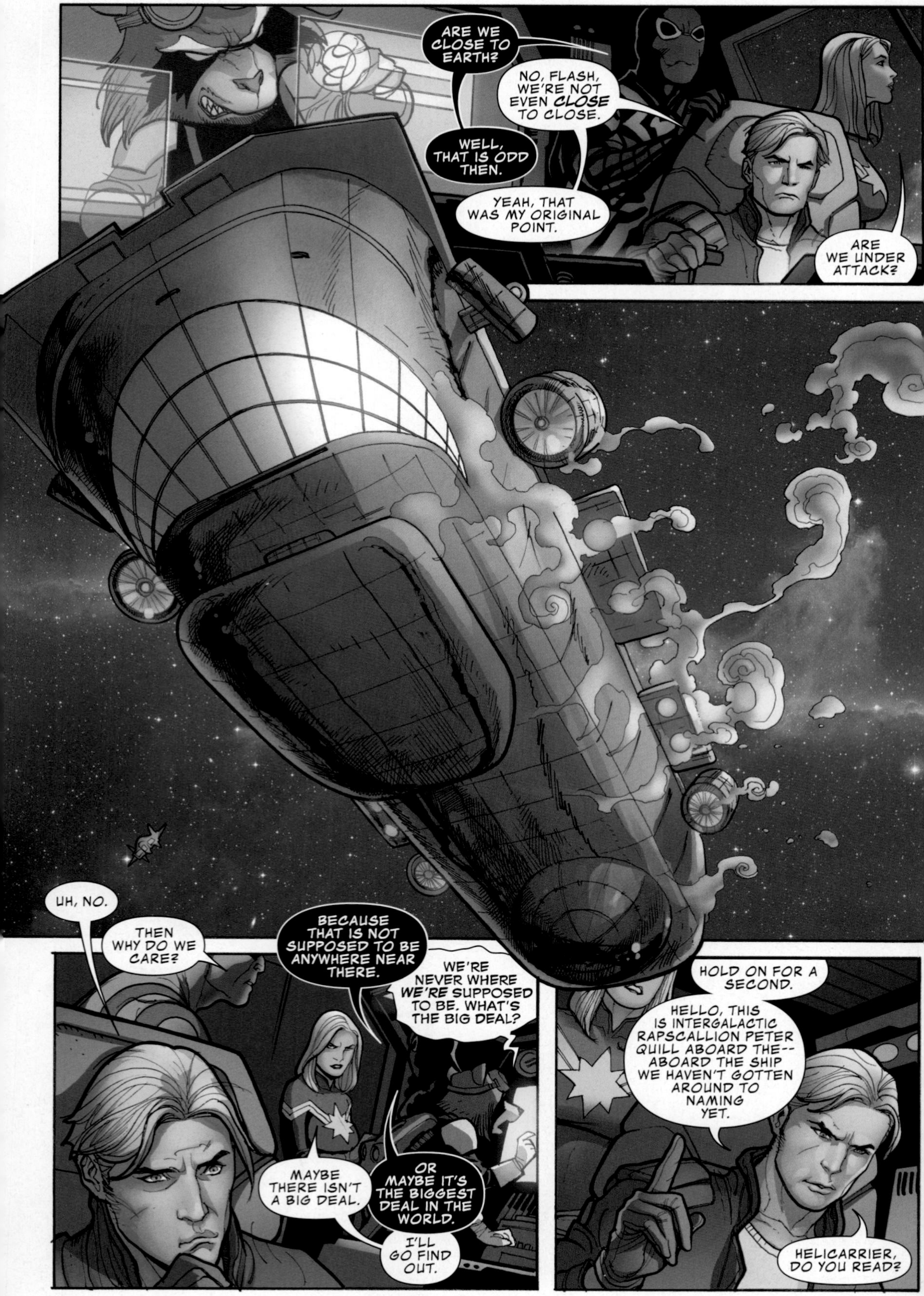

ARE WE CLOSE TO EARTH?
NO, FLASH, WE'RE NOT EVEN CLOSE TO CLOSE.
WELL, THAT IS ODD THEN.
YEAH, THAT WAS MY ORIGINAL POINT.
ARE WE UNDER ATTACK?
UH, NO.
THEN WHY DO WE CARE?
BECAUSE THAT IS NOT SUPPOSED TO BE ANYWHERE NEAR THERE.
WE'RE NEVER WHERE WE'RE SUPPOSED TO BE. WHAT'S THE BIG DEAL?
MAYBE THERE ISN'T A BIG DEAL.
OR MAYBE IT'S THE BIGGEST DEAL IN THE WORLD.
I'LL GO FIND OUT.
HOLD ON FOR A SECOND.
HELLO, THIS IS INTERGALACTIC RAPSCALLION PETER QUILL ABOARD THE-- ABOARD THE SHIP WE HAVEN'T GOTTEN AROUND TO NAMING YET.
HELICARRIER, DO YOU READ?

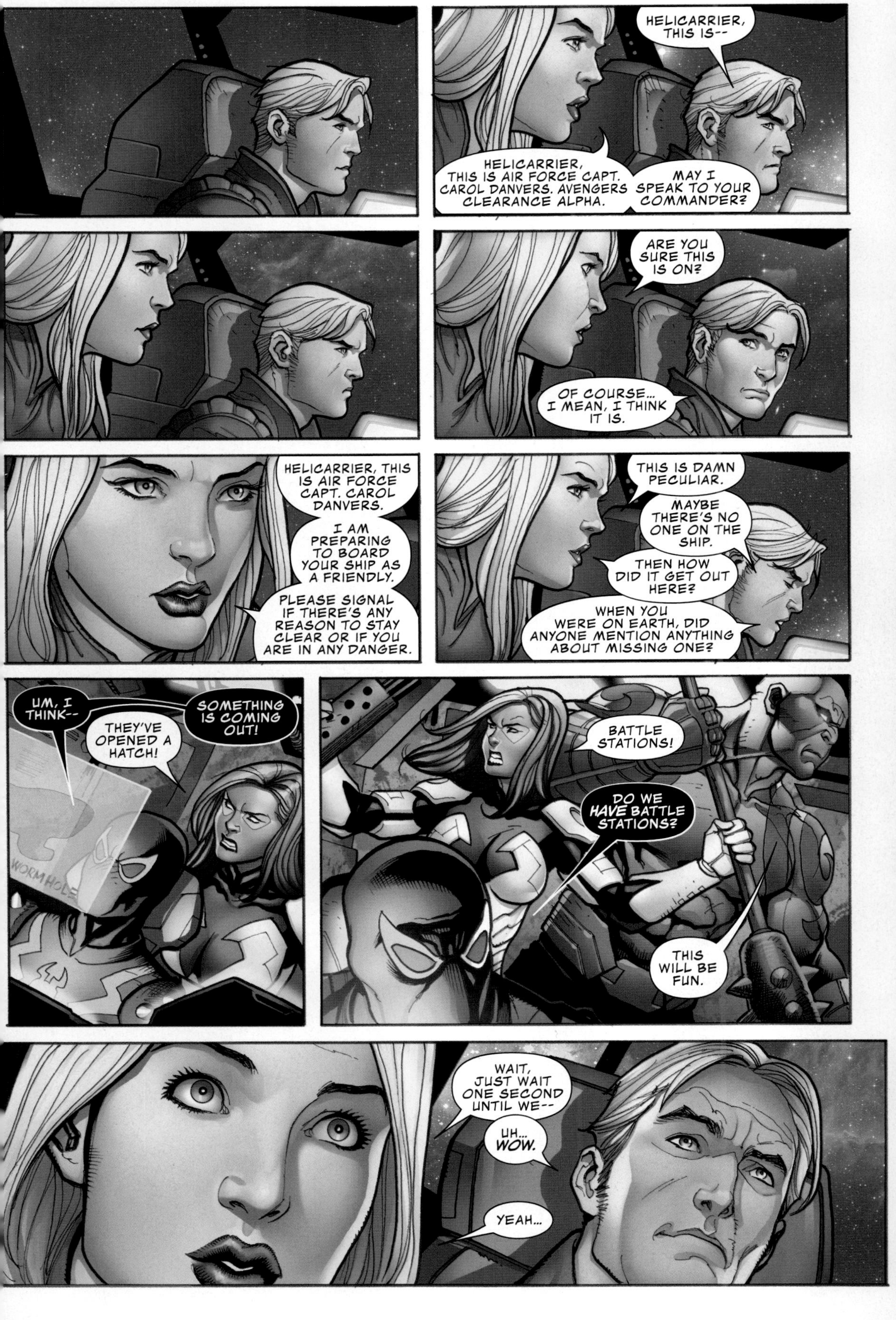
HELICARRIER, THIS IS--
HELICARRIER, THIS IS AIR FORCE CAPT. CAROL DANVERS. AVENGERS CLEARANCE ALPHA.
MAY I SPEAK TO YOUR COMMANDER?
ARE YOU SURE THIS IS ON?
OF COURSE... I MEAN, I THINK IT IS.
HELICARRIER, THIS IS AIR FORCE CAPT. CAROL DANVERS.
I AM PREPARING TO BOARD YOUR SHIP AS A FRIENDLY.
PLEASE SIGNAL IF THERE'S ANY REASON TO STAY CLEAR OR IF YOU ARE IN ANY DANGER.
THIS IS DAMN PECULIAR.
MAYBE THERE'S NO ONE ON THE SHIP.
THEN HOW DID IT GET OUT HERE?
WHEN YOU WERE ON EARTH, DID ANYONE MENTION ANYTHING ABOUT MISSING ONE?
UM, I THINK--
SOMETHING IS COMING OUT!
THEY'VE OPENED A HATCH!
WORMHOLE
BATTLE STATIONS!
DO WE HAVE BATTLE STATIONS?
THIS WILL BE FUN.
WAIT, JUST WAIT ONE SECOND UNTIL WE--
UH... WOW.
YEAH...

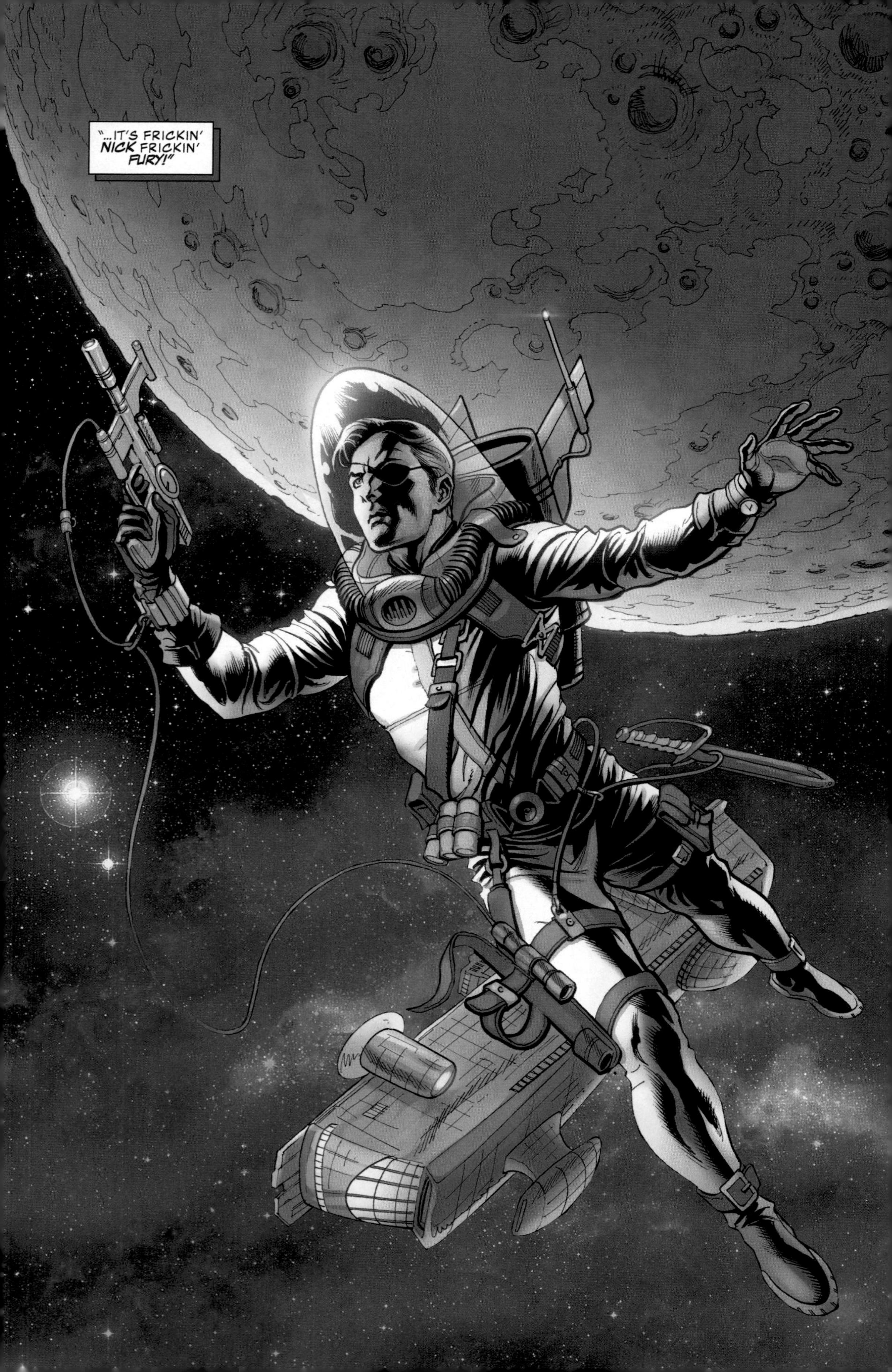
"...IT'S FRICKIN' NICK FRICKIN' FURY!"

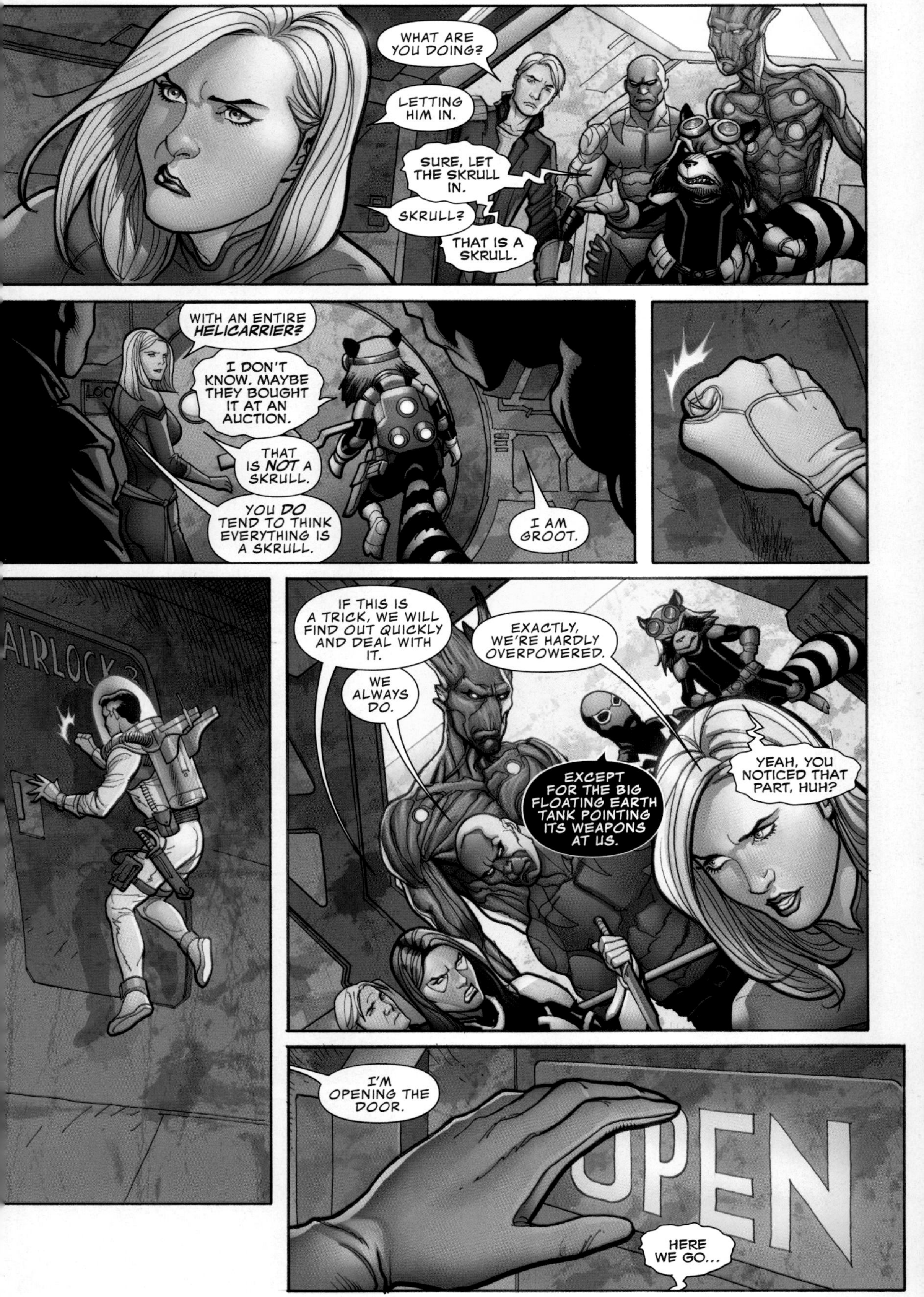
WHAT ARE YOU DOING?
LETTING HIM IN.
SURE, LET THE SKRULL IN.
SKRULL?
THAT IS A SKRULL.
WITH AN ENTIRE HELICARRIER?
I DON'T KNOW. MAYBE THEY BOUGHT IT AT AN AUCTION.
THAT IS NOT A SKRULL.
YOU DO TEND TO THINK EVERYTHING IS A SKRULL.
I AM GROOT.
AIRLOCK 3
IF THIS IS A TRICK, WE WILL FIND OUT QUICKLY AND DEAL WITH IT.
WE ALWAYS DO.
EXACTLY, WE'RE HARDLY OVERPOWERED.
EXCEPT FOR THE BIG FLOATING EARTH TANK POINTING ITS WEAPONS AT US.
YEAH, YOU NOTICED THAT PART, HUH?
I'M OPENING THE DOOR.
OPEN
HERE WE GO...

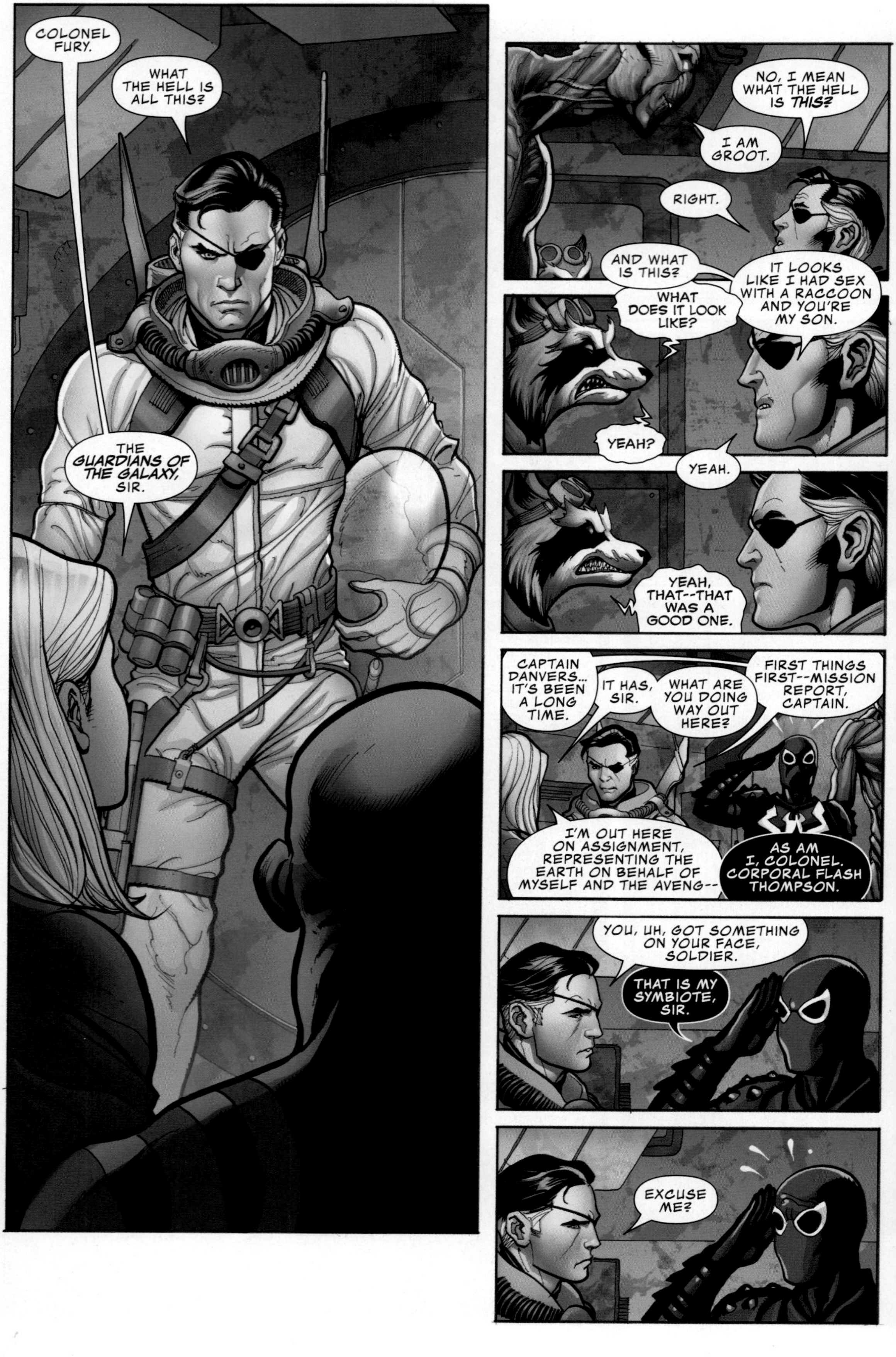
COLONEL FURY.
WHAT THE HELL IS ALL THIS?
THE GUARDIANS OF THE GALAXY, SIR.
NO, I MEAN WHAT THE HELL IS THIS?
I AM GROOT.
RIGHT.
AND WHAT IS THIS?
WHAT DOES IT LOOK LIKE?
IT LOOKS LIKE I HAD SEX WITH A RACCOON AND YOU'RE MY SON.
YEAH?
YEAH.
YEAH, THAT--THAT WAS A GOOD ONE.
CAPTAIN DANVERS... IT'S BEEN A LONG TIME.
IT HAS, SIR.
WHAT ARE YOU DOING WAY OUT HERE?
FIRST THINGS FIRST--MISSION REPORT, CAPTAIN.
I'M OUT HERE ON ASSIGNMENT, REPRESENTING THE EARTH ON BEHALF OF MYSELF AND THE AVENG--
AS AM I, COLONEL. CORPORAL FLASH THOMPSON.
YOU, UH, GOT SOMETHING ON YOUR FACE, SOLDIER.
THAT IS MY SYMBIOTE, SIR.
EXCUSE ME?

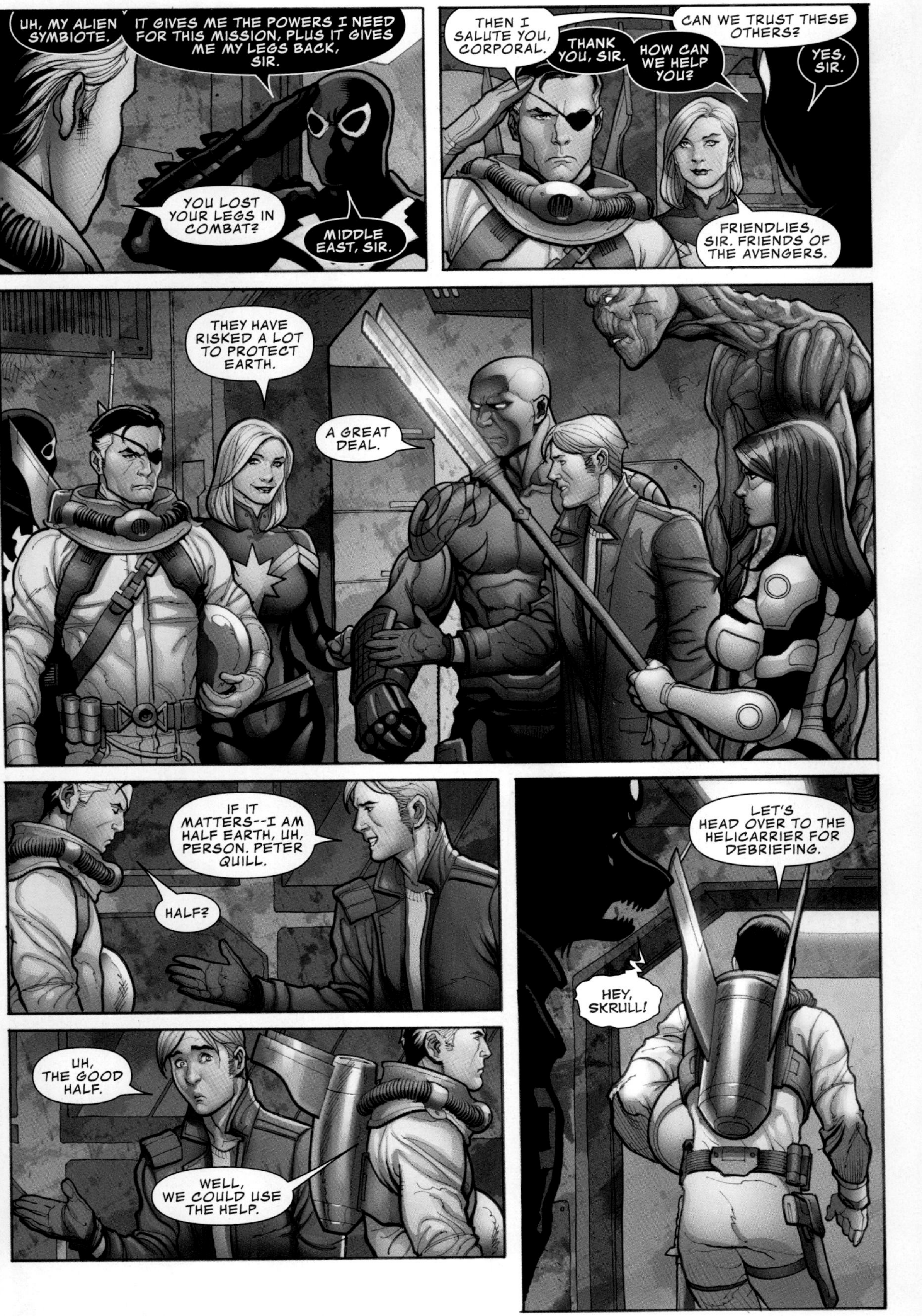
UH, MY ALIEN SYMBIOTE.
IT GIVES ME THE POWERS I NEED FOR THIS MISSION, PLUS IT GIVES ME MY LEGS BACK, SIR.
YOU LOST YOUR LEGS IN COMBAT?
MIDDLE EAST, SIR.
THEN I SALUTE YOU, CORPORAL.
THANK YOU, SIR.
CAN WE TRUST THESE OTHERS?
HOW CAN WE HELP YOU?
YES, SIR.
FRIENDLIES, SIR. FRIENDS OF THE AVENGERS.
THEY HAVE RISKED A LOT TO PROTECT EARTH.
A GREAT DEAL.
IF IT MATTERS--I AM HALF EARTH, UH, PERSON. PETER QUILL.
HALF?
UH, THE GOOD HALF.
WELL, WE COULD USE THE HELP.
LET'S HEAD OVER TO THE HELICARRIER FOR DEBRIEFING.
HEY, SKRULL!

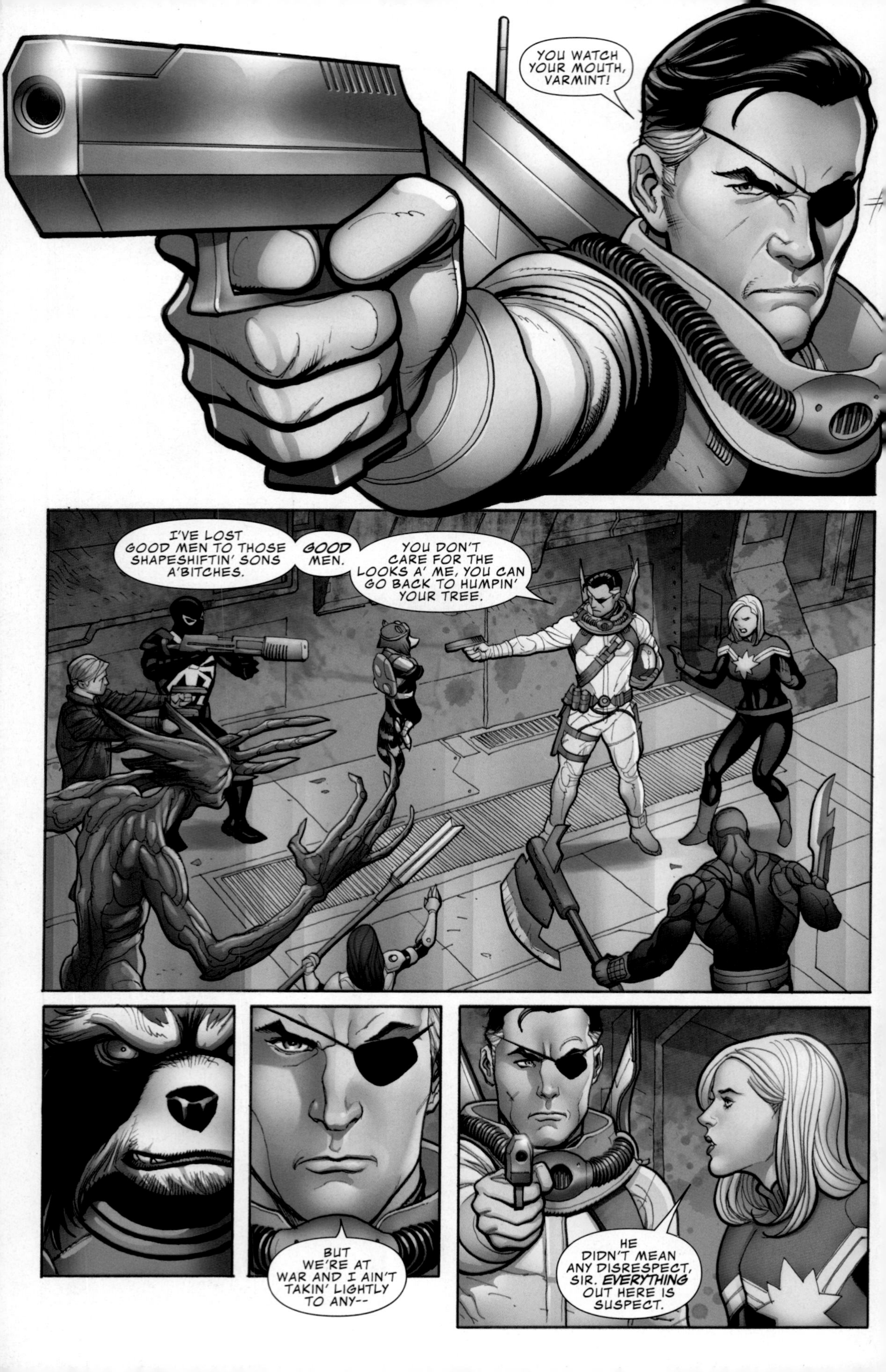

YOU WATCH YOUR MOUTH, VARMINT!
I'VE LOST GOOD MEN TO THOSE SHAPESHIFTIN' SONS A'BITCHES.
GOOD MEN.
YOU DON'T CARE FOR THE LOOKS A' ME, YOU CAN GO BACK TO HUMPIN' YOUR TREE.
BUT WE'RE AT WAR AND I AIN'T TAKIN' LIGHTLY TO ANY--
HE DIDN'T MEAN ANY DISRESPECT, SIR. **EVERYTHING** OUT HERE IS SUSPECT.

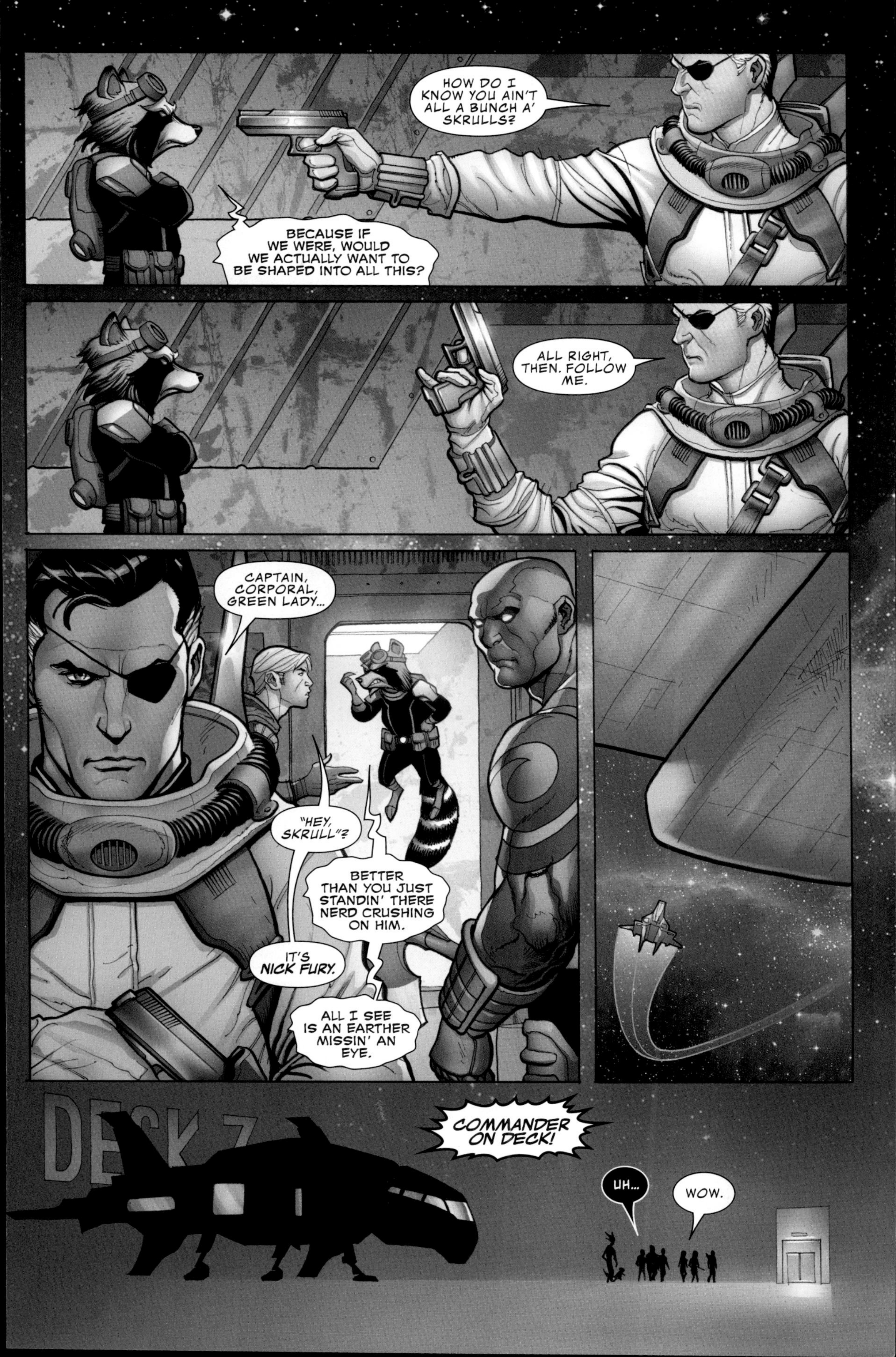
HOW DO I KNOW YOU AIN'T ALL A BUNCH A' SKRULLS?
BECAUSE IF WE WERE, WOULD WE ACTUALLY WANT TO BE SHAPED INTO ALL THIS?
ALL RIGHT, THEN. FOLLOW ME.
CAPTAIN, CORPORAL, GREEN LADY...
"HEY, SKRULL"?
BETTER THAN YOU JUST STANDIN' THERE NERD CRUSHING ON HIM.
IT'S NICK FURY.
ALL I SEE IS AN EARTHER MISSIN' AN EYE.
DECK 7
COMMANDER ON DECK!
UH...
WOW.

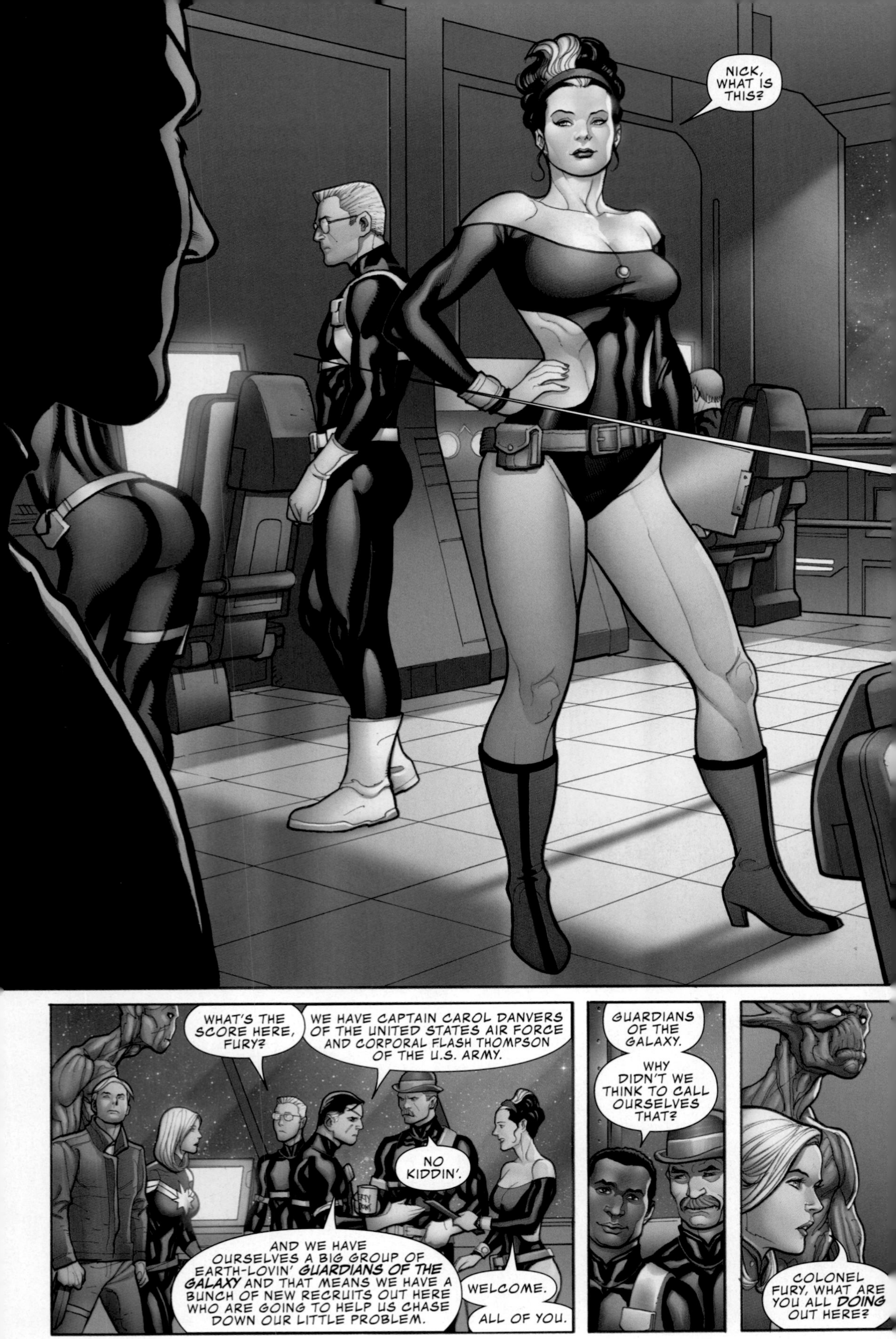
NICK, WHAT IS THIS?
WHAT'S THE SCORE HERE, FURY?
WE HAVE CAPTAIN CAROL DANVERS OF THE UNITED STATES AIR FORCE AND CORPORAL FLASH THOMPSON OF THE U.S. ARMY.
NO KIDDIN'.
AND WE HAVE OURSELVES A BIG GROUP OF EARTH-LOVIN' ***GUARDIANS OF THE GALAXY*** AND THAT MEANS WE HAVE A BUNCH OF NEW RECRUITS OUT HERE WHO ARE GOING TO HELP US CHASE DOWN OUR LITTLE PROBLEM.
WELCOME.
ALL OF YOU.
GUARDIANS OF THE GALAXY.
WHY DIDN'T WE THINK TO CALL OURSELVES THAT?
COLONEL FURY, WHAT ARE YOU ALL ***DOING*** OUT HERE?

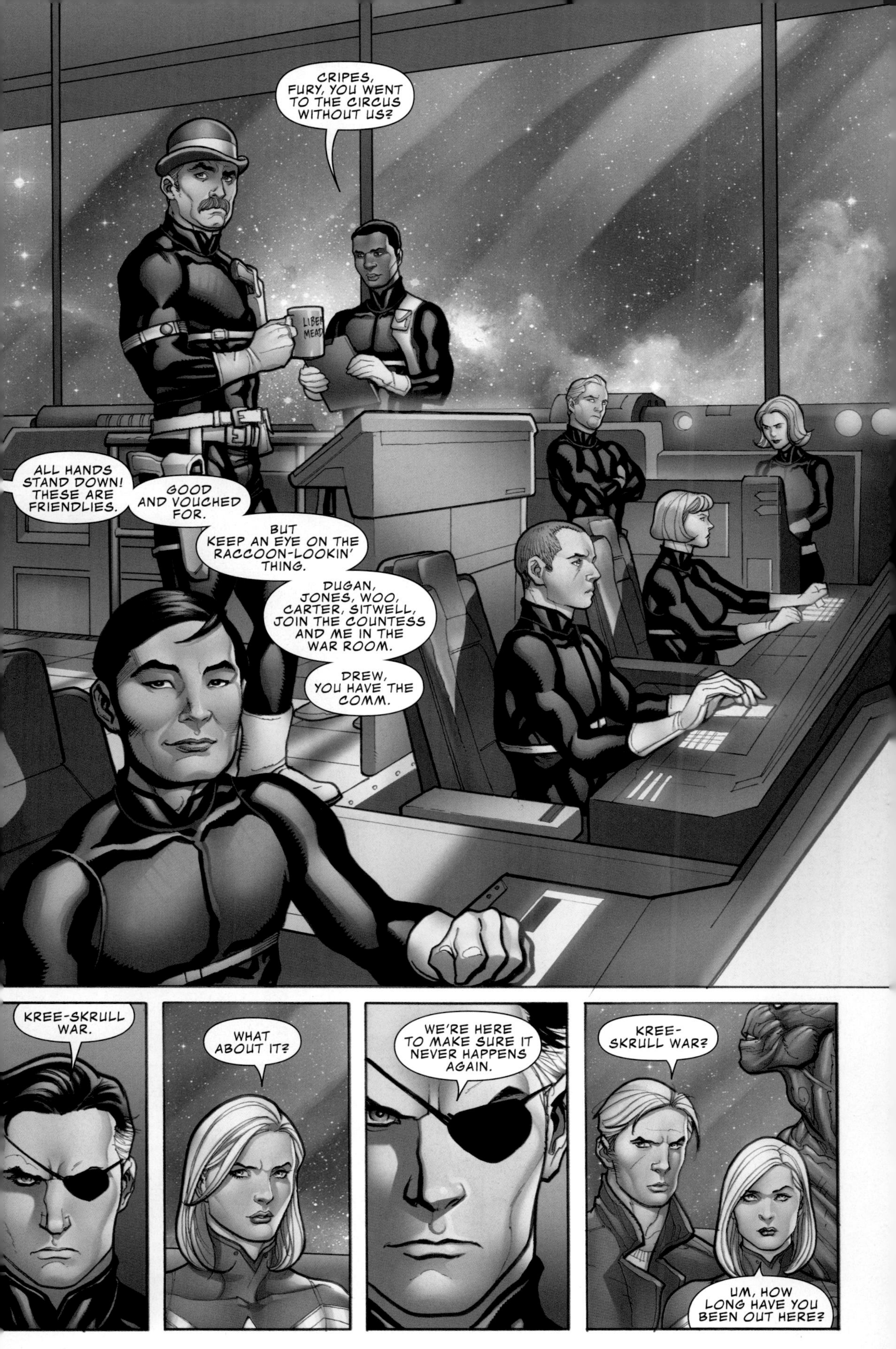
CRIPES, FURY, YOU WENT TO THE CIRCUS WITHOUT US?
ALL HANDS STAND DOWN! THESE ARE FRIENDLIES.
GOOD AND VOUCHED FOR.
BUT KEEP AN EYE ON THE RACCOON-LOOKIN' THING.
DUGAN, JONES, WOO, CARTER, SITWELL, JOIN THE COUNTESS AND ME IN THE WAR ROOM.
DREW, YOU HAVE THE COMM.
KREE-SKRULL WAR.
WHAT ABOUT IT?
WE'RE HERE TO MAKE SURE IT NEVER HAPPENS AGAIN.
KREE-SKRULL WAR?
UM, HOW LONG HAVE YOU BEEN OUT HERE?

THE KREE AND THE SKRULLS BOTH PLANTED THEIR FLAG ON EARTH.

JUST DECIDED IT WAS THEIRS.

WHEN WAS THIS?

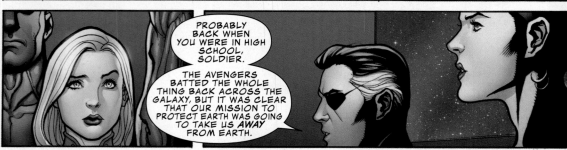

PROBABLY BACK WHEN YOU WERE IN HIGH SCHOOL, SOLDIER.

THE AVENGERS BATTED THE WHOLE THING BACK ACROSS THE GALAXY, BUT IT WAS CLEAR THAT OUR MISSION TO PROTECT EARTH WAS GOING TO TAKE US *AWAY* FROM EARTH.

THE THREAT TO OUR FREEDOM AIN'T JUST COMIN' FROM MOTHER RUSSIA AND HYDRA...

...IT'S COMIN' FROM ALL ANGLES AND ALL SPACES.

THERE ARE PLAYERS OUT HERE WE DON'T EVEN KNOW ABOUT YET.

SO WE SET OUT TO TAKE THE FIGHT HEAD ON.

WE GAVE UP A LOT TO BE HERE.

ALL OF US.

THESE ARE THE FINEST, MOST DEDICATED SOLDIERS I HAVE EVER HAD THE DAMN HONOR OF SERVIN' WITH.

NO ONE ON EARTH KNOWS ABOUT THIS, DO THEY?

I DON'T KNOW WHAT THEY KNOW.

BUT PROBABLY NOT.

HAVE YOU HAD ANY RUN-INS WITH SKRULLS?

BECAUSE WE'RE HUNTIN' THEM DOWN, EACH AND EVERY ONE.

AND THEY AIN'T THAT EASY TO SPOT.

BATTLE STATIONS!

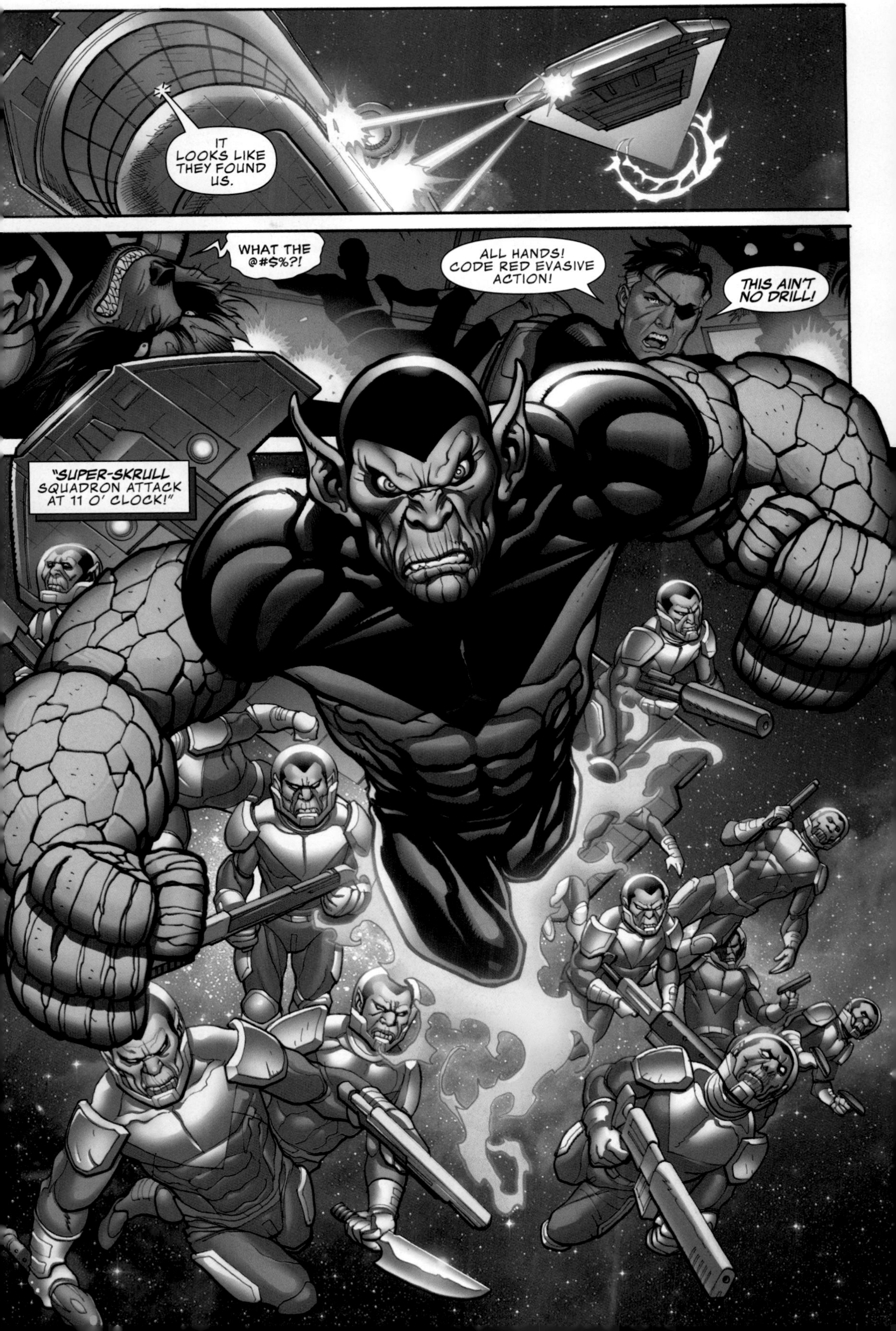
IT LOOKS LIKE THEY FOUND US.
WHAT THE @#$%?!
ALL HANDS! CODE RED EVASIVE ACTION!
THIS AIN'T NO DRILL!
"SUPER-SKRULL SQUADRON ATTACK AT 11 O' CLOCK!"

SKRULLS? FOR REAL?!

MY FAVORITE SPORT.

WE SHOULD HAVE NEVER LEFT OUR SHIP! THIS IS WHY YOU NEVER LEAVE THE SHIP!

THE SHIP IS CLOAKED! STOP YOUR WHINING.

YEAH, BUT I'M NOT!

GUYS, THIS ALL FEELS REALLY OFF TO ME!

HEY! STOP THEM! THEY MIGHT BE SKRULLS SENT HERE TO DISTRACT US!

STOP RIGHT THERE, SKRULLS!

WE'RE NOT SKRULLS, YA DUMB FRATAKI! IF WE WERE SKRULLS, WOULD WE BE SHAPESHIFTING INTO THIS?!

YOU USED THAT LINE ALREADY.

MAYBE THAT'S EXACTLY WHAT YOU'D SHAPESHIFT INTO. SOMETHING WE WOULDN'T--

GET OUT OF THE WAY. WE CAN HELP YOU.

GET BACK!

IF I WAS HERE TO HARM YOU, YOU'D BE HARMED!

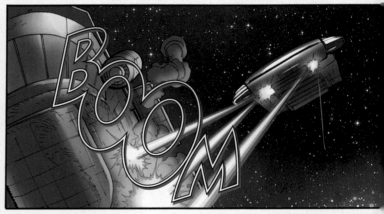

BOOM

AGH!

GUARDIANS!

WE'RE OKAY!

LET'S GO!

I AM GROOT!

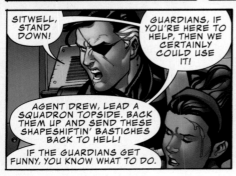

SITWELL, STAND DOWN!

GUARDIANS, IF YOU'RE HERE TO HELP, THEN WE CERTAINLY COULD USE IT!

AGENT DREW, LEAD A SQUADRON TOPSIDE. BACK THEM UP AND SEND THESE SHAPESHIFTIN' BASTICHES BACK TO HELL!

IF THE GUARDIANS GET FUNNY, YOU KNOW WHAT TO DO.

I'M ON IT, COLONEL!

AGENT DREW?!

FOLLOW ME! WE'LL STOP THEM ON THE AIRFIELD.

JESSICA?

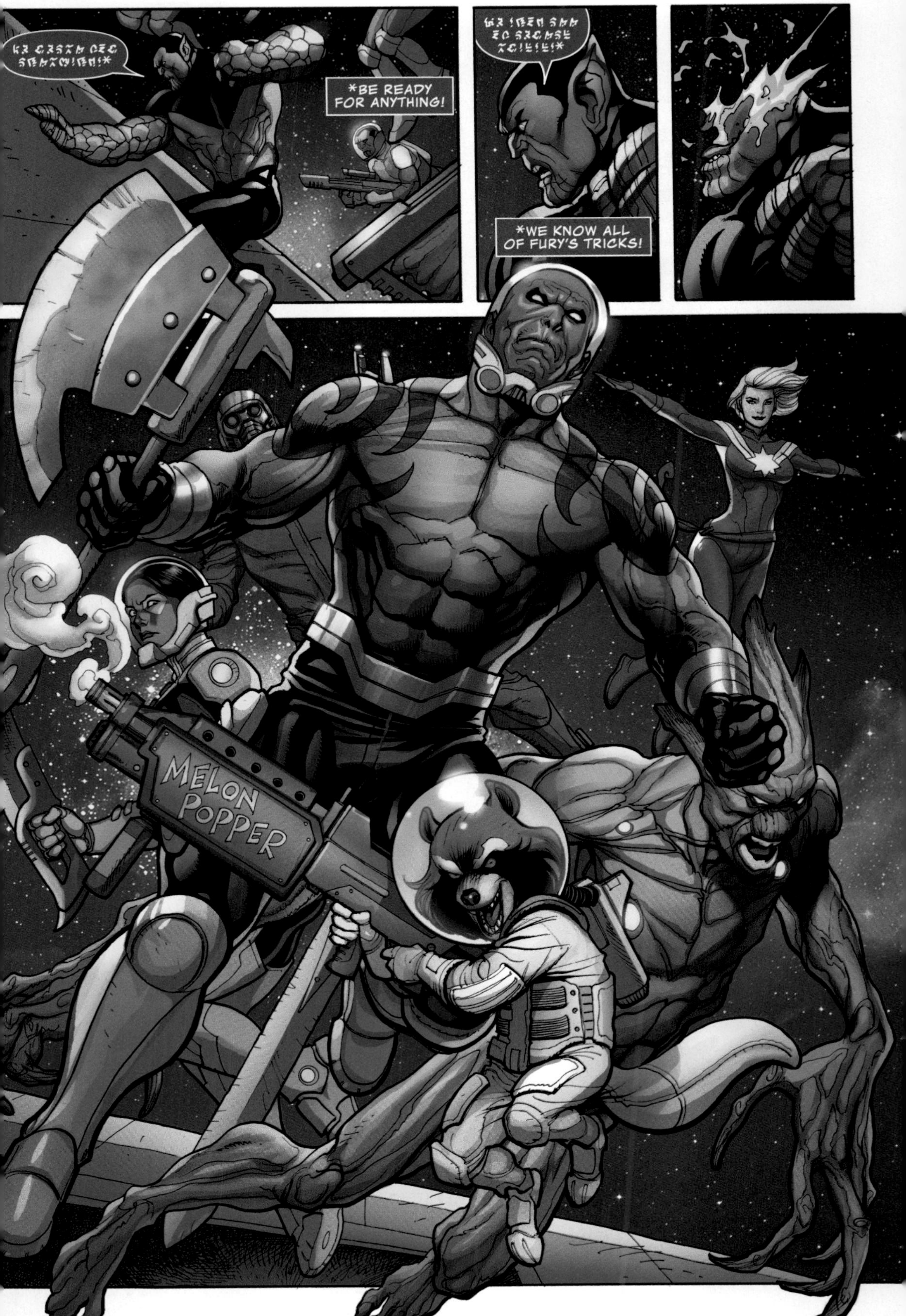
*BE READY FOR ANYTHING!
*WE KNOW ALL OF FURY'S TRICKS!
MELON POPPER

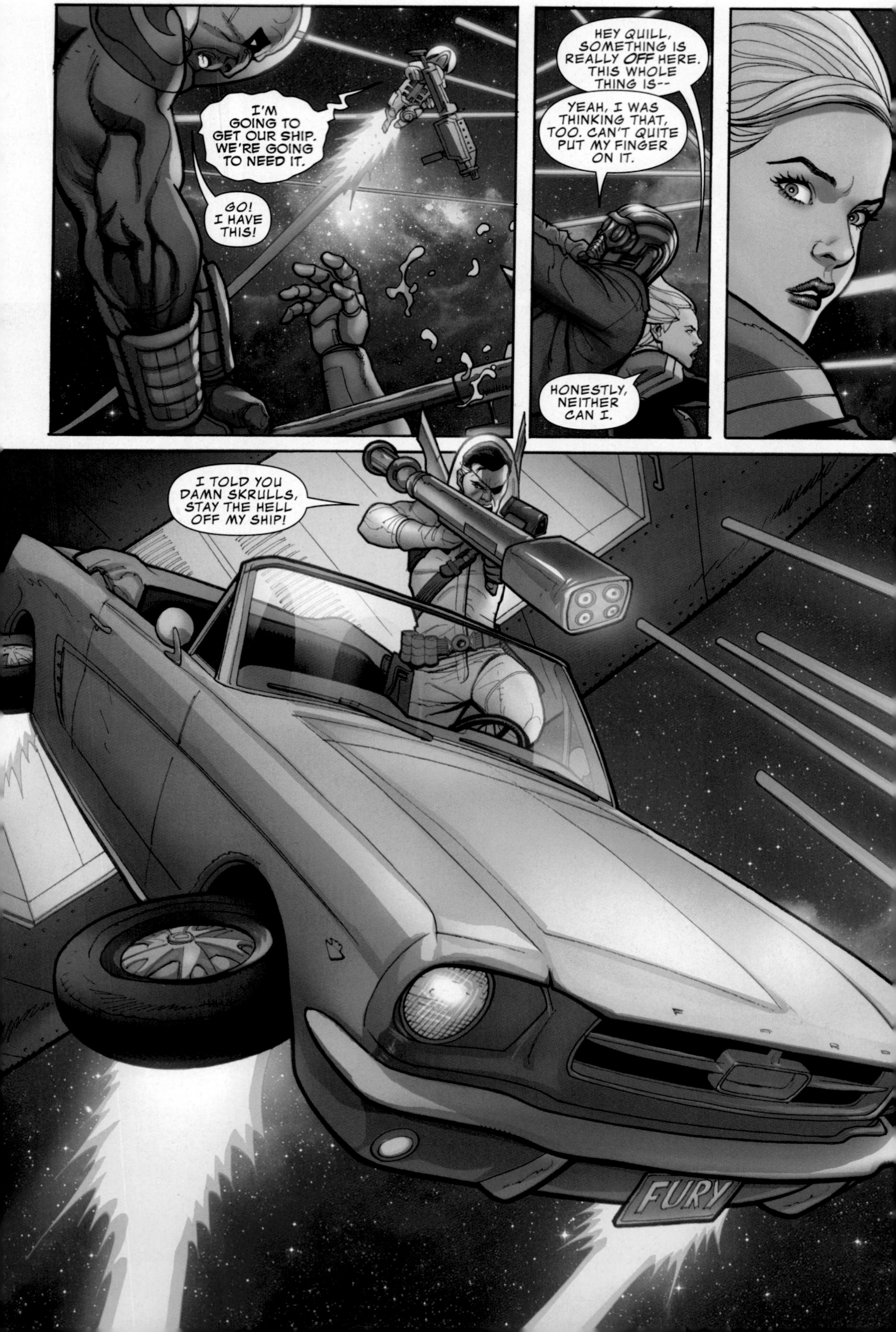
I'M GOING TO GET OUR SHIP. WE'RE GOING TO NEED IT.
GO! I HAVE THIS!
HEY QUILL, SOMETHING IS REALLY OFF HERE. THIS WHOLE THING IS--
YEAH, I WAS THINKING THAT, TOO. CAN'T QUITE PUT MY FINGER ON IT.
HONESTLY, NEITHER CAN I.
I TOLD YOU DAMN SKRULLS, STAY THE HELL OFF MY SHIP!
FORD
FURY

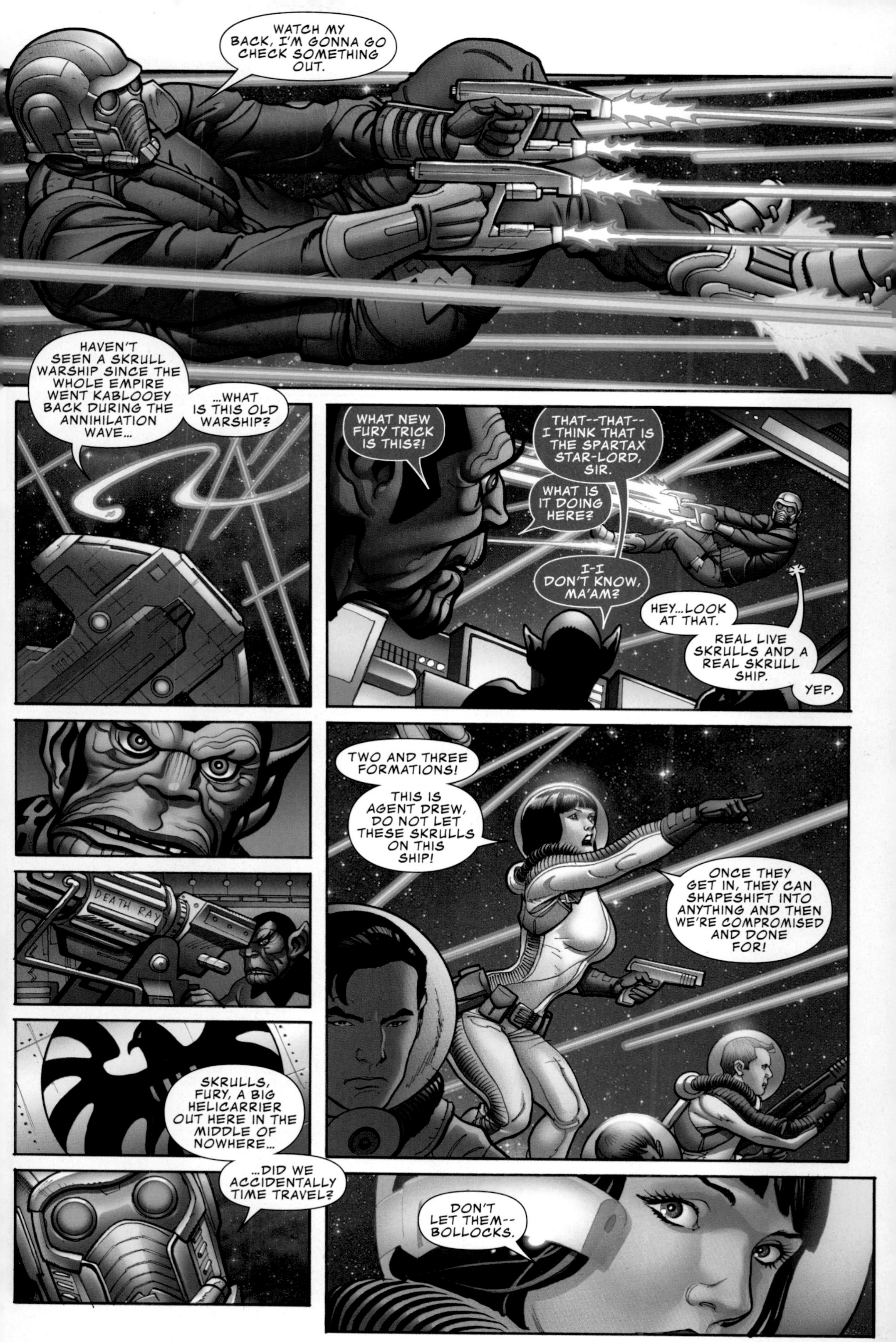
WATCH MY BACK, I'M GONNA GO CHECK SOMETHING OUT.
HAVEN'T SEEN A SKRULL WARSHIP SINCE THE WHOLE EMPIRE WENT KABLOOEY BACK DURING THE ANNIHILATION WAVE...
...WHAT IS THIS OLD WARSHIP?
WHAT NEW FURY TRICK IS THIS?!
THAT--THAT--I THINK THAT IS THE SPARTAX STAR-LORD, SIR.
WHAT IS IT DOING HERE?
I-I DON'T KNOW, MA'AM?
HEY...LOOK AT THAT.
REAL LIVE SKRULLS AND A REAL SKRULL SHIP.
YEP.
TWO AND THREE FORMATIONS!
THIS IS AGENT DREW, DO NOT LET THESE SKRULLS ON THIS SHIP!
ONCE THEY GET IN, THEY CAN SHAPESHIFT INTO ANYTHING AND THEN WE'RE COMPROMISED AND DONE FOR!
DEATH RAY
SKRULLS, FURY, A BIG HELICARRIER OUT HERE IN THE MIDDLE OF NOWHERE...
...DID WE ACCIDENTALLY TIME TRAVEL?
DON'T LET THEM--BOLLOCKS.

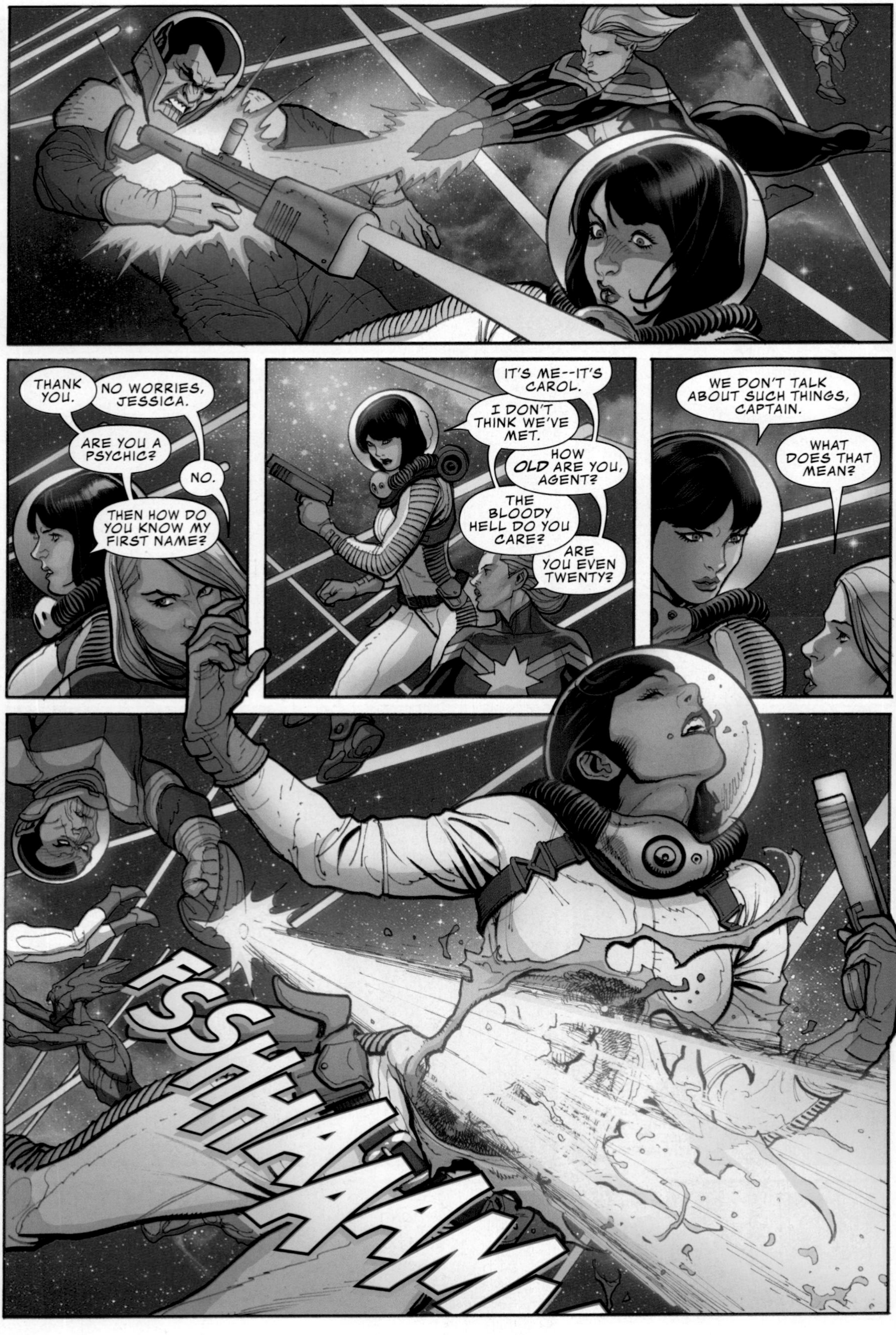
THANK YOU.
NO WORRIES, JESSICA.
ARE YOU A PSYCHIC?
NO.
THEN HOW DO YOU KNOW MY FIRST NAME?
IT'S ME--IT'S CAROL.
I DON'T THINK WE'VE MET.
HOW OLD ARE YOU, AGENT?
THE BLOODY HELL DO YOU CARE?
ARE YOU EVEN TWENTY?
WE DON'T TALK ABOUT SUCH THINGS, CAPTAIN.
WHAT DOES THAT MEAN?
FSSHHAAAM!

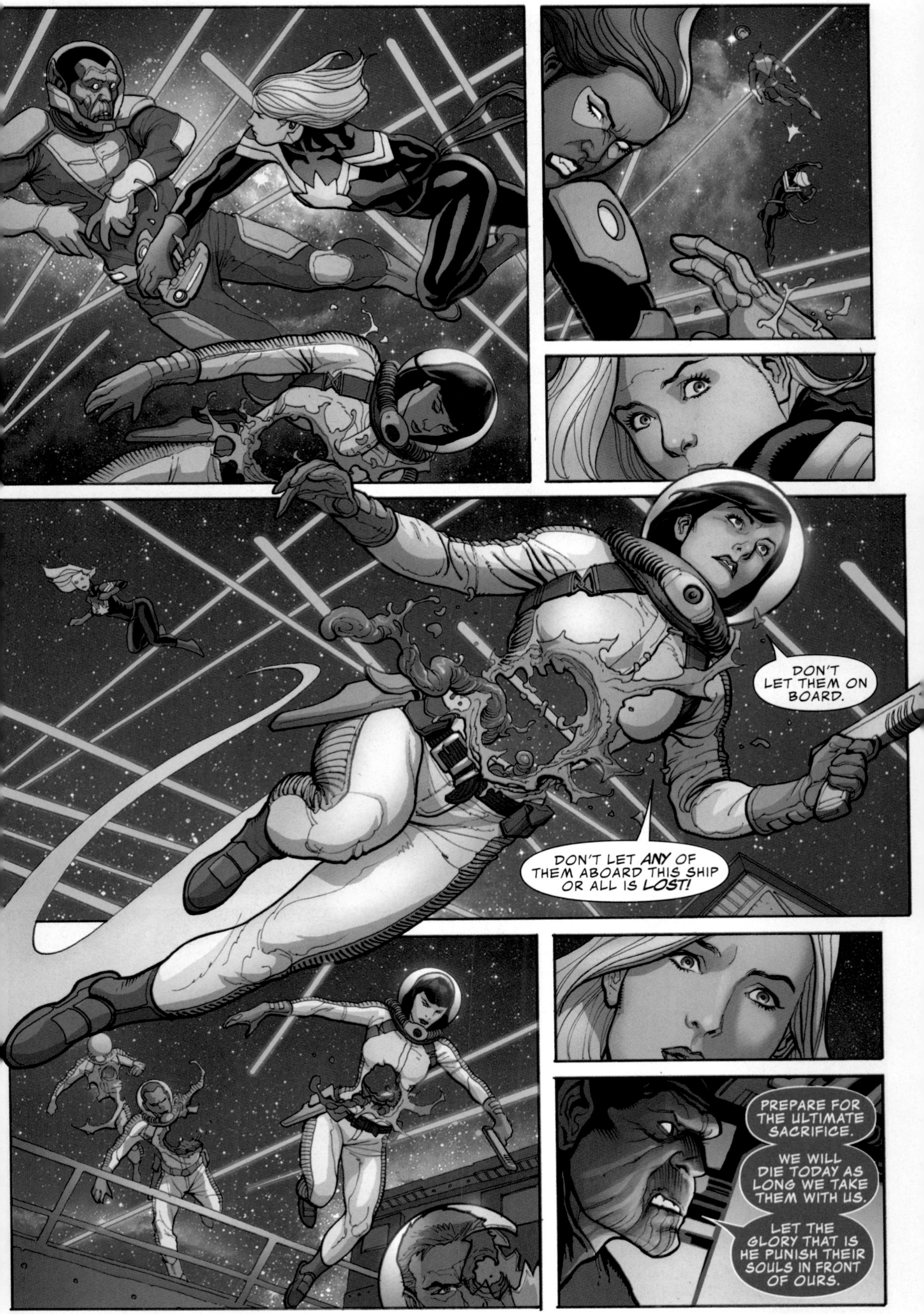
DON'T LET THEM ON BOARD.
DON'T LET ANY OF THEM ABOARD THIS SHIP OR ALL IS LOST!
PREPARE FOR THE ULTIMATE SACRIFICE.
WE WILL DIE TODAY AS LONG WE TAKE THEM WITH US.
LET THE GLORY THAT IS HE PUNISH THEIR SOULS IN FRONT OF OURS.

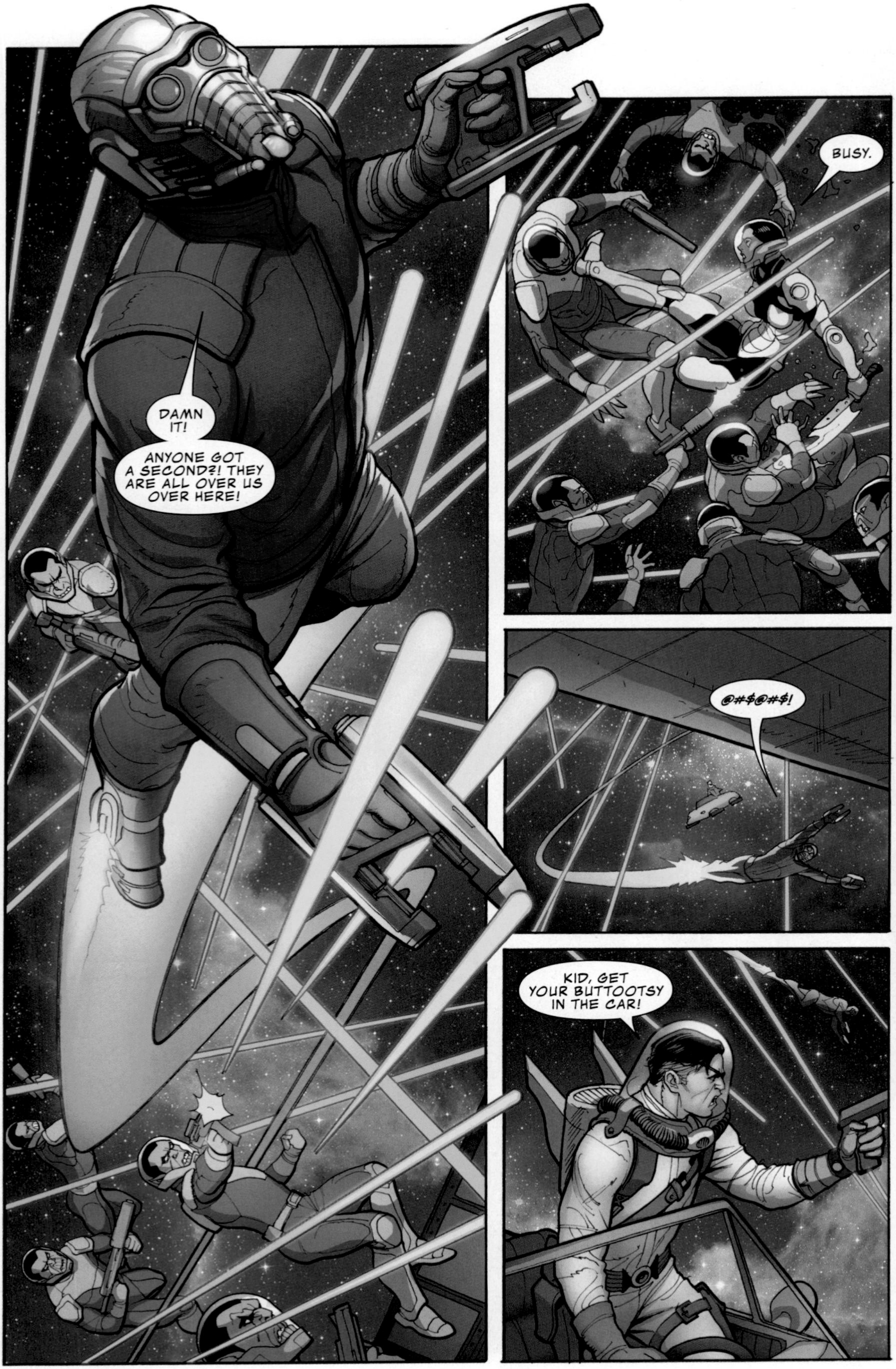
DAMN IT!
ANYONE GOT A SECOND?! THEY ARE ALL OVER US OVER HERE!
BUSY.
@#$@#$!
KID, GET YOUR BUTTOOTSY IN THE CAR!

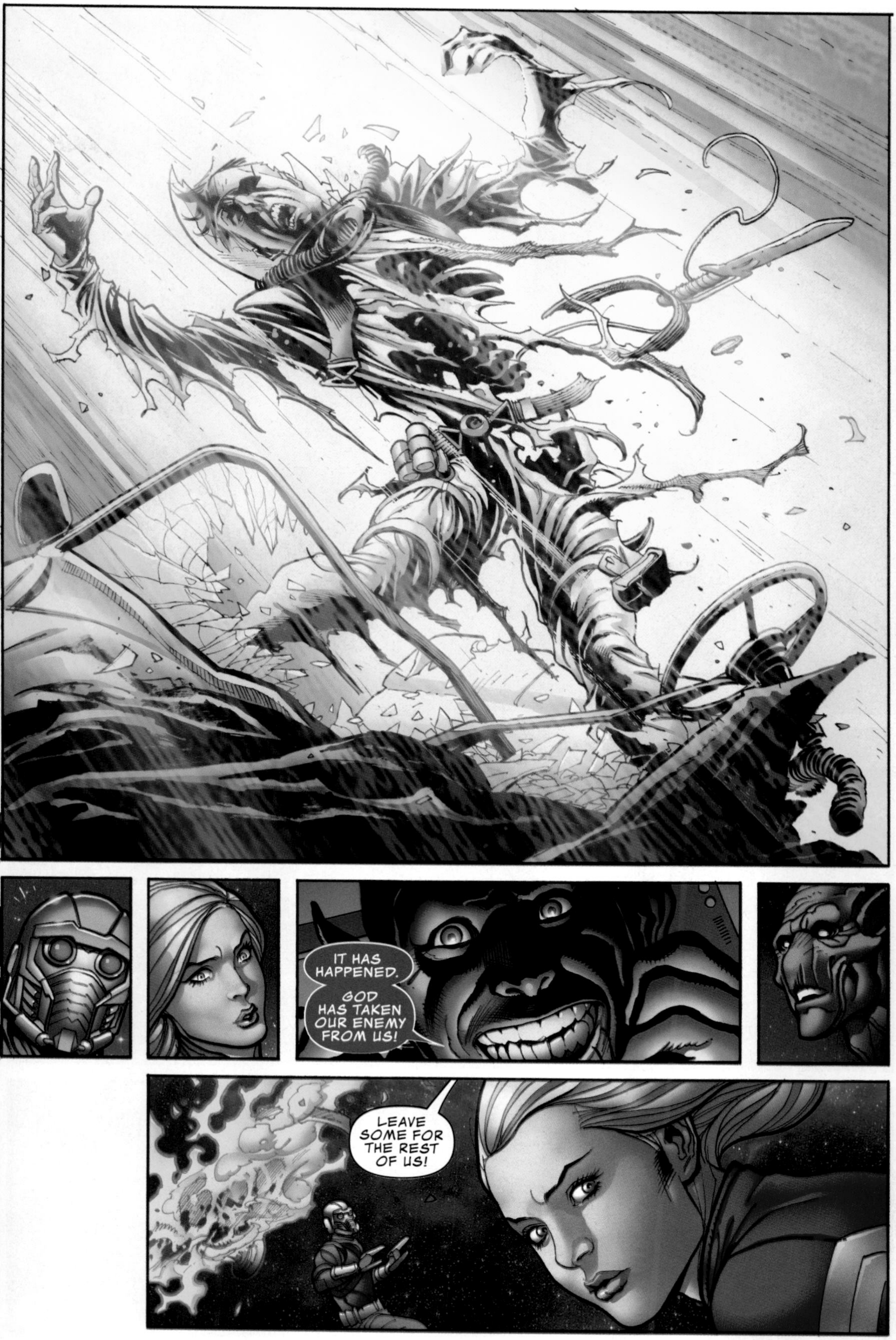
IT HAS HAPPENED.
GOD HAS TAKEN OUR ENEMY FROM US!
LEAVE SOME FOR THE REST OF US!

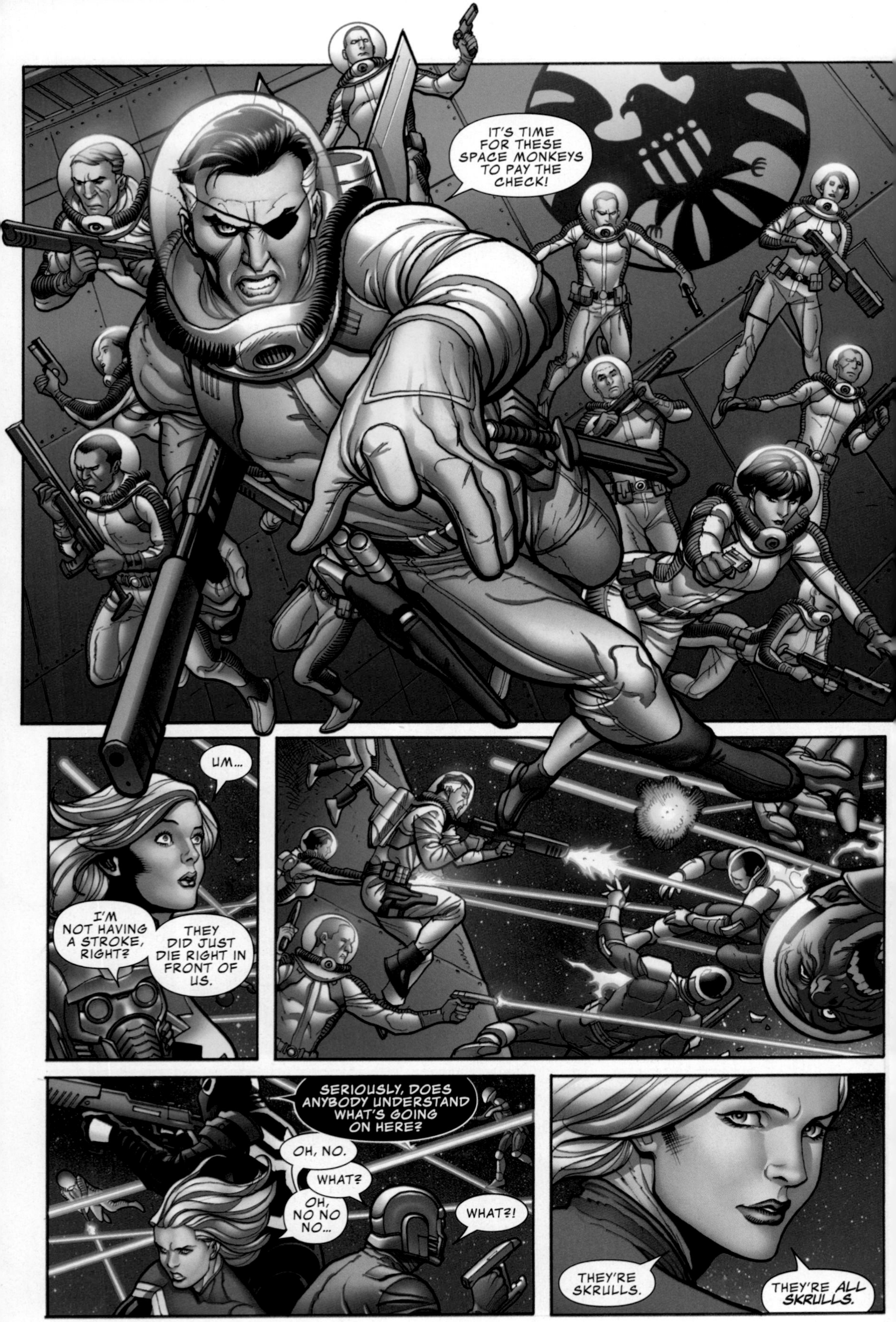

IT'S TIME FOR THESE SPACE MONKEYS TO PAY THE CHECK!
UM...
I'M NOT HAVING A STROKE, RIGHT?
THEY DID JUST DIE RIGHT IN FRONT OF US.
SERIOUSLY, DOES ANYBODY UNDERSTAND WHAT'S GOING ON HERE?
OH, NO.
WHAT?
OH, NO NO NO...
WHAT?!
THEY'RE SKRULLS.
THEY'RE *ALL* *SKRULLS*.

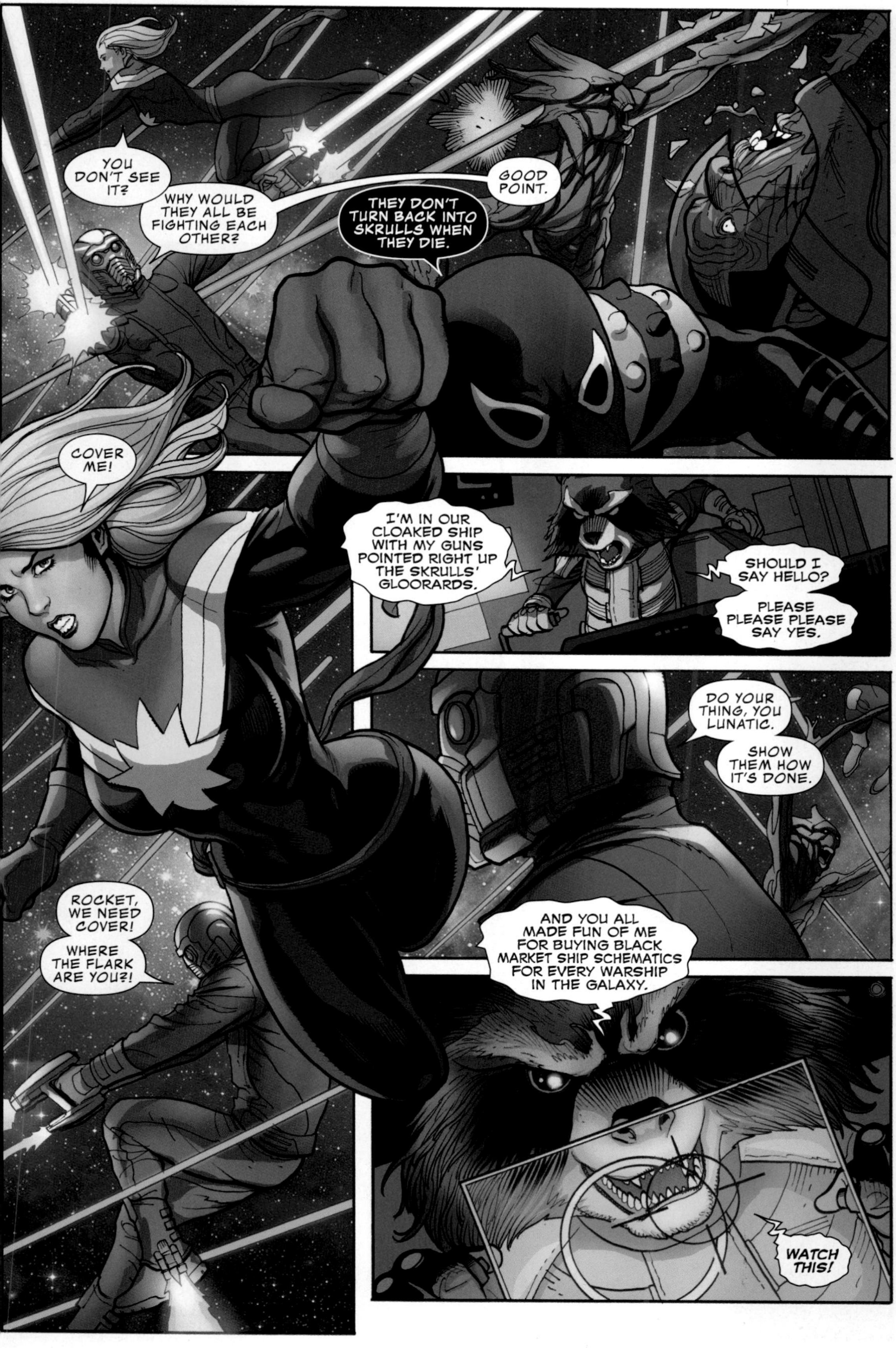
YOU DON'T SEE IT?
WHY WOULD THEY ALL BE FIGHTING EACH OTHER?
GOOD POINT.
THEY DON'T TURN BACK INTO SKRULLS WHEN THEY DIE.
COVER ME!
I'M IN OUR CLOAKED SHIP WITH MY GUNS POINTED RIGHT UP THE SKRULLS' GLOORARDS.
SHOULD I SAY HELLO?
PLEASE PLEASE PLEASE SAY YES.
DO YOUR THING, YOU LUNATIC.
SHOW THEM HOW IT'S DONE.
ROCKET, WE NEED COVER!
WHERE THE FLARK ARE YOU?!
AND YOU ALL MADE FUN OF ME FOR BUYING BLACK MARKET SHIP SCHEMATICS FOR EVERY WARSHIP IN THE GALAXY.
WATCH THIS!

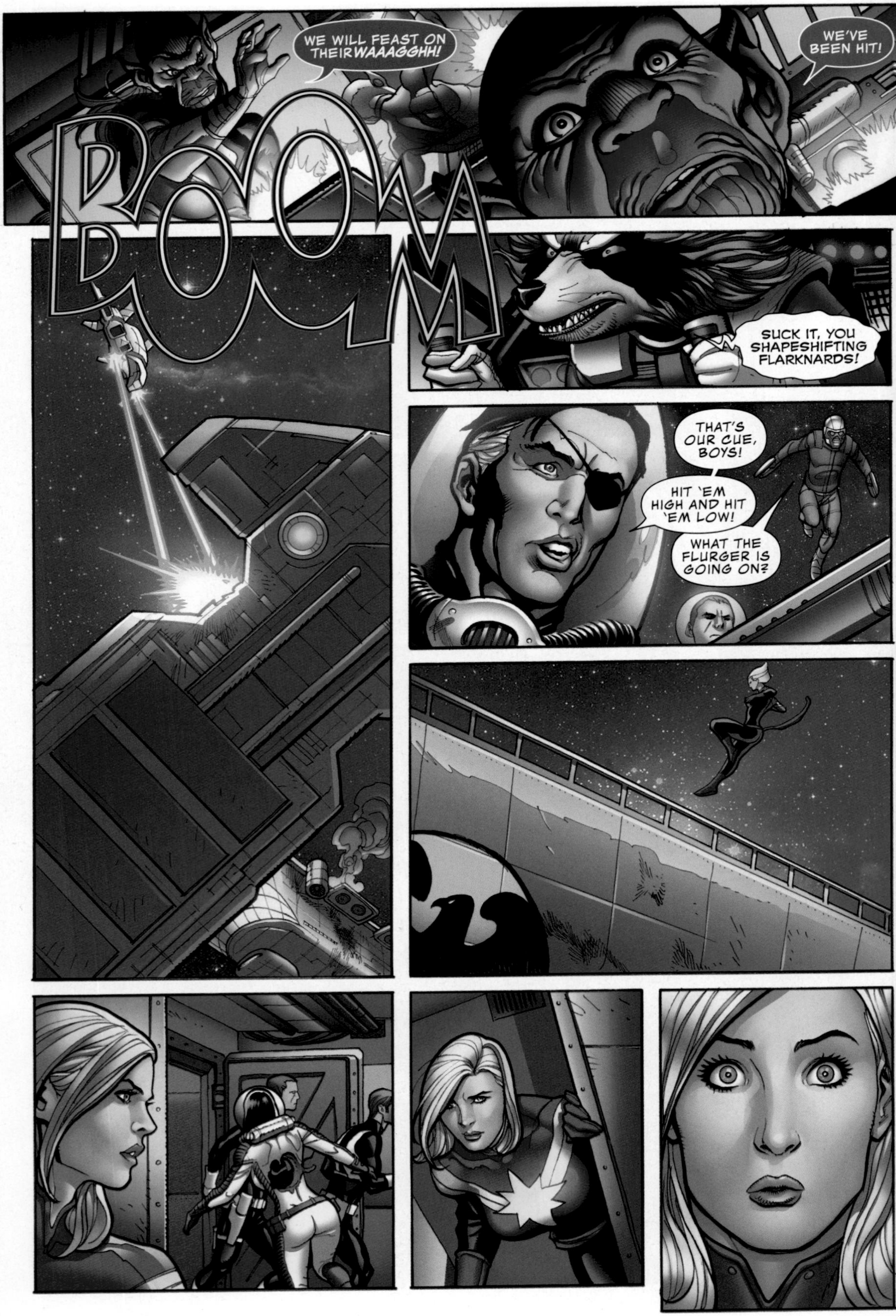
WE WILL FEAST ON THEIRWAAAGGHH!
WE'VE BEEN HIT!
BOOM
SUCK IT, YOU SHAPESHIFTING FLARKNARDS!
THAT'S OUR CUE, BOYS!
HIT 'EM HIGH AND HIT 'EM LOW!
WHAT THE FLURGER IS GOING ON?

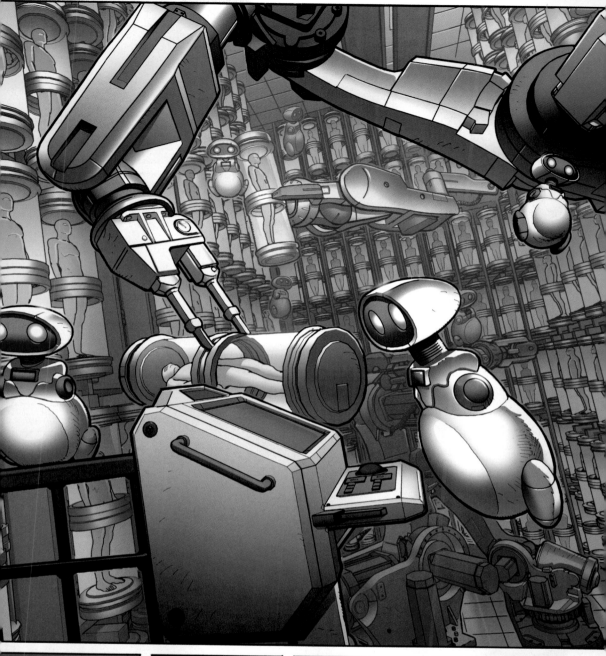

TIMOTHY ALOYSIUS
CADWALLANDER DUGAN

ALIAS: DUM DUM

RANK: S.H.I.E.L.D.
DEPUTY DIRECTOR

TIMOTHY ALOYSIUS
CADWALLANDER DUGAN

DECEASED

RANK: S.H.I.E.L.D.
DEPUTY DIRECTOR

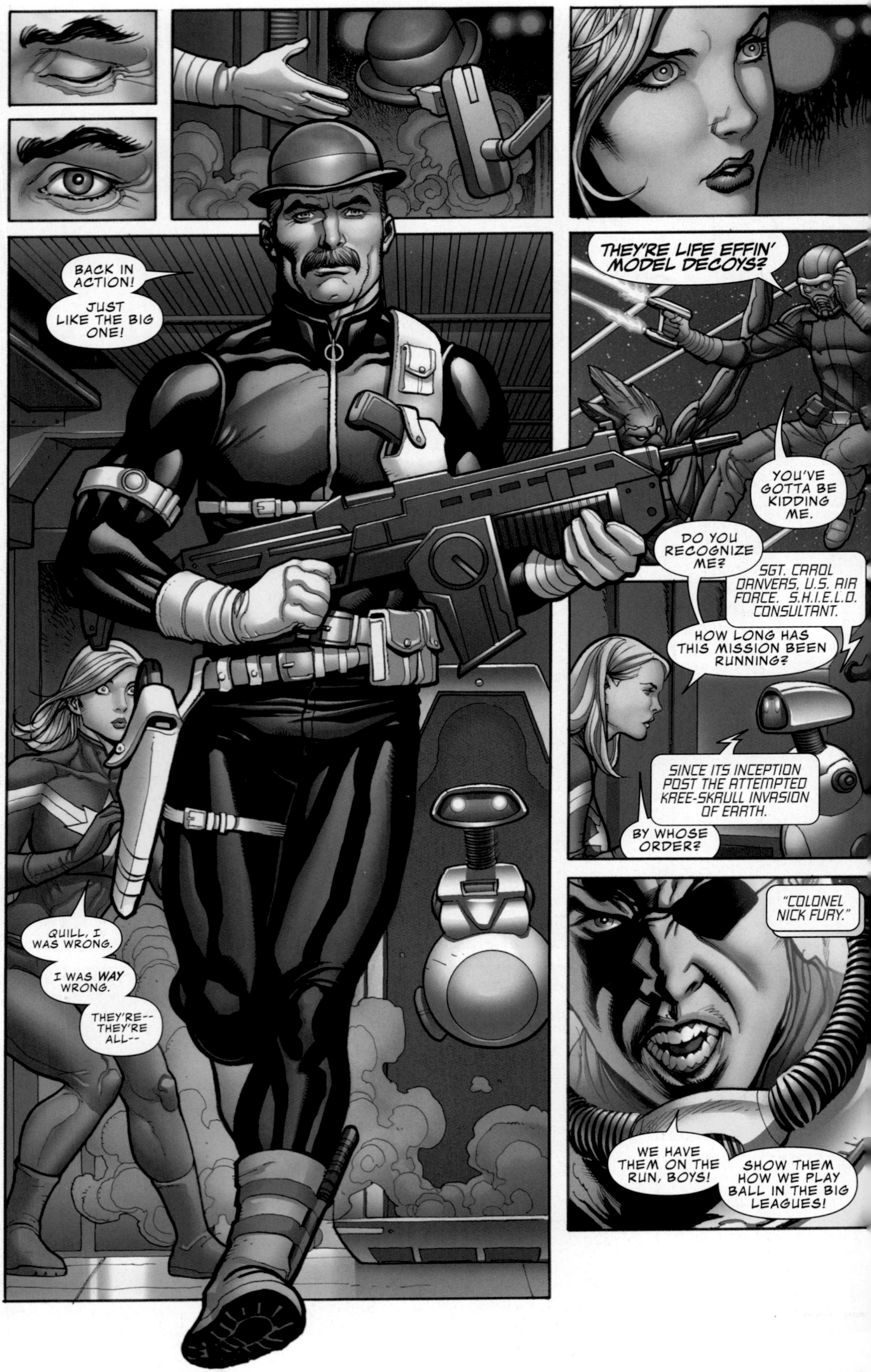
THEY'RE LIFE EFFIN' MODEL DECOYS?
YOU'VE GOTTA BE KIDDING ME.
DO YOU RECOGNIZE ME?
SGT. CAROL DANVERS, U.S. AIR FORCE. S.H.I.E.L.D. CONSULTANT.
HOW LONG HAS THIS MISSION BEEN RUNNING?
SINCE ITS INCEPTION POST THE ATTEMPTED KREE-SKRULL INVASION OF EARTH.
BY WHOSE ORDER?
"COLONEL NICK FURY."
BACK IN ACTION!
JUST LIKE THE BIG ONE!
QUILL, I WAS WRONG.
I WAS WAY WRONG.
THEY'RE-- THEY'RE ALL--
WE HAVE THEM ON THE RUN, BOYS!
SHOW THEM HOW WE PLAY BALL IN THE BIG LEAGUES!

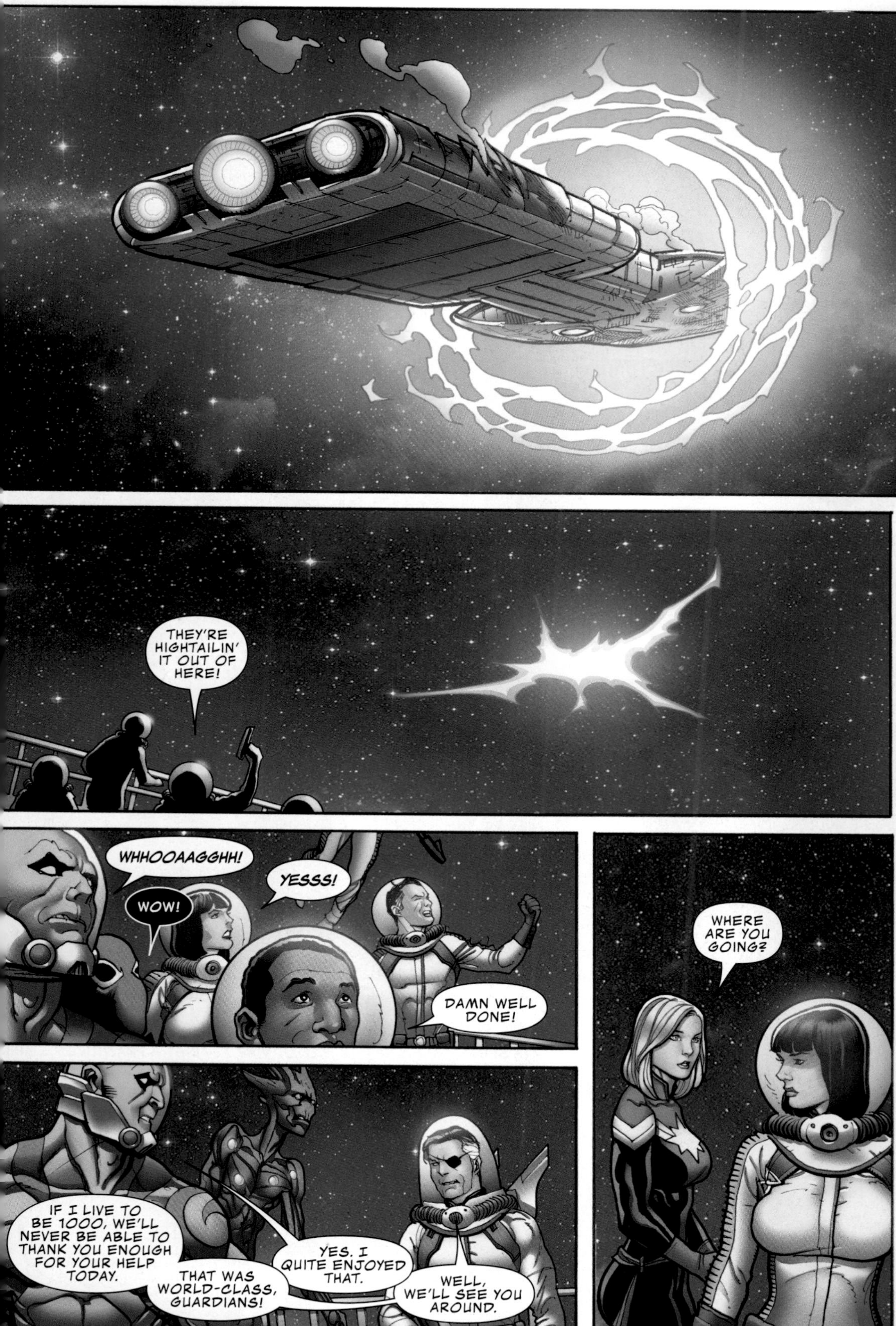
THEY'RE HIGHTAILIN' IT OUT OF HERE!
WHHOOAAGGHH!
WOW!
YESSS!
DAMN WELL DONE!
WHERE ARE YOU GOING?
IF I LIVE TO BE 1000, WE'LL NEVER BE ABLE TO THANK YOU ENOUGH FOR YOUR HELP TODAY.
THAT WAS WORLD-CLASS, GUARDIANS!
YES. I QUITE ENJOYED THAT.
WELL, WE'LL SEE YOU AROUND.

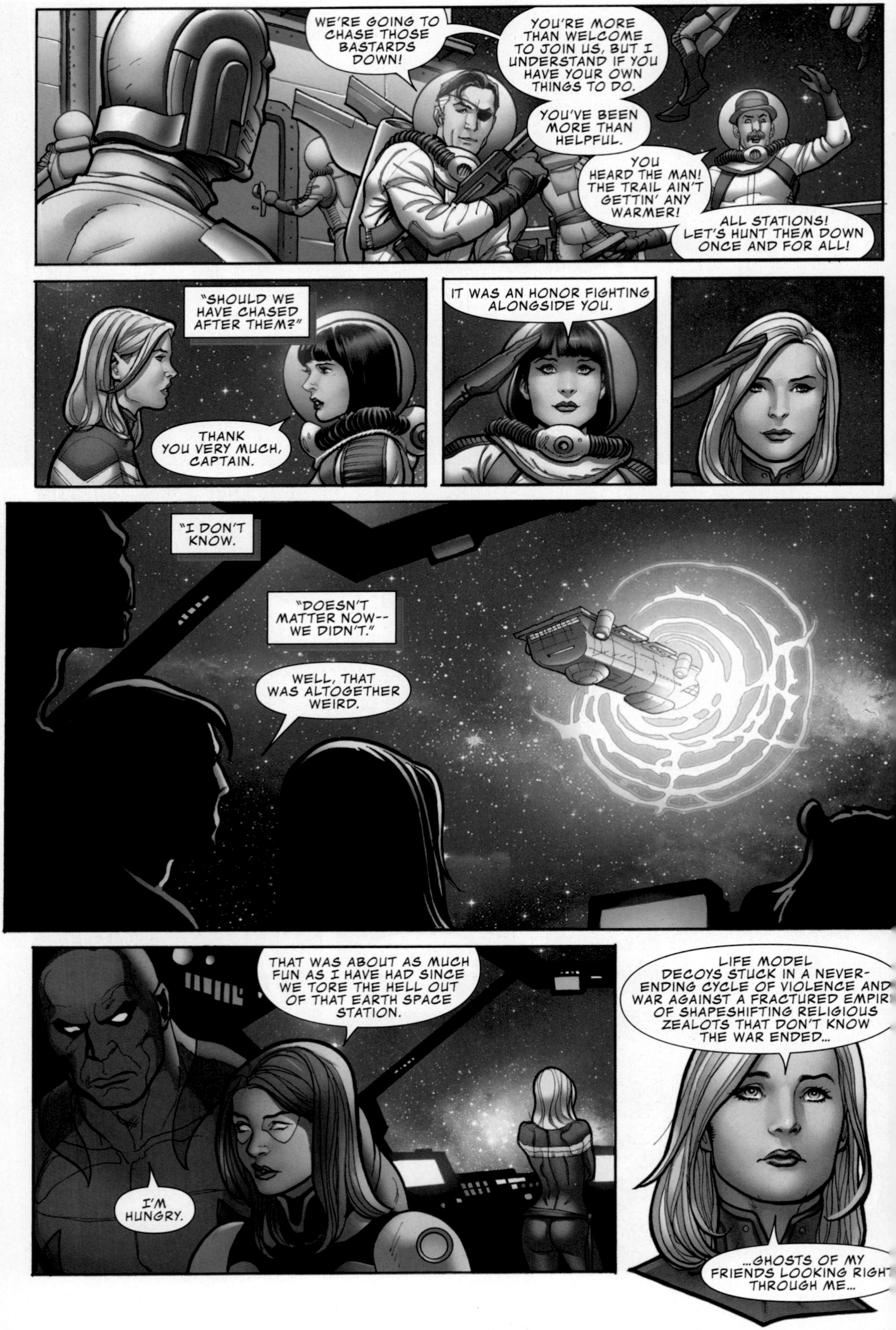
WE'RE GOING TO CHASE THOSE BASTARDS DOWN!
YOU'RE MORE THAN WELCOME TO JOIN US, BUT I UNDERSTAND IF YOU HAVE YOUR OWN THINGS TO DO.
YOU'VE BEEN MORE THAN HELPFUL.
YOU HEARD THE MAN! THE TRAIL AIN'T GETTIN' ANY WARMER!
ALL STATIONS! LET'S HUNT THEM DOWN ONCE AND FOR ALL!
"SHOULD WE HAVE CHASED AFTER THEM?"
THANK YOU VERY MUCH, CAPTAIN.
IT WAS AN HONOR FIGHTING ALONGSIDE YOU.
"I DON'T KNOW.
"DOESN'T MATTER NOW-- WE DIDN'T."
WELL, THAT WAS ALTOGETHER WEIRD.
THAT WAS ABOUT AS MUCH FUN AS I HAVE HAD SINCE WE TORE THE HELL OUT OF THAT EARTH SPACE STATION.
I'M HUNGRY.
LIFE MODEL DECOYS STUCK IN A NEVER-ENDING CYCLE OF VIOLENCE AND WAR AGAINST A FRACTURED EMPIR OF SHAPESHIFTING RELIGIOUS ZEALOTS THAT DON'T KNOW THE WAR ENDED...
...GHOSTS OF MY FRIENDS LOOKING RIGH THROUGH ME...

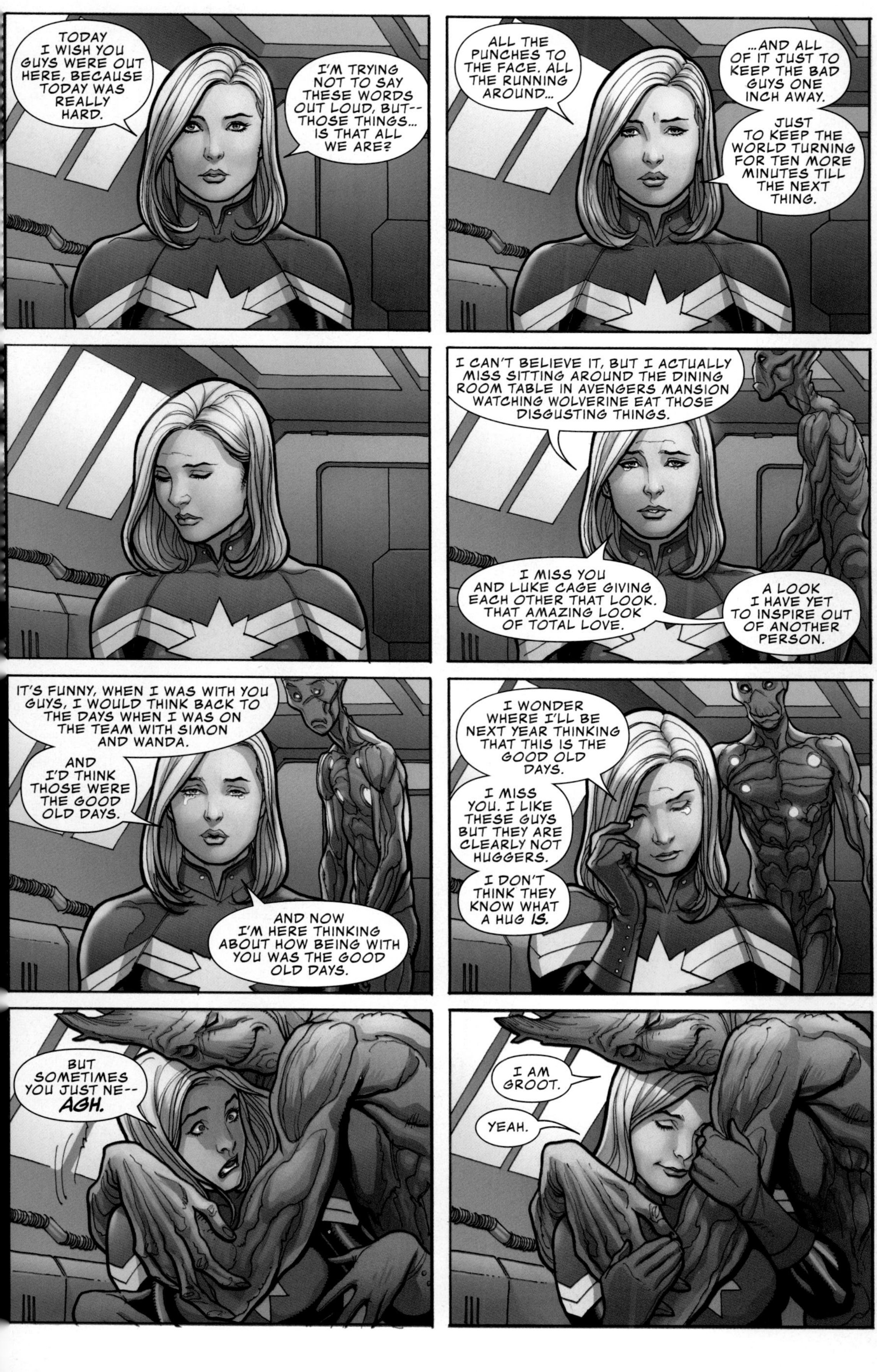
TODAY I WISH YOU GUYS WERE OUT HERE, BECAUSE TODAY WAS REALLY HARD.
I'M TRYING NOT TO SAY THESE WORDS OUT LOUD, BUT-- THOSE THINGS... IS THAT ALL WE ARE?
ALL THE PUNCHES TO THE FACE. ALL THE RUNNING AROUND...
...AND ALL OF IT JUST TO KEEP THE BAD GUYS ONE INCH AWAY.
JUST TO KEEP THE WORLD TURNING FOR TEN MORE MINUTES TILL THE NEXT THING.
I CAN'T BELIEVE IT, BUT I ACTUALLY MISS SITTING AROUND THE DINING ROOM TABLE IN AVENGERS MANSION WATCHING WOLVERINE EAT THOSE DISGUSTING THINGS.
I MISS YOU AND LUKE CAGE GIVING EACH OTHER THAT LOOK. THAT AMAZING LOOK OF TOTAL LOVE.
A LOOK I HAVE YET TO INSPIRE OUT OF ANOTHER PERSON.
IT'S FUNNY, WHEN I WAS WITH YOU GUYS, I WOULD THINK BACK TO THE DAYS WHEN I WAS ON THE TEAM WITH SIMON AND WANDA.
AND I'D THINK THOSE WERE THE GOOD OLD DAYS.
AND NOW I'M HERE THINKING ABOUT HOW BEING WITH YOU WAS THE GOOD OLD DAYS.
I WONDER WHERE I'LL BE NEXT YEAR THINKING THAT THIS IS THE GOOD OLD DAYS.
I MISS YOU. I LIKE THESE GUYS BUT THEY ARE CLEARLY NOT HUGGERS.
I DON'T THINK THEY KNOW WHAT A HUG *IS.*
BUT SOMETIMES YOU JUST NE-- **AGH.**
I AM GROOT.
YEAH.

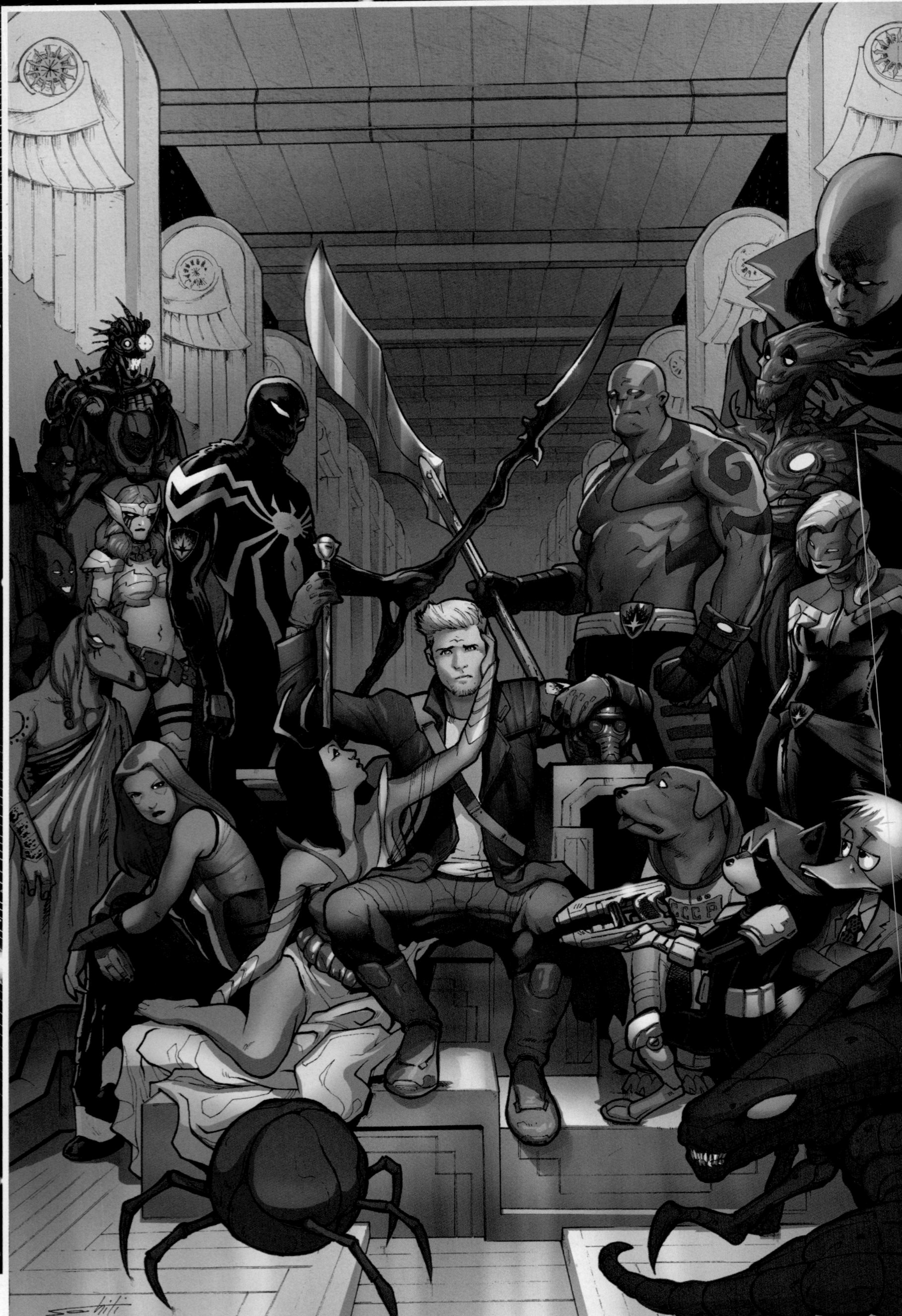
CCCP

GUARDIANS OF THE GALAXY & X-MEN

THE BLACK VORTEX

CHAPTER 2

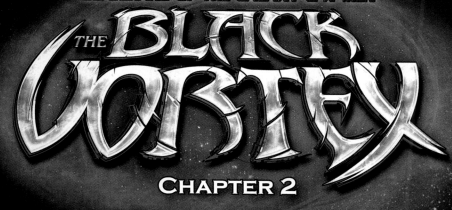

Previously in *The Black Vortex*...

Billions of years ago, an ancient race named the Viscardi were gifted an object of immense cosmic power by a Celestial. This artifact, known as the Black Vortex, transforms the user, imbuing them with cosmic energy. However, the power of this object caused the Viscardi to turn on each other, annihilating their own race from within.

In the present day, Peter Quill has been hounded by a mysterious villain named Mister Knife. Upon being captured by Knife, Peter discovered him to actually be his father, J-Son, the deposed Emperor of Spartax. With the help of Kitty Pryde, Peter escaped Knife's clutches. Seeking revenge, Peter and Kitty returned to Knife's fortress. However, while spying on Mister Knife's conversations, they discovered that he had recovered the Black Vortex and watched as he used it to enhance his henchmen, christening them, in their new forms, as the Slaughter Lords. Not willing to leave such power in the hands of his father, Peter stole the Black Vortex. In need of help, Peter and Kitty summoned the Guardians of the Galaxy and members of the X-Men. But while they argued over what to do with the object, the Slaughter Lords arrived and began to lay waste to the heroes. Seeking to save her friends, Gamora took matters into her own hands and submitted to the power of the Black Vortex.

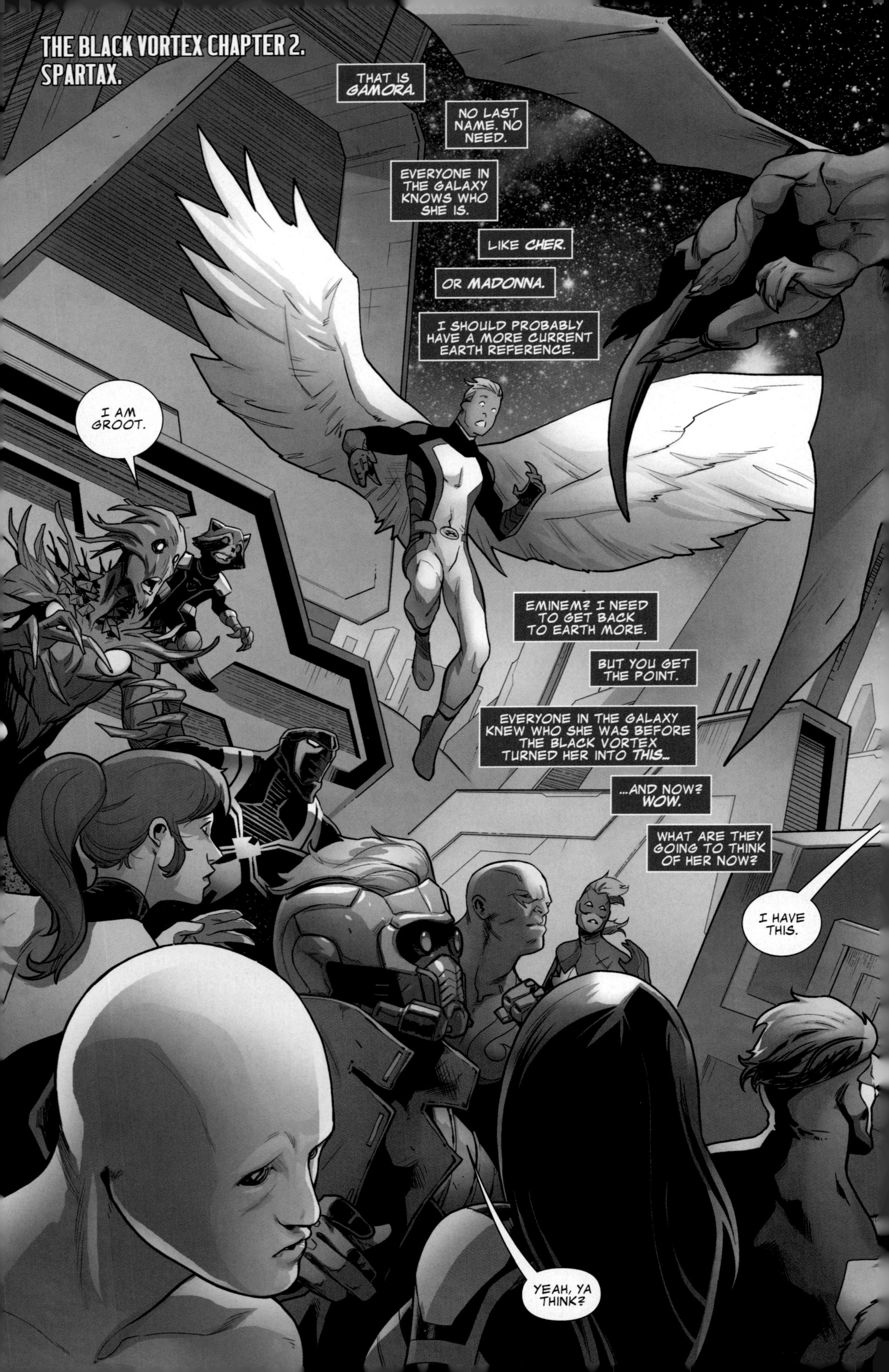
THE BLACK VORTEX CHAPTER 2.
SPARTAX.
THAT IS GAMORA.
NO LAST NAME. NO NEED.
EVERYONE IN THE GALAXY KNOWS WHO SHE IS.
LIKE CHER.
OR MADONNA.
I SHOULD PROBABLY HAVE A MORE CURRENT EARTH REFERENCE.
I AM GROOT.
EMINEM? I NEED TO GET BACK TO EARTH MORE.
BUT YOU GET THE POINT.
EVERYONE IN THE GALAXY KNEW WHO SHE WAS BEFORE THE BLACK VORTEX TURNED HER INTO THIS...
...AND NOW? WOW.
WHAT ARE THEY GOING TO THINK OF HER NOW?
I HAVE THIS.
YEAH, YA THINK?

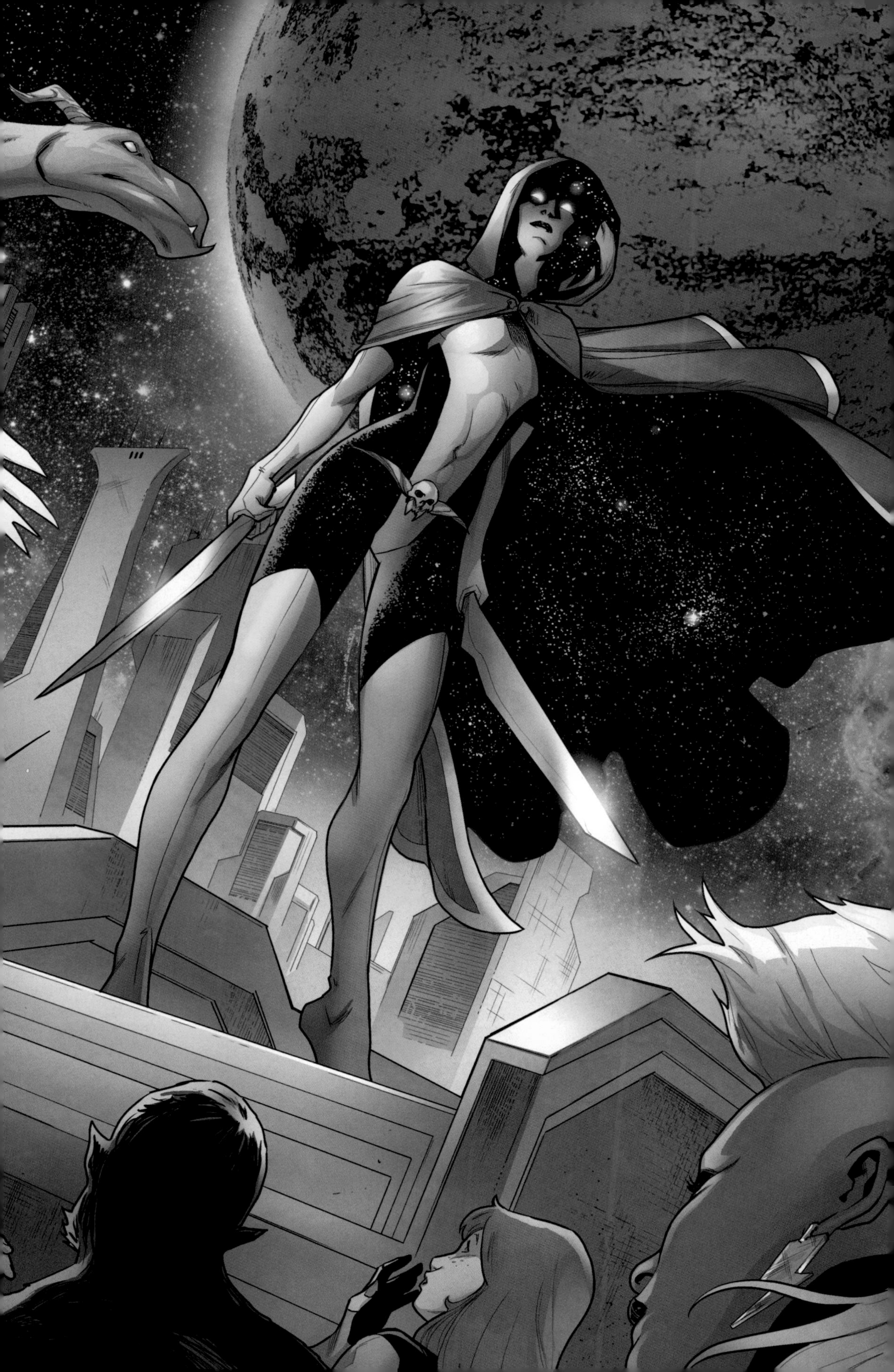

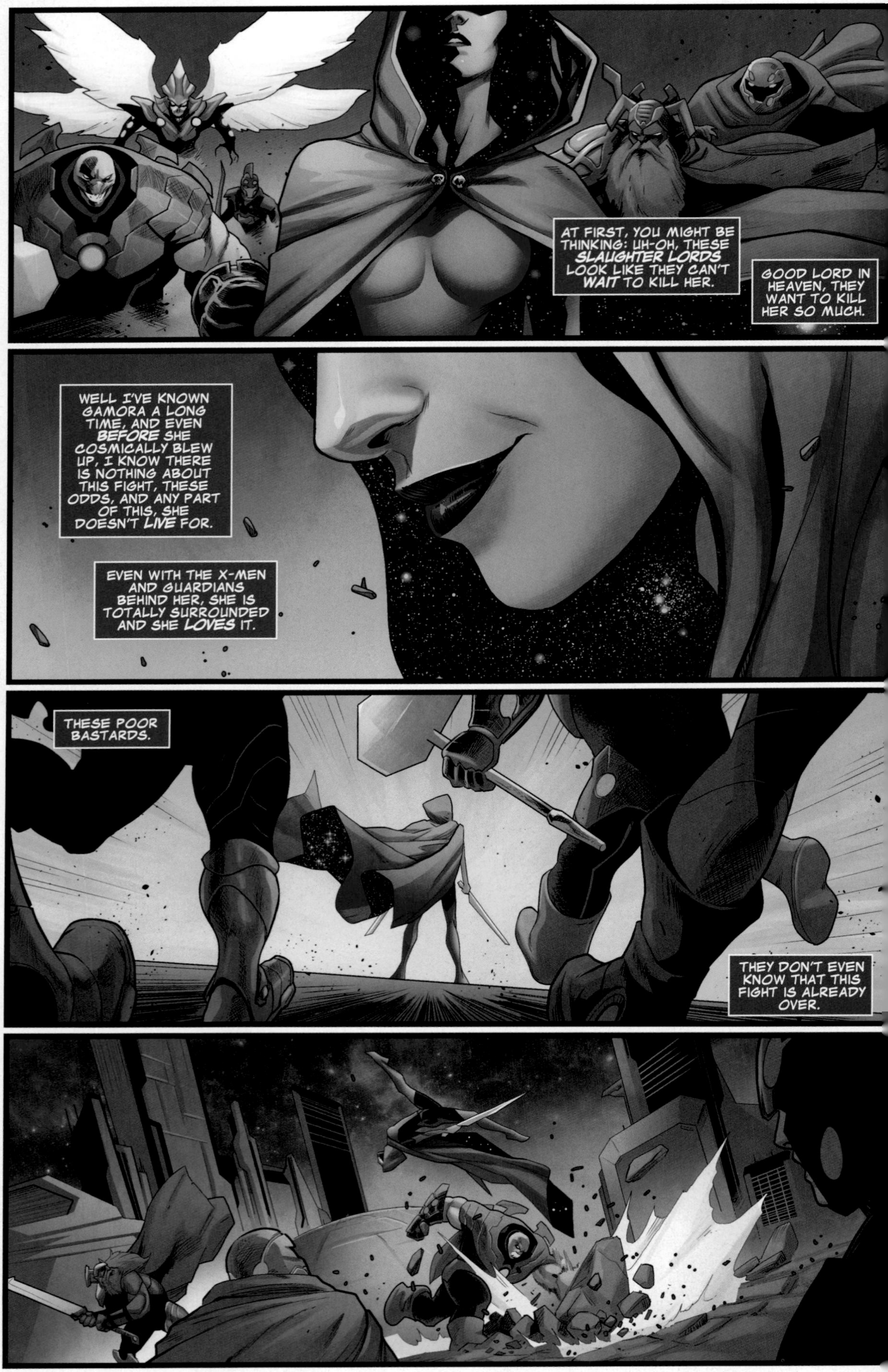
AT FIRST, YOU MIGHT BE THINKING: UH-OH, THESE SLAUGHTER LORDS LOOK LIKE THEY CAN'T WAIT TO KILL HER.
GOOD LORD IN HEAVEN, THEY WANT TO KILL HER SO MUCH.
WELL I'VE KNOWN GAMORA A LONG TIME, AND EVEN BEFORE SHE COSMICALLY BLEW UP, I KNOW THERE IS NOTHING ABOUT THIS FIGHT, THESE ODDS, AND ANY PART OF THIS, SHE DOESN'T LIVE FOR.
EVEN WITH THE X-MEN AND GUARDIANS BEHIND HER, SHE IS TOTALLY SURROUNDED AND SHE LOVES IT.
THESE POOR BASTARDS.
THEY DON'T EVEN KNOW THAT THIS FIGHT IS ALREADY OVER.

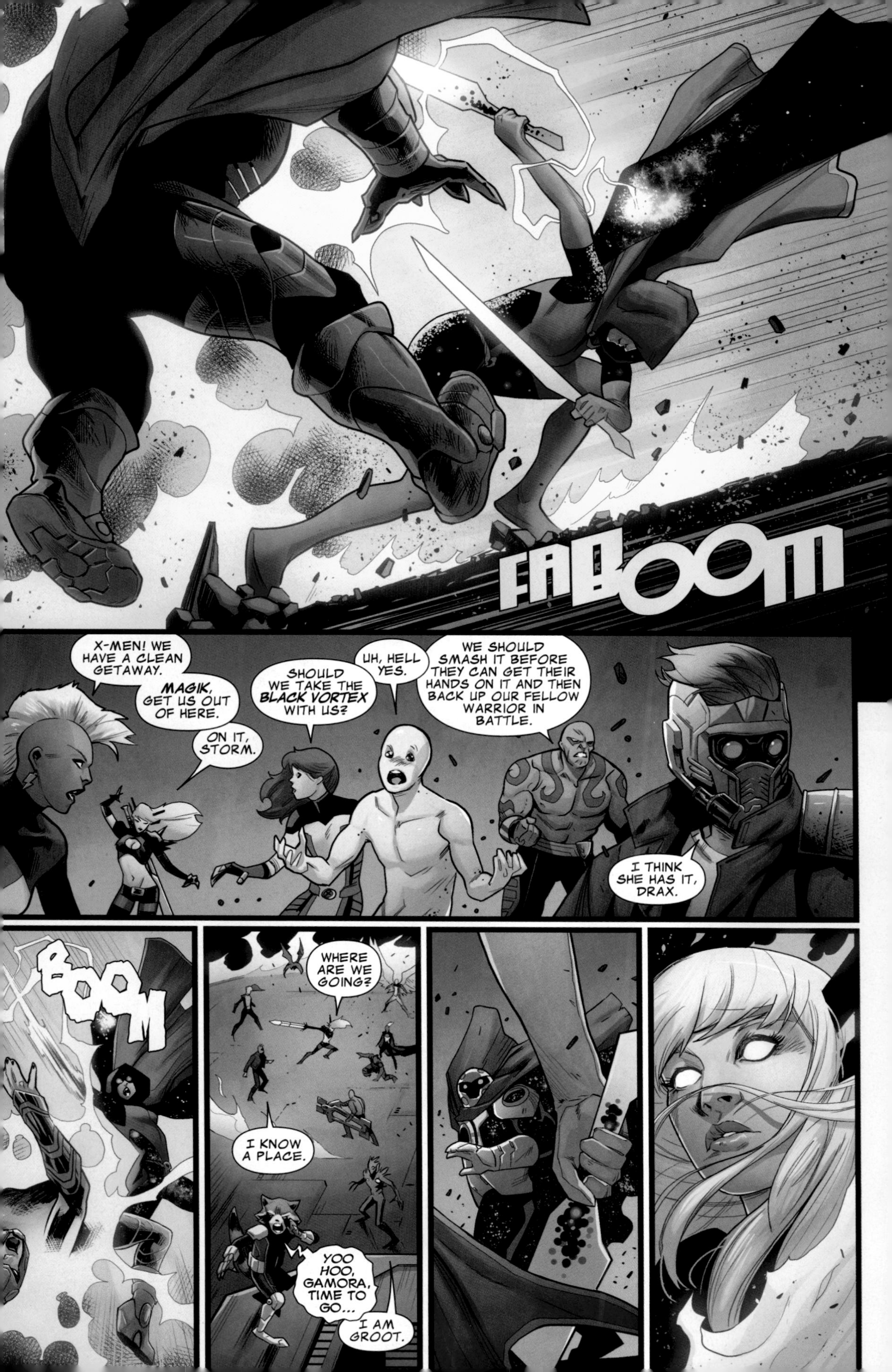

FABOOM
X-MEN! WE HAVE A CLEAN GETAWAY.
MAGIK, GET US OUT OF HERE.
ON IT, STORM.
SHOULD WE TAKE THE BLACK VORTEX WITH US?
UH, HELL YES.
WE SHOULD SMASH IT BEFORE THEY CAN GET THEIR HANDS ON IT AND THEN BACK UP OUR FELLOW WARRIOR IN BATTLE.
I THINK SHE HAS IT, DRAX.
BOOM
WHERE ARE WE GOING?
I KNOW A PLACE.
YOO HOO, GAMORA, TIME TO GO...
I AM GROOT.

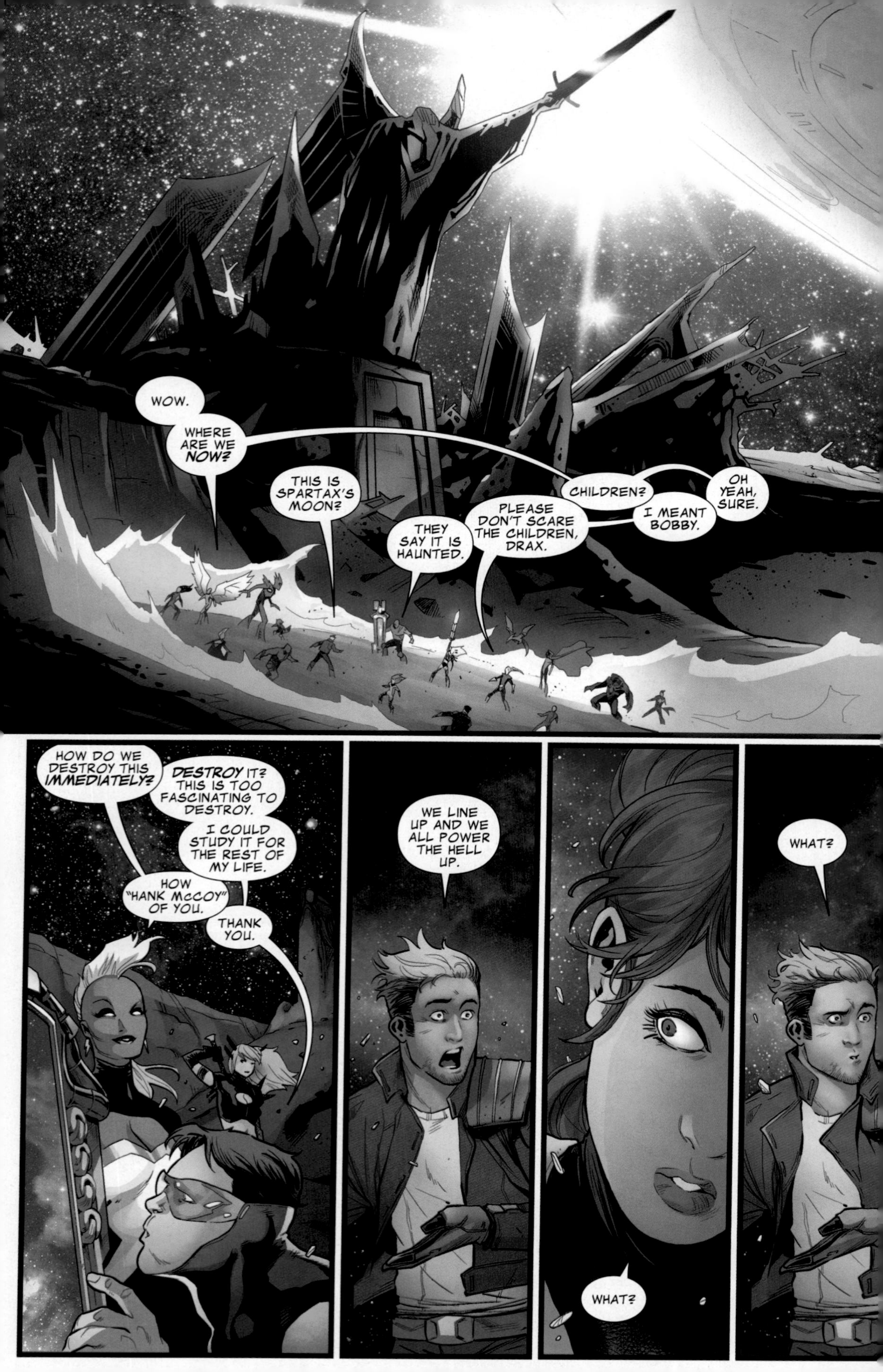
WOW.
WHERE ARE WE NOW?
THIS IS SPARTAX'S MOON?
THEY SAY IT IS HAUNTED.
PLEASE DON'T SCARE THE CHILDREN, DRAX.
CHILDREN?
I MEANT BOBBY.
OH YEAH, SURE.
HOW DO WE DESTROY THIS IMMEDIATELY?
DESTROY IT? THIS IS TOO FASCINATING TO DESTROY.
I COULD STUDY IT FOR THE REST OF MY LIFE.
HOW "HANK McCOY" OF YOU.
THANK YOU.
WE LINE UP AND WE ALL POWER THE HELL UP.
WHAT?
WHAT?

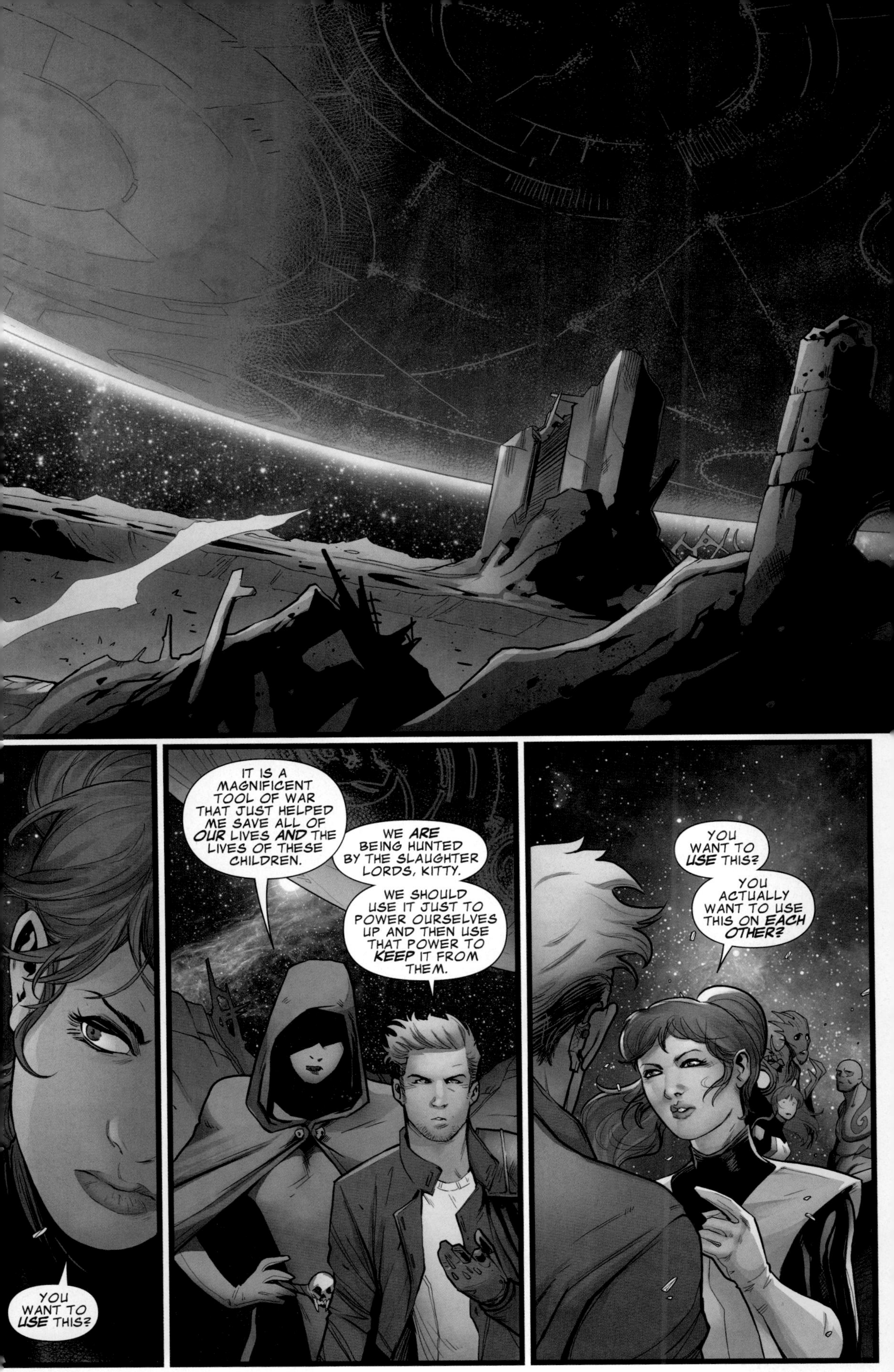
YOU WANT TO USE THIS?
IT IS A MAGNIFICENT TOOL OF WAR THAT JUST HELPED ME SAVE ALL OF OUR LIVES AND THE LIVES OF THESE CHILDREN.
WE ARE BEING HUNTED BY THE SLAUGHTER LORDS, KITTY.
WE SHOULD USE IT JUST TO POWER OURSELVES UP AND THEN USE THAT POWER TO KEEP IT FROM THEM.
YOU WANT TO USE THIS?
YOU ACTUALLY WANT TO USE THIS ON EACH OTHER?

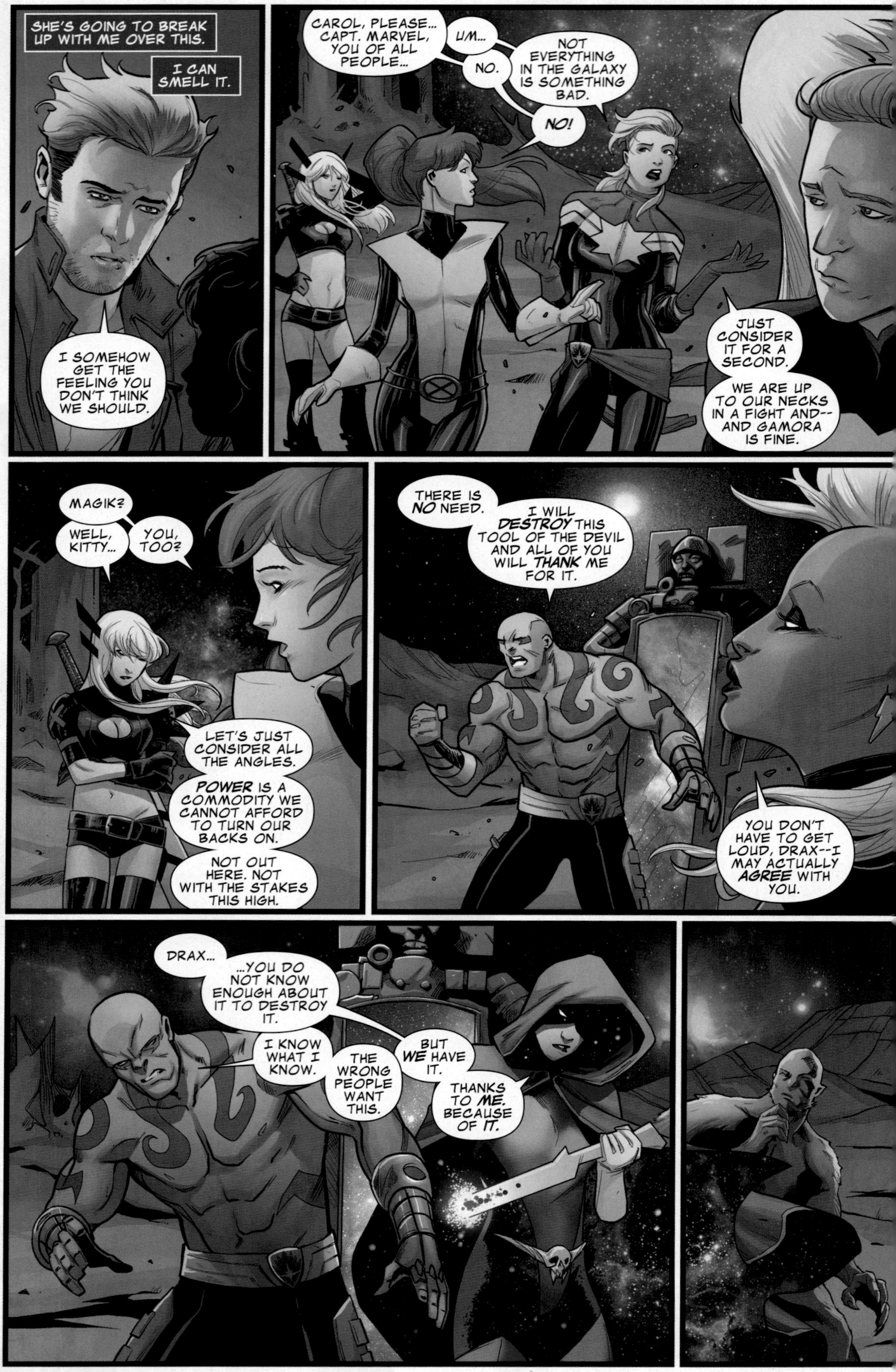
SHE'S GOING TO BREAK UP WITH ME OVER THIS.
I CAN SMELL IT.
I SOMEHOW GET THE FEELING YOU DON'T THINK WE SHOULD.
CAROL, PLEASE... CAPT. MARVEL, YOU OF ALL PEOPLE...
UM...
NO.
NOT EVERYTHING IN THE GALAXY IS SOMETHING BAD.
NO!
JUST CONSIDER IT FOR A SECOND.
WE ARE UP TO OUR NECKS IN A FIGHT AND-- AND GAMORA IS FINE.
MAGIK?
WELL, KITTY...
YOU, TOO?
LET'S JUST CONSIDER ALL THE ANGLES.
POWER IS A COMMODITY WE CANNOT AFFORD TO TURN OUR BACKS ON.
NOT OUT HERE. NOT WITH THE STAKES THIS HIGH.
THERE IS NO NEED.
I WILL DESTROY THIS TOOL OF THE DEVIL AND ALL OF YOU WILL THANK ME FOR IT.
YOU DON'T HAVE TO GET LOUD, DRAX--I MAY ACTUALLY AGREE WITH YOU.
DRAX...
...YOU DO NOT KNOW ENOUGH ABOUT IT TO DESTROY IT.
I KNOW WHAT I KNOW.
THE WRONG PEOPLE WANT THIS.
BUT WE HAVE IT.
THANKS TO ME. BECAUSE OF IT.

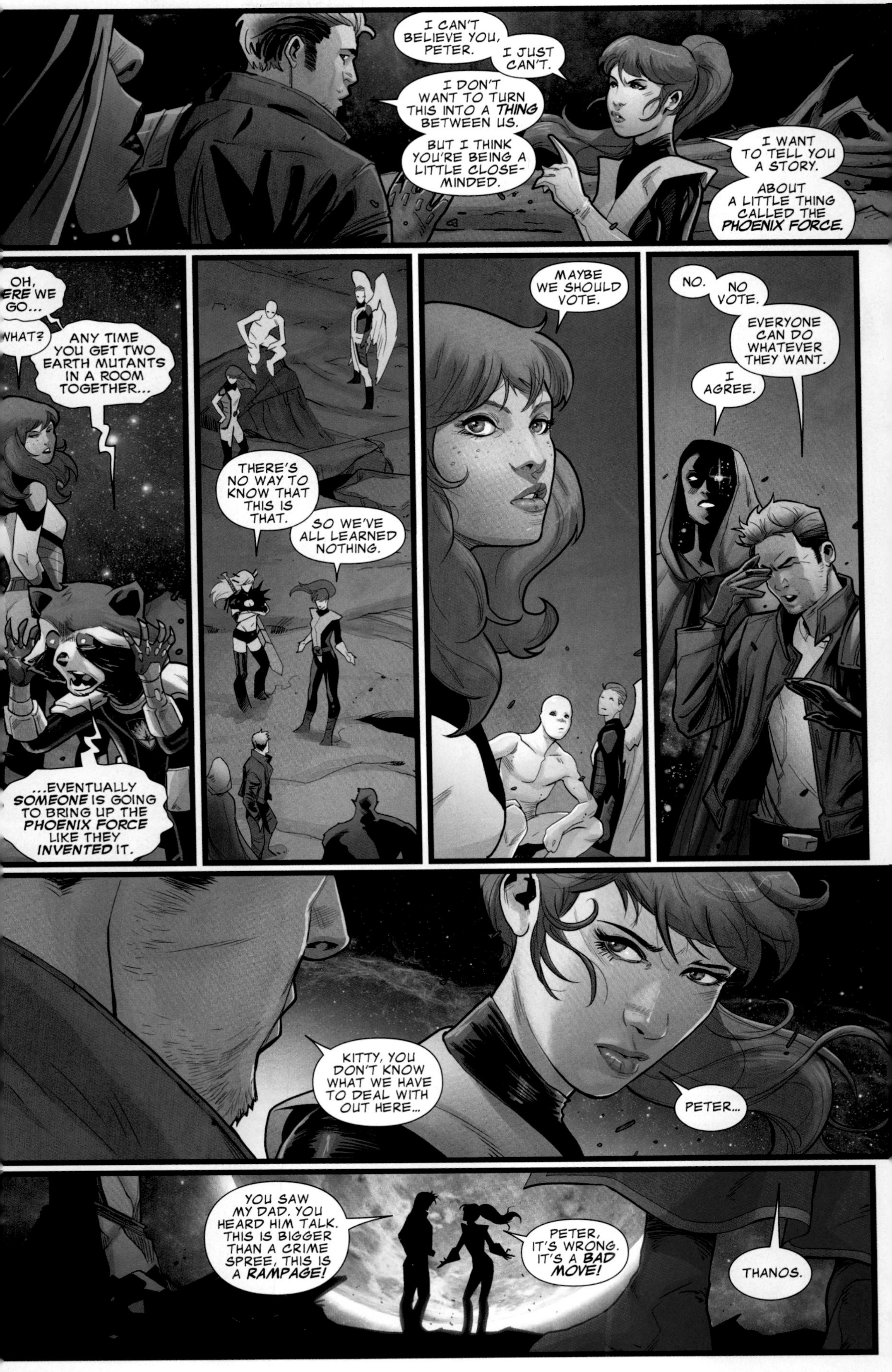
I CAN'T BELIEVE YOU, PETER.
I JUST CAN'T.
I DON'T WANT TO TURN THIS INTO A *THING* BETWEEN US.
BUT I THINK YOU'RE BEING A LITTLE CLOSE-MINDED.
I WANT TO TELL YOU A STORY.
ABOUT A LITTLE THING CALLED THE *PHOENIX FORCE.*
OH, *ERE* WE GO...
WHAT?
ANY TIME YOU GET TWO EARTH MUTANTS IN A ROOM TOGETHER...
...EVENTUALLY *SOMEONE* IS GOING TO BRING UP THE *PHOENIX FORCE* LIKE THEY *INVENTED* IT.
THERE'S NO WAY TO KNOW THAT THIS IS THAT.
SO WE'VE ALL LEARNED NOTHING.
MAYBE WE SHOULD VOTE.
NO.
NO VOTE.
EVERYONE CAN DO WHATEVER THEY WANT.
I AGREE.
KITTY, YOU DON'T KNOW WHAT WE HAVE TO DEAL WITH OUT HERE...
PETER...
YOU SAW MY DAD. YOU HEARD HIM TALK. THIS IS BIGGER THAN A CRIME SPREE, THIS IS A *RAMPAGE!*
PETER, IT'S WRONG. IT'S A *BAD MOVE!*
THANOS.

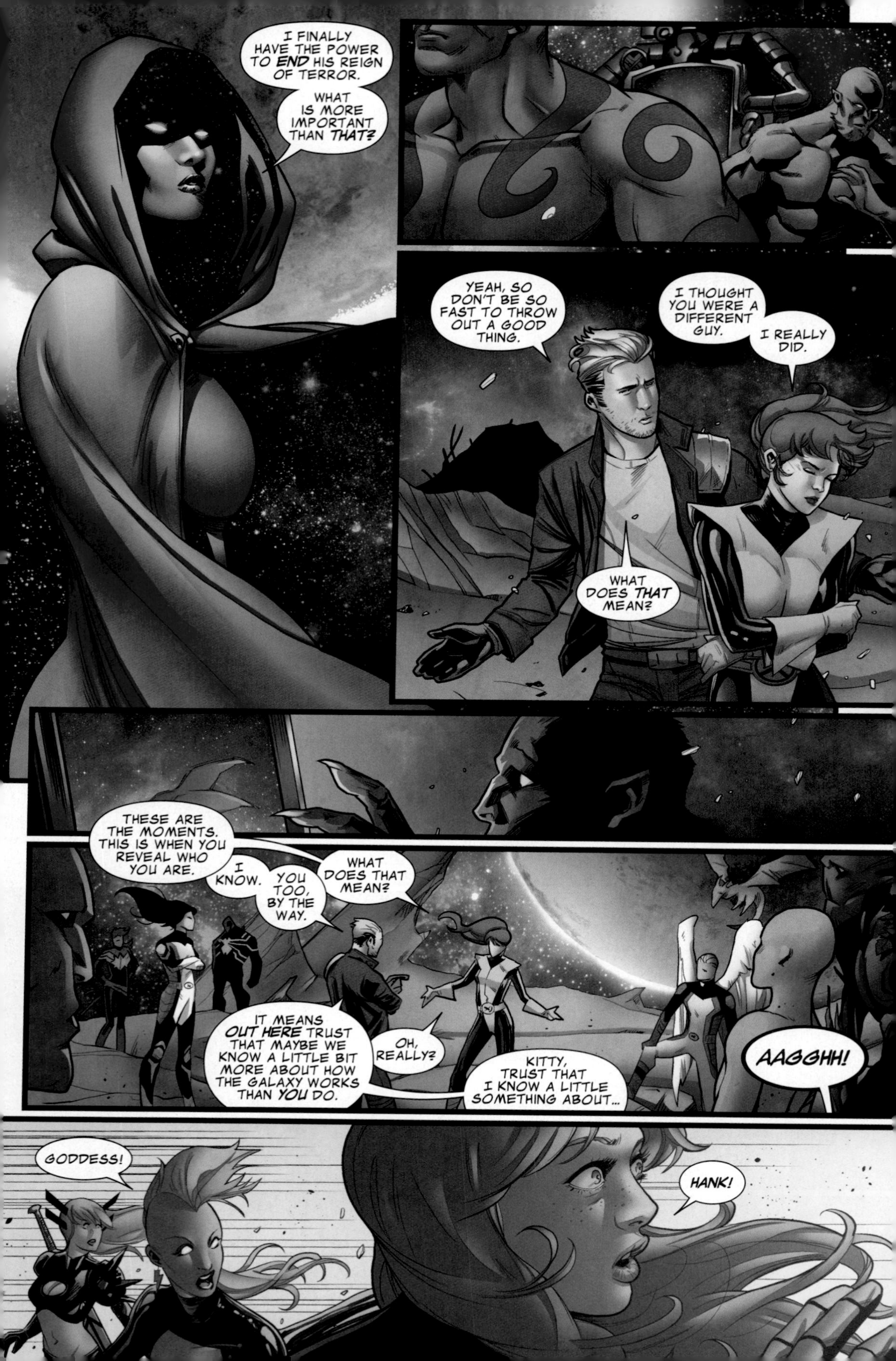
I FINALLY HAVE THE POWER TO END HIS REIGN OF TERROR.
WHAT IS MORE IMPORTANT THAN THAT?
YEAH, SO DON'T BE SO FAST TO THROW OUT A GOOD THING.
I THOUGHT YOU WERE A DIFFERENT GUY.
I REALLY DID.
WHAT DOES THAT MEAN?
THESE ARE THE MOMENTS. THIS IS WHEN YOU REVEAL WHO YOU ARE.
I KNOW.
YOU TOO, BY THE WAY.
WHAT DOES THAT MEAN?
IT MEANS OUT HERE TRUST THAT MAYBE WE KNOW A LITTLE BIT MORE ABOUT HOW THE GALAXY WORKS THAN YOU DO.
OH, REALLY?
KITTY, TRUST THAT I KNOW A LITTLE SOMETHING ABOUT...
AAGGHH!
GODDESS!
HANK!

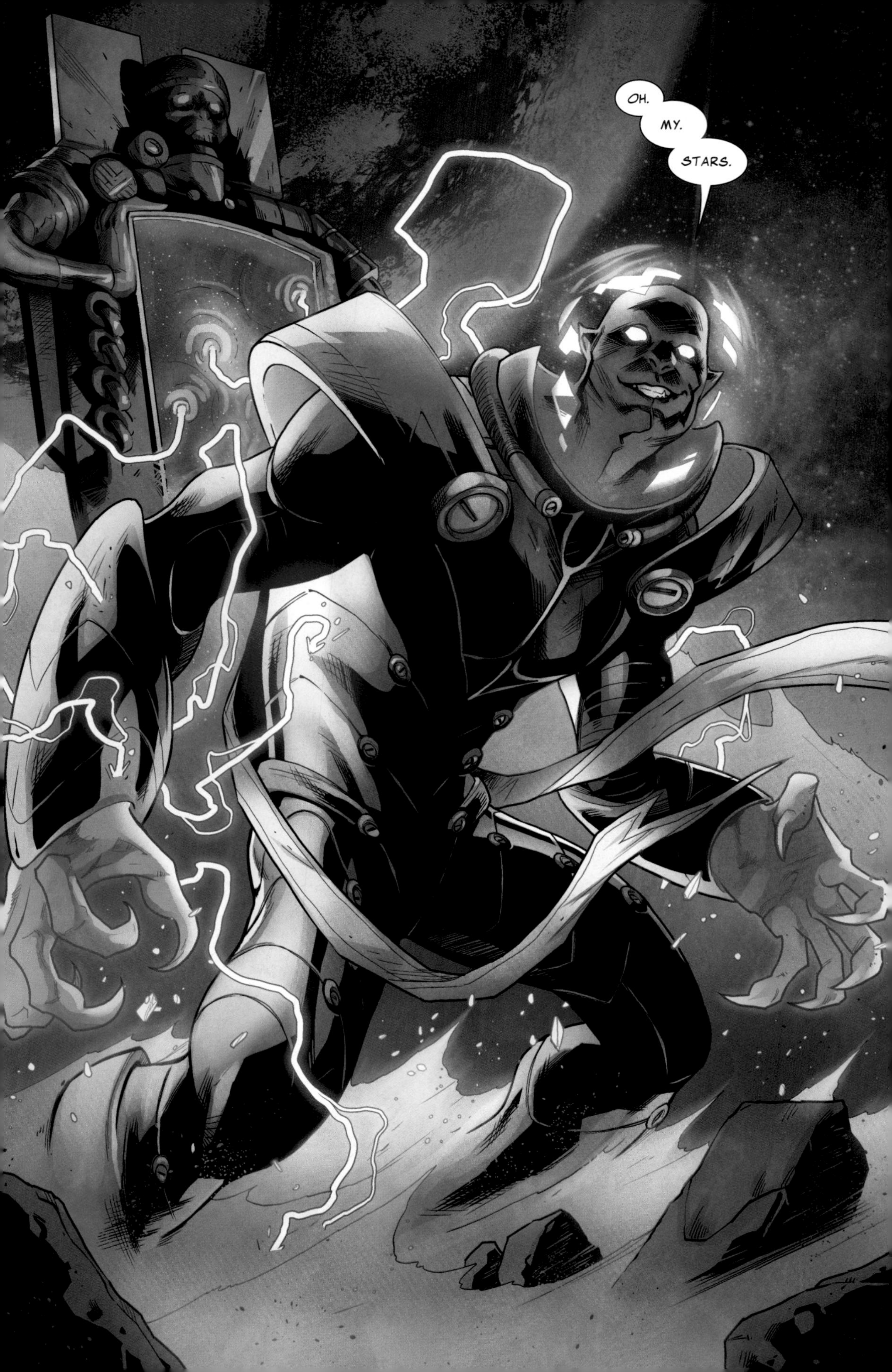
OH.
MY.
STARS.

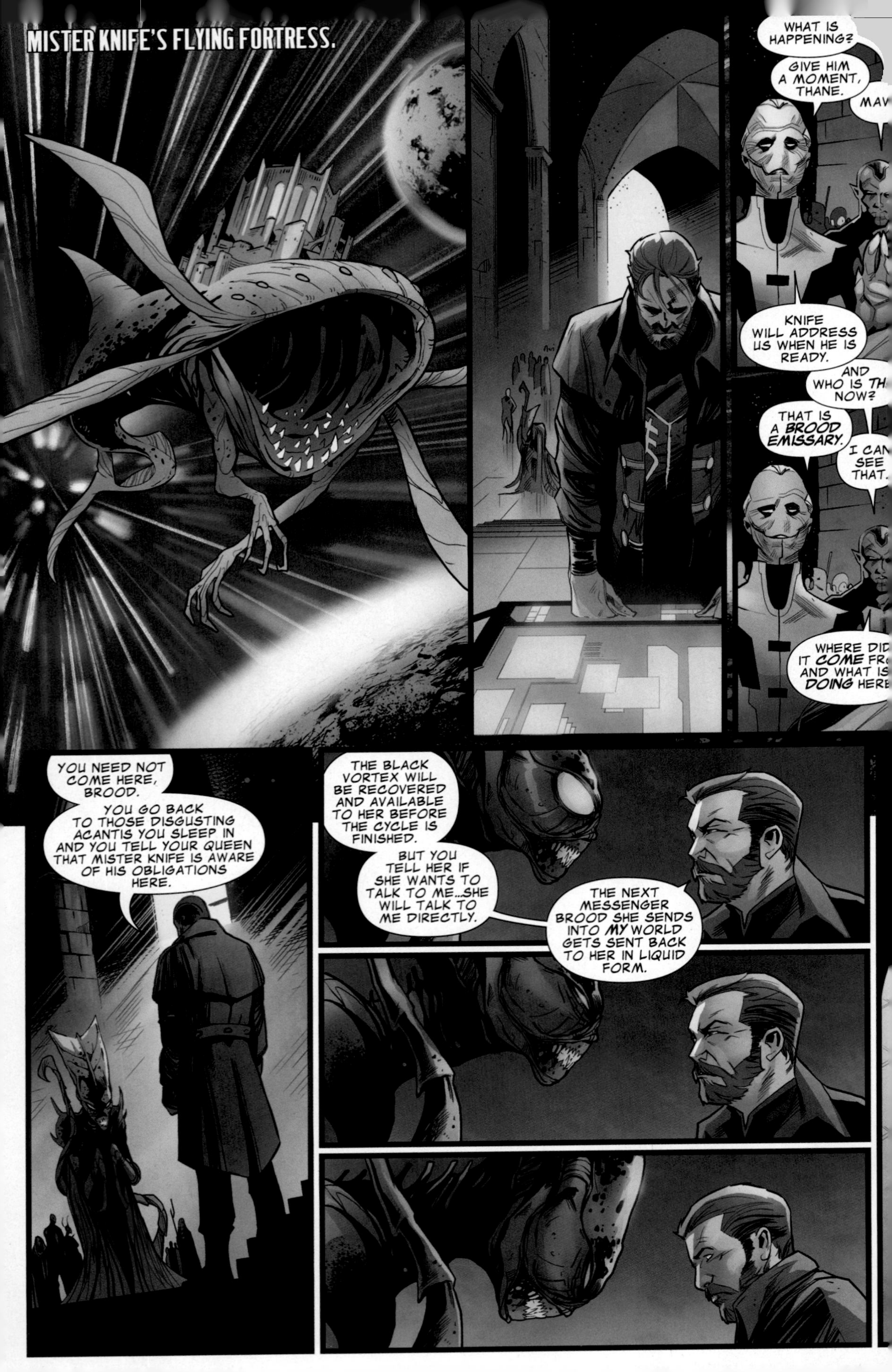
MISTER KNIFE'S FLYING FORTRESS.
WHAT IS HAPPENING?
GIVE HIM A MOMENT, THANE.
MAV
KNIFE WILL ADDRESS US WHEN HE IS READY.
AND WHO IS TH NOW?
THAT IS A BROOD EMISSARY.
I CAN SEE THAT.
WHERE DID IT COME FR AND WHAT IS DOING HERE
YOU NEED NOT COME HERE, BROOD.
YOU GO BACK TO THOSE DISGUSTING ACANTIS YOU SLEEP IN AND YOU TELL YOUR QUEEN THAT MISTER KNIFE IS AWARE OF HIS OBLIGATIONS HERE.
THE BLACK VORTEX WILL BE RECOVERED AND AVAILABLE TO HER BEFORE THE CYCLE IS FINISHED.
BUT YOU TELL HER IF SHE WANTS TO TALK TO ME...SHE WILL TALK TO ME DIRECTLY.
THE NEXT MESSENGER BROOD SHE SENDS INTO MY WORLD GETS SENT BACK TO HER IN LIQUID FORM.

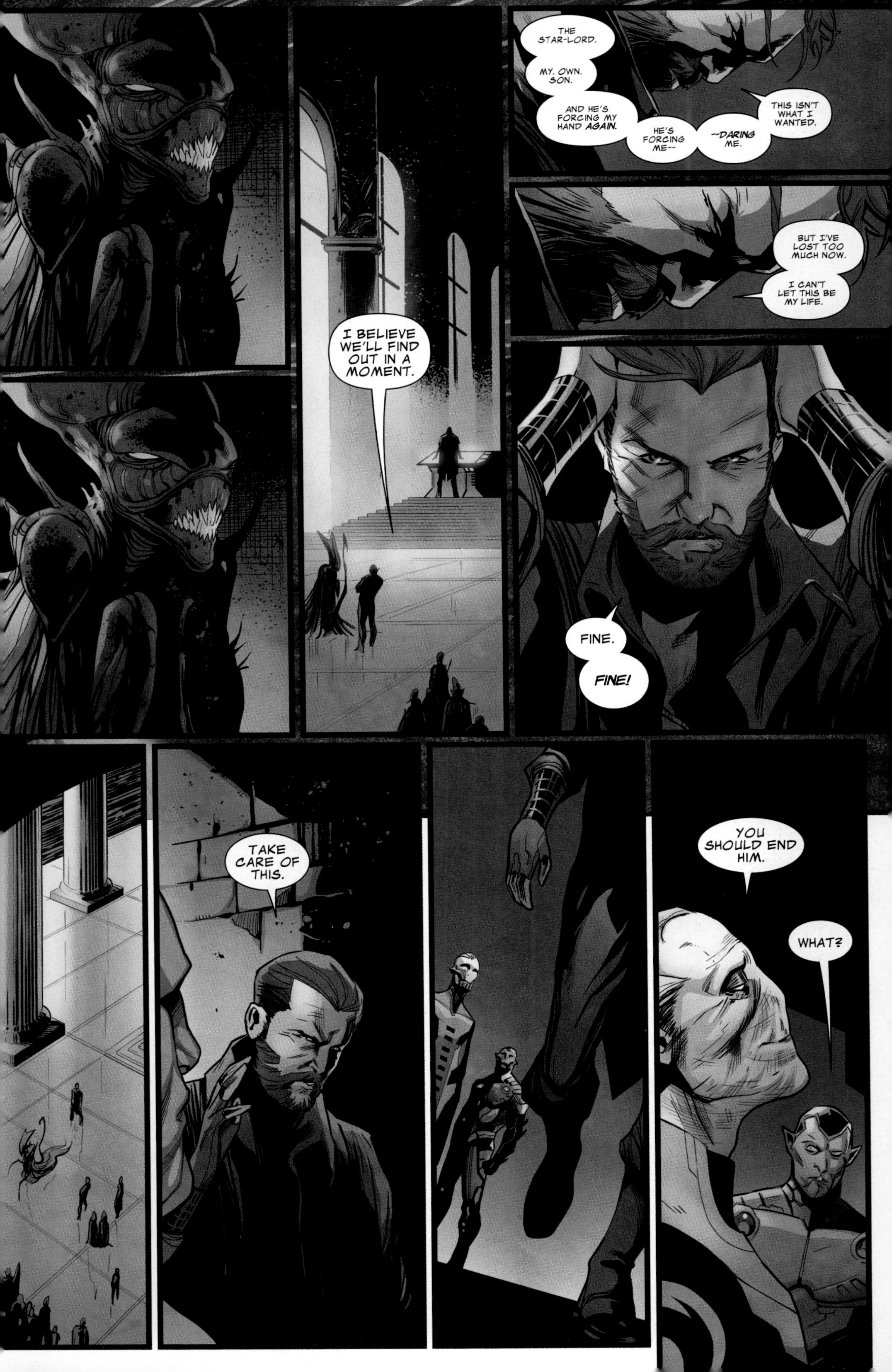
I BELIEVE WE'LL FIND OUT IN A MOMENT.
THE STAR-LORD.
MY. OWN. SON.
AND HE'S FORCING MY HAND AGAIN.
HE'S FORCING ME--
--DARING ME.
THIS ISN'T WHAT I WANTED.
BUT I'VE LOST TOO MUCH NOW.
I CAN'T LET THIS BE MY LIFE.
FINE.
FINE!
TAKE CARE OF THIS.
YOU SHOULD END HIM.
WHAT?

YOU HEARD ME. WE ARE BUILDING SOMETHING HERE.

SOMETHING TO FEAR. SOMETHING OF MATTER.

OF IMPORT.

WE ARE CHANGING THE BALANCE OF POWER IN THE GALAXY AND THAT IS SOMETHING THIS GALAXY DESPERATELY NEEDS.

AND HE, THAT MAN, WITH EVERY STEP FORWARD IS REVEALING THAT HE IS NOT THE MAN TO TAKE US THERE.

SO WE KILL HIM?

THAT'S NOT NICE.

YOUR FATHER IS A MAD TITAN. NO ONE WOULD ARGUE THAT.

BUT IF HE HAD THE VISION AND CLARITY YOU HAVE...HE WOULD OWN THIS GALAXY.

HE WOULD ABSOLUTELY OWN IT.

THANE... YOU HAVE ALL OF YOUR FATHER'S STRENGTH OF SPIRIT AND NONE OF HIS DEFECTS.

YOU...CAN LEAD.

GO BACK TO WHEREVER YOU DISAPPEAR TO.

YOU WILL NOT SPEAK THE WORDS T ME AGAIN

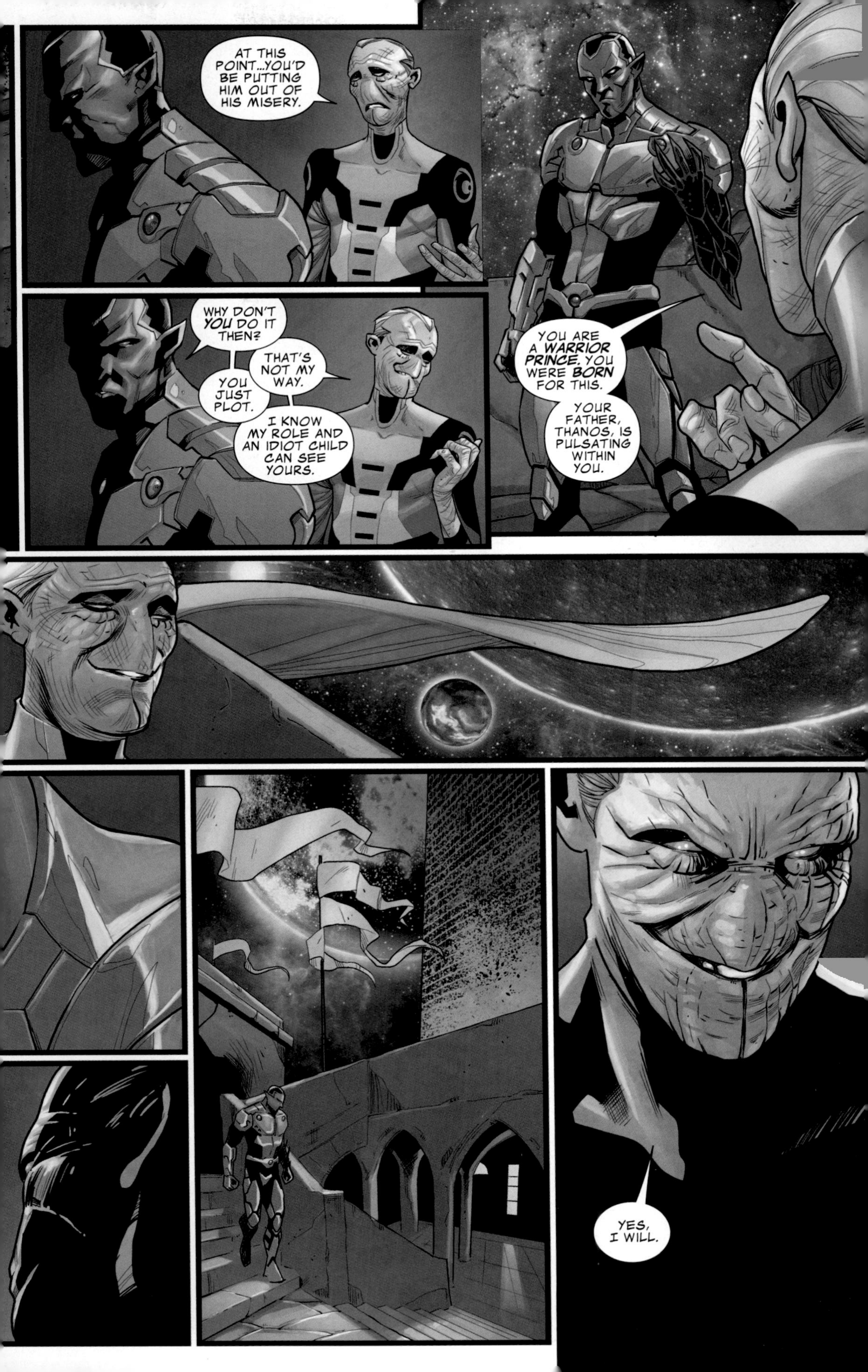
AT THIS POINT...YOU'D BE PUTTING HIM OUT OF HIS MISERY.
WHY DON'T YOU DO IT THEN?
THAT'S NOT MY WAY.
YOU JUST PLOT.
I KNOW MY ROLE AND AN IDIOT CHILD CAN SEE YOURS.
YOU ARE A WARRIOR PRINCE. YOU WERE BORN FOR THIS.
YOUR FATHER, THANOS, IS PULSATING WITHIN YOU.
YES, I WILL.

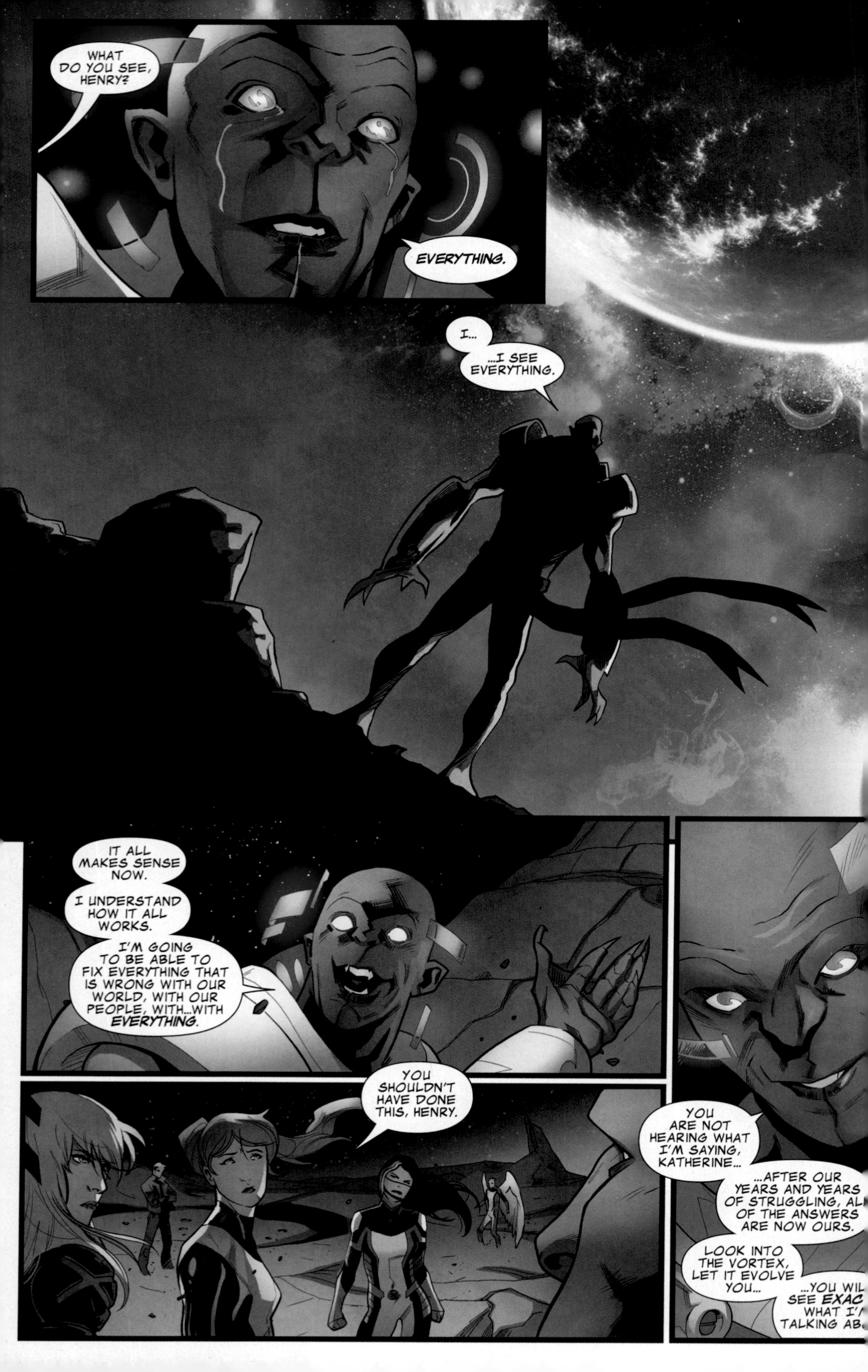
WHAT DO YOU SEE, HENRY?
EVERYTHING.
I...
...I SEE EVERYTHING.
IT ALL MAKES SENSE NOW.
I UNDERSTAND HOW IT ALL WORKS.
I'M GOING TO BE ABLE TO FIX EVERYTHING THAT IS WRONG WITH OUR WORLD, WITH OUR PEOPLE, WITH...WITH *EVERYTHING*.
YOU SHOULDN'T HAVE DONE THIS, HENRY.
YOU ARE NOT HEARING WHAT I'M SAYING, KATHERINE...
...AFTER OUR YEARS AND YEARS OF STRUGGLING, AL
OF THE ANSWERS ARE NOW OURS.
LOOK INTO THE VORTEX, LET IT EVOLVE YOU...
...YOU WIL
SEE *EXAC*
WHAT I'
TALKING AB

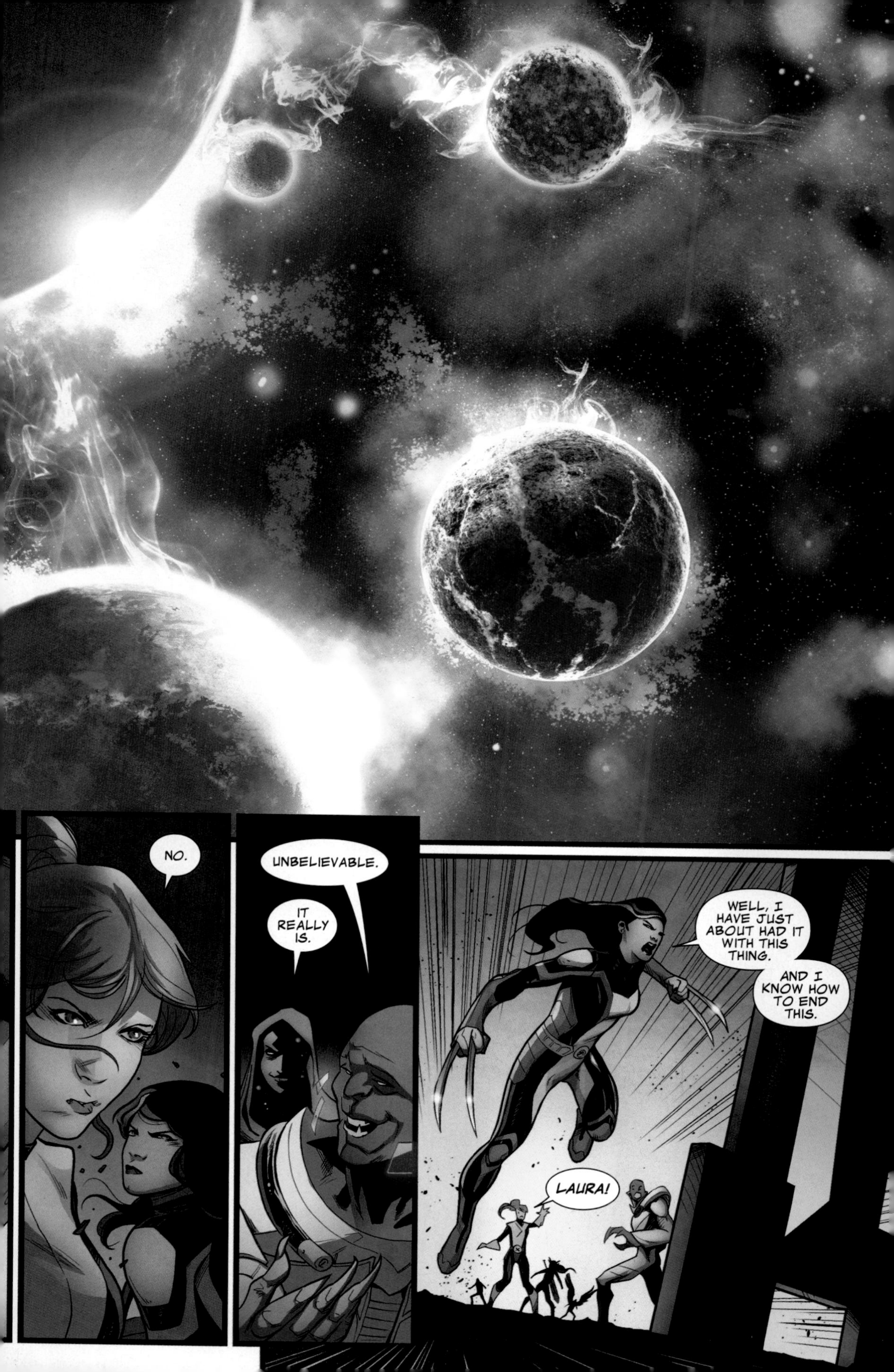
NO.
UNBELIEVABLE.
IT REALLY IS.
WELL, I HAVE JUST ABOUT HAD IT WITH THIS THING.
AND I KNOW HOW TO END THIS.
LAURA!

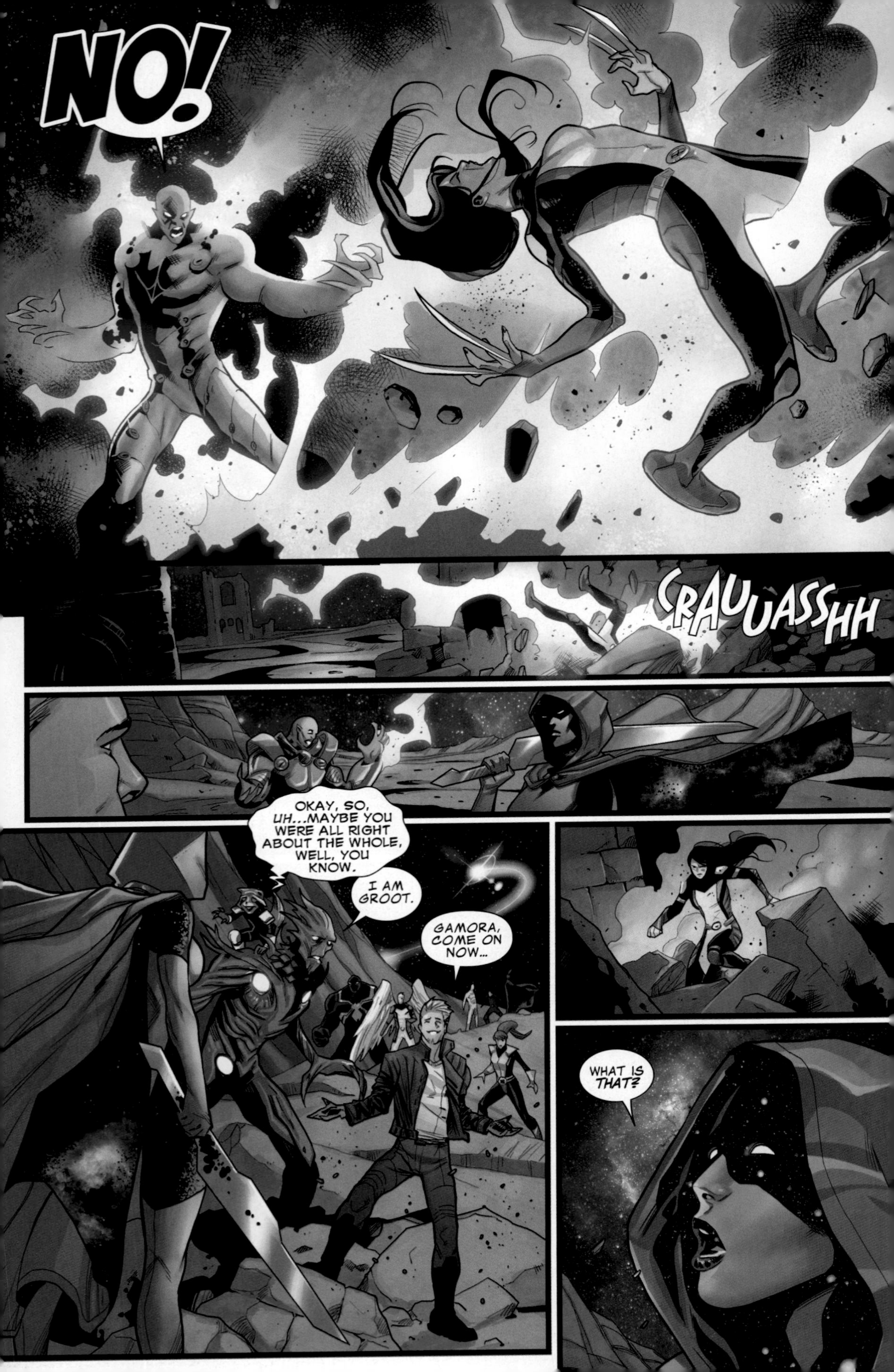
NO!
CRAUUASSHH
OKAY, SO, UH...MAYBE YOU WERE ALL RIGHT ABOUT THE WHOLE, WELL, YOU KNOW.
I AM GROOT.
GAMORA, COME ON NOW...
WHAT IS THAT?

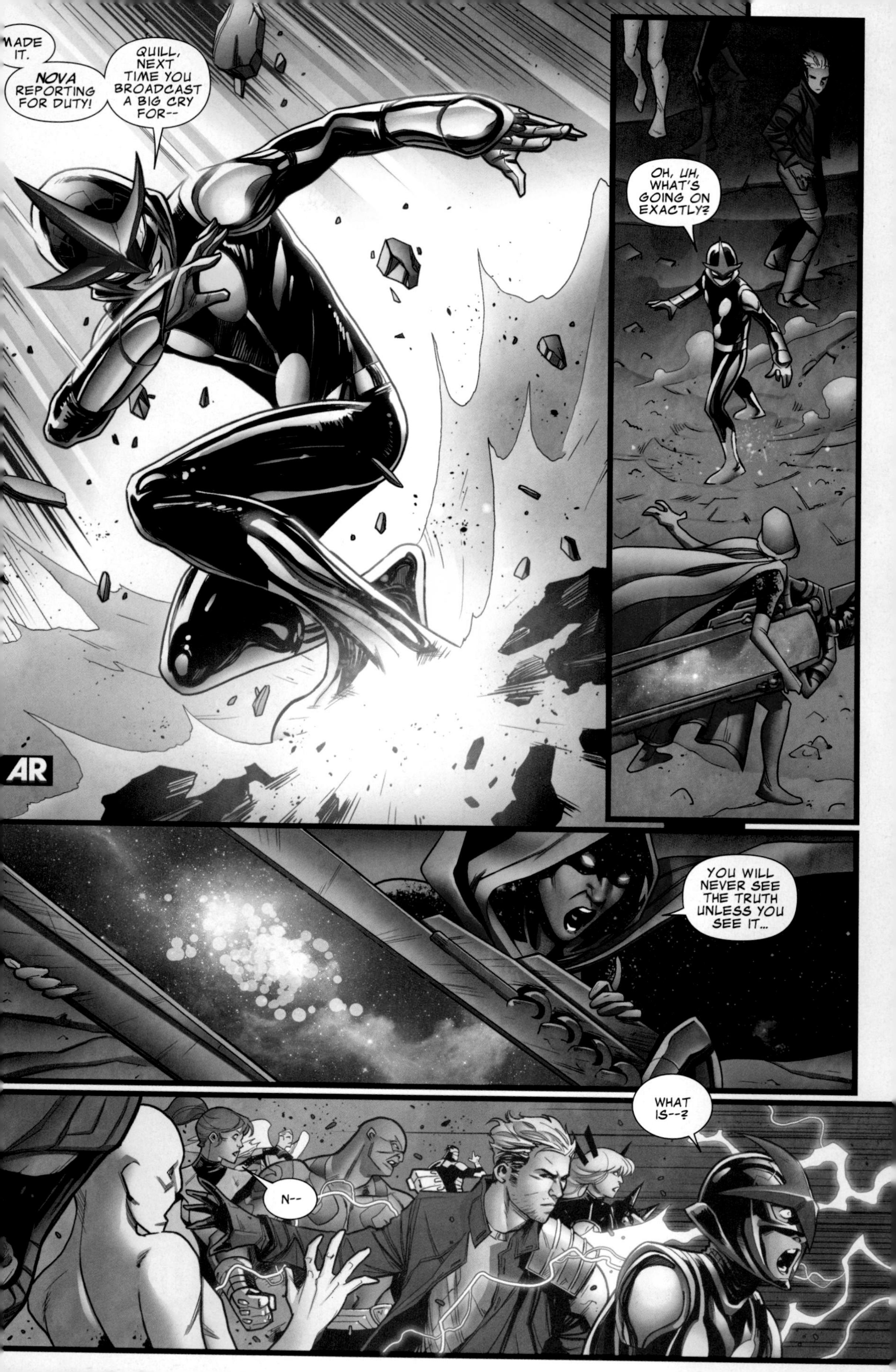
MADE IT. NOVA REPORTING FOR DUTY!
QUILL, NEXT TIME YOU BROADCAST A BIG CRY FOR--
AR
OH, UH, WHAT'S GOING ON EXACTLY?
YOU WILL NEVER SEE THE TRUTH UNLESS YOU SEE IT...
WHAT IS--?
N--

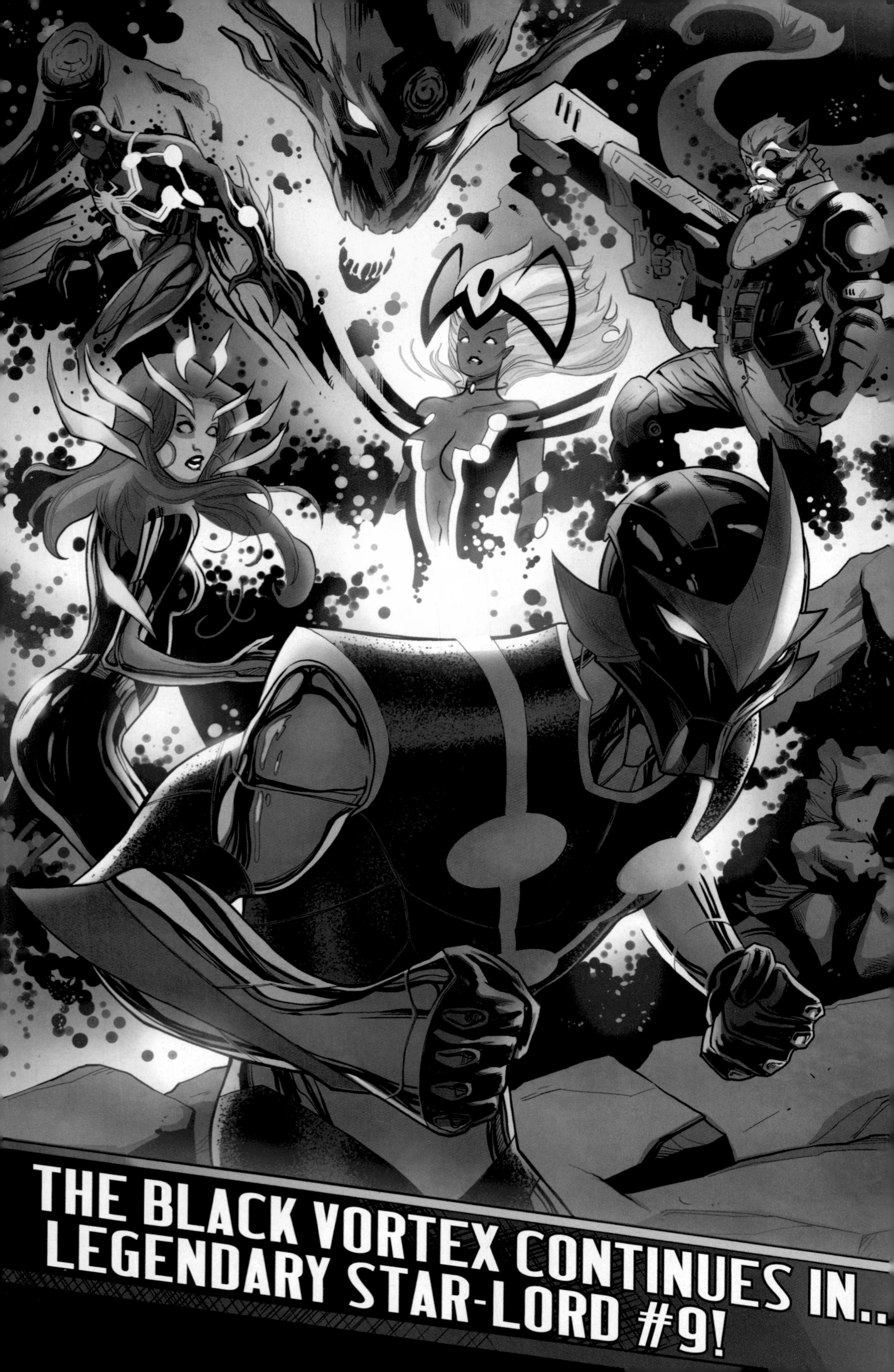
THE BLACK VORTEX CONTINUES IN...
LEGENDARY STAR-LORD #9!

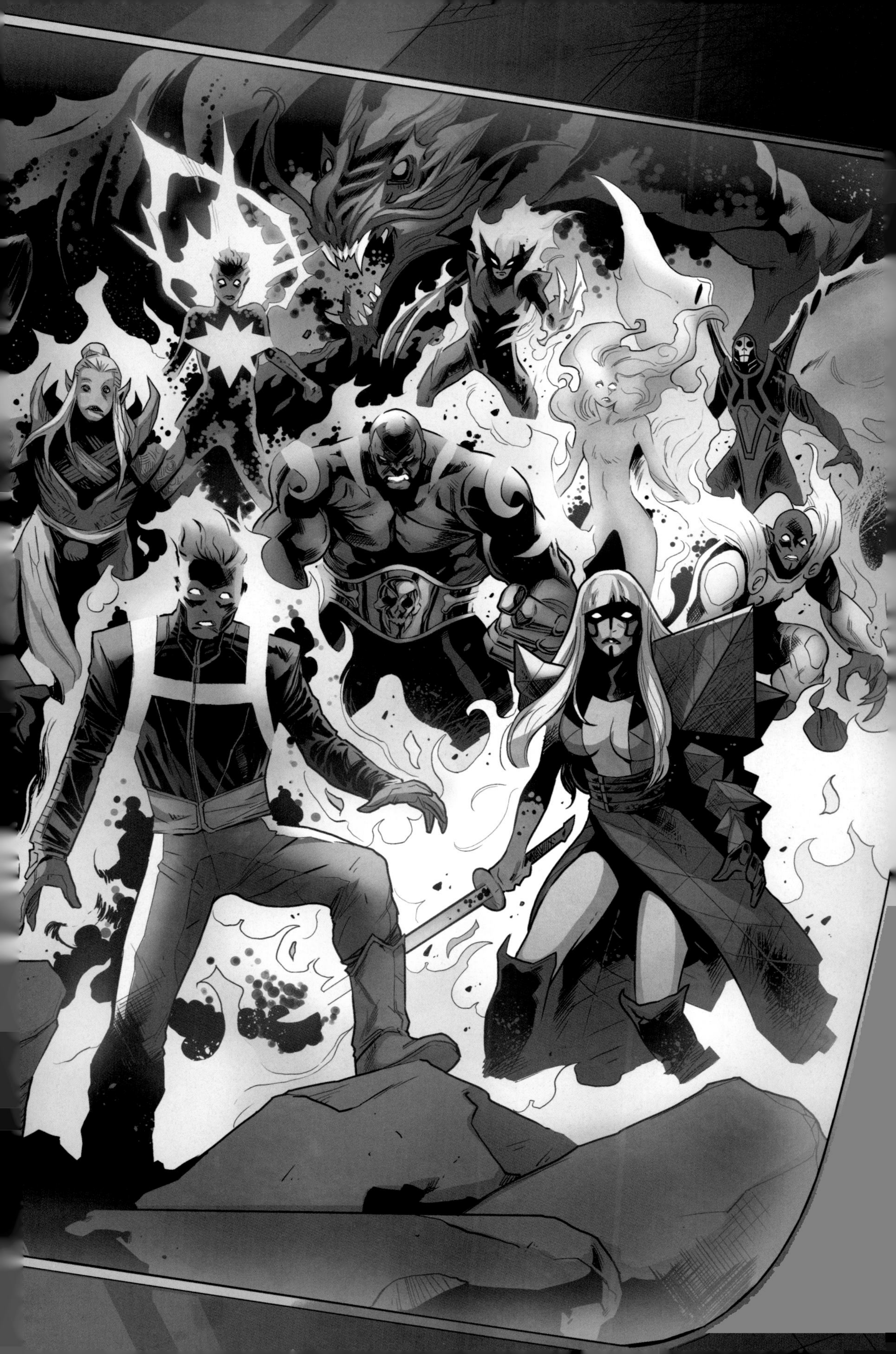

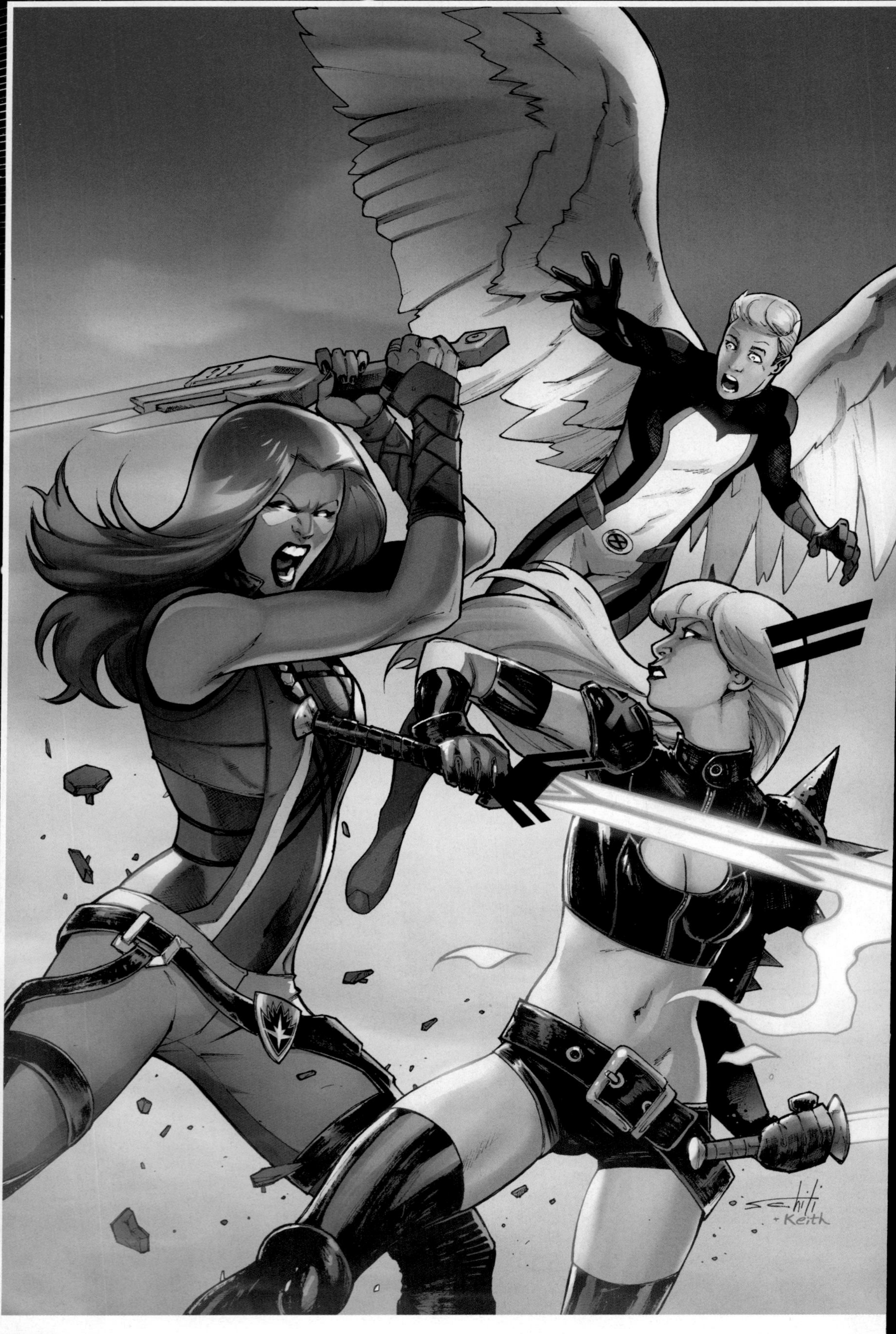
Schiti
+Keith

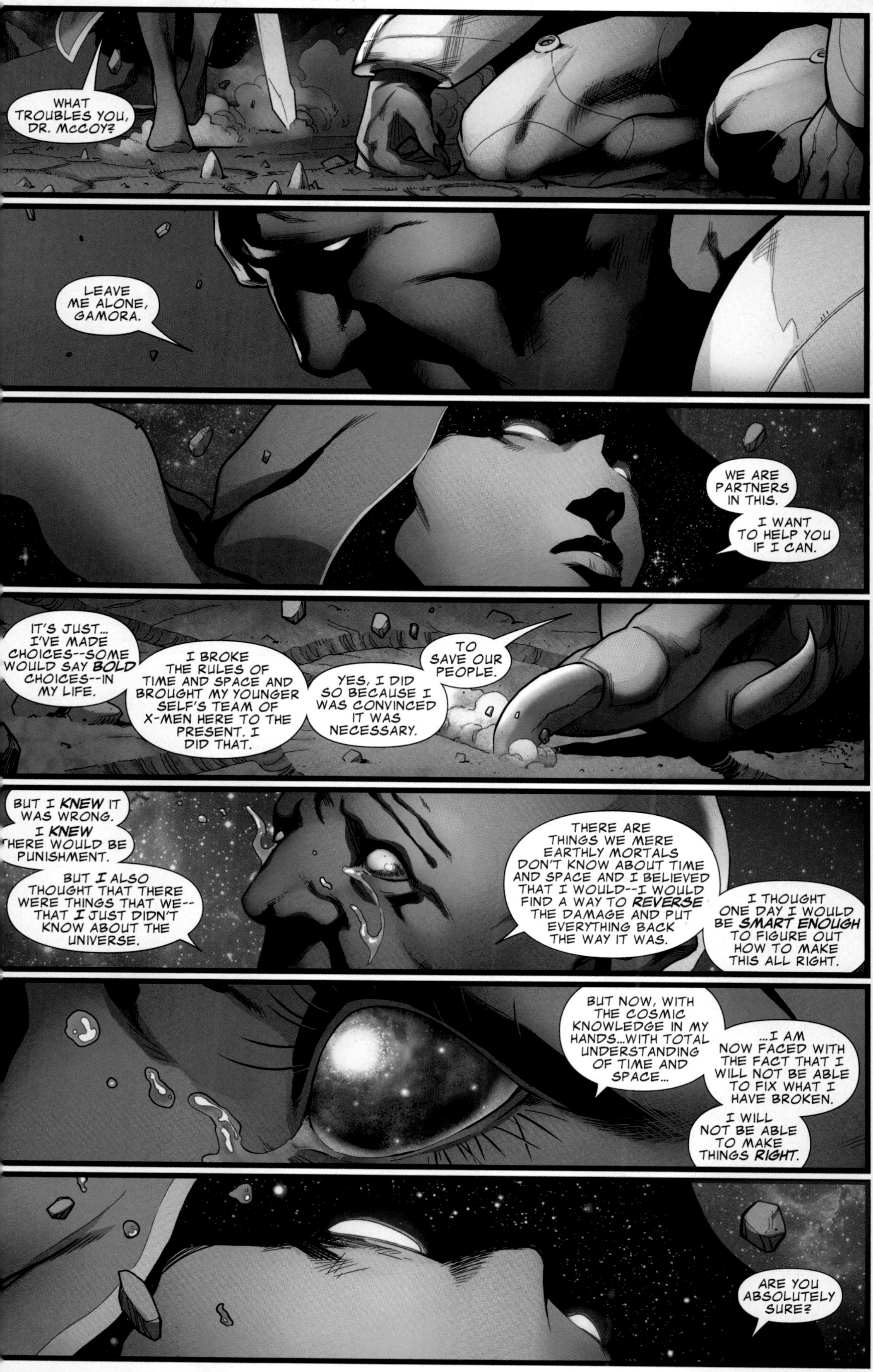
WHAT TROUBLES YOU, DR. McCOY?
LEAVE ME ALONE, GAMORA.
WE ARE PARTNERS IN THIS.
I WANT TO HELP YOU IF I CAN.
IT'S JUST... I'VE MADE CHOICES--SOME WOULD SAY BOLD CHOICES--IN MY LIFE.
I BROKE THE RULES OF TIME AND SPACE AND BROUGHT MY YOUNGER SELF'S TEAM OF X-MEN HERE TO THE PRESENT. I DID THAT.
YES, I DID SO BECAUSE I WAS CONVINCED IT WAS NECESSARY.
TO SAVE OUR PEOPLE.
BUT I KNEW IT WAS WRONG.
I KNEW THERE WOULD BE PUNISHMENT.
BUT I ALSO THOUGHT THAT THERE WERE THINGS THAT WE-- THAT I JUST DIDN'T KNOW ABOUT THE UNIVERSE.
THERE ARE THINGS WE MERE EARTHLY MORTALS DON'T KNOW ABOUT TIME AND SPACE AND I BELIEVED THAT I WOULD--I WOULD FIND A WAY TO REVERSE THE DAMAGE AND PUT EVERYTHING BACK THE WAY IT WAS.
I THOUGHT ONE DAY I WOULD BE SMART ENOUGH TO FIGURE OUT HOW TO MAKE THIS ALL RIGHT.
BUT NOW, WITH THE COSMIC KNOWLEDGE IN MY HANDS...WITH TOTAL UNDERSTANDING OF TIME AND SPACE...
...I AM NOW FACED WITH THE FACT THAT I WILL NOT BE ABLE TO FIX WHAT I HAVE BROKEN.
I WILL NOT BE ABLE TO MAKE THINGS RIGHT.
ARE YOU ABSOLUTELY SURE?

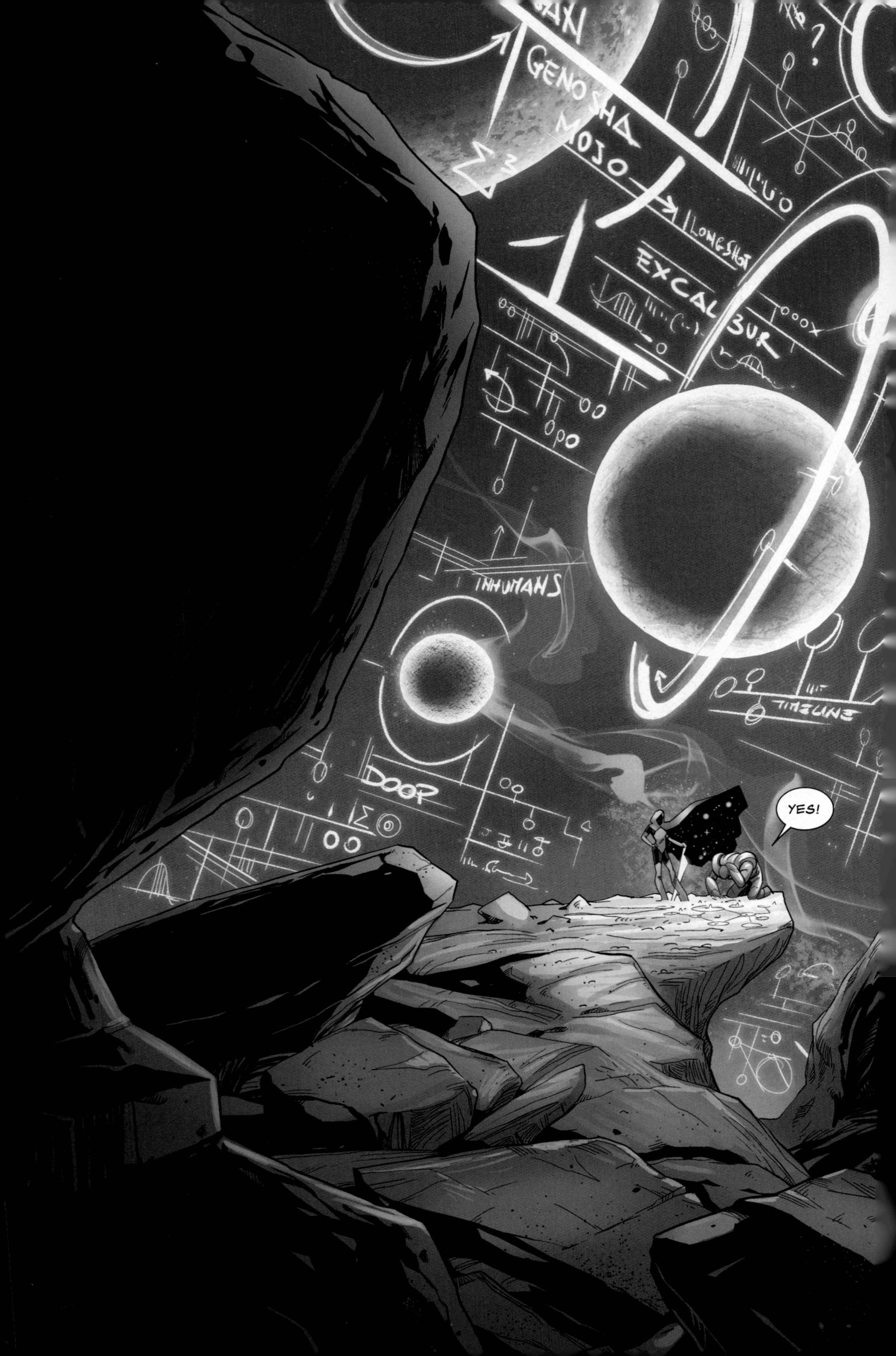
GENOSHA
MOJO
LONGSHOT
EXCALIBUR
INHUMANS
TIMELINE
DOOP
YES!

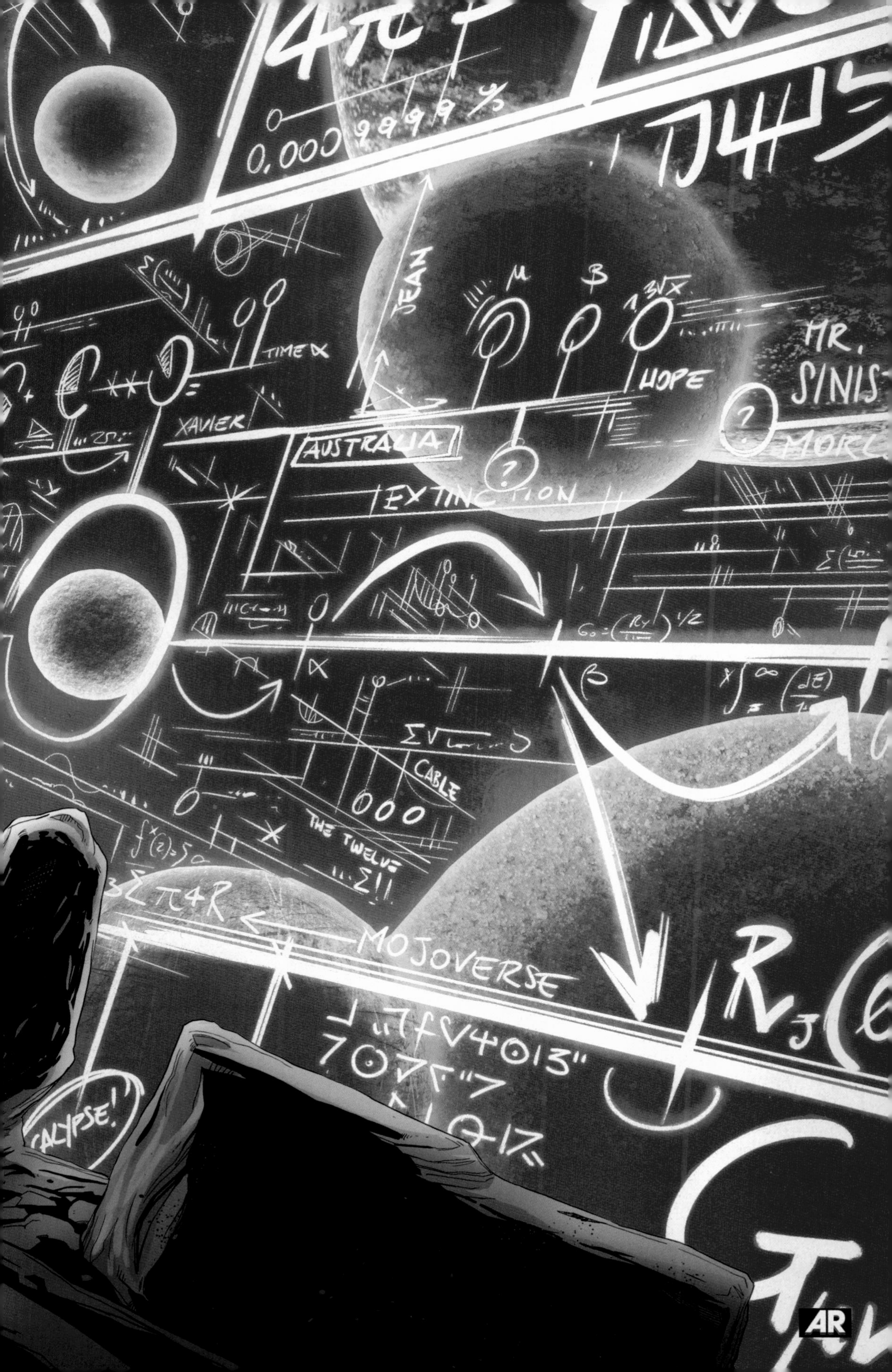
0,000 9999 %
JEAN
μ
β
TIME
XAVIER
HOPE
MR. SINIS-
AUSTRALIA
EXTINCTION
CABLE
THE TWELVE
MOJOVERSE
CALYPSE!

GUARDIANS OF THE GALAXY & X-MEN

THE BLACK VORTEX

CHAPTER 7

Previously in *The Black Vortex*. . .

Billions of years ago, an ancient race named the Viscardi were gifted an object of immense cosmic power by a Celestial. This artifact, known as the Black Vortex, transformed the user, imbuing them with cosmic energy. However, the power of this object caused the Viscardi to turn on each other, annihilating their own race from within.

When Mister Knife, a.k.a. J'Son, Peter Quill's father, obtained the Black Vortex, Peter and Kitty Pryde stole the artifact and recruited the Guardians of the Galaxy and the X-Men for help. Gamora, the elder Beast, and Angel chose to submit to the Vortex and the three cosmically enhanced heroes took the artifact and left, intending to reshape the universe in their image. But when Ronan the Accuser stole the Vortex from them, they retaliated by assaulting the Kree homeworld, Hala. Fearing total annihilation, Ronan used the Vortex to enhance himself against the Supreme Intelligence's wishes. As Ronan used his new powers to hold off the three enhanced heroes, the elder Beast was horrified to discover that he could not fix the damage he had done to space-time and fled with the other two in tow.

Meanwhile, the Guardians and X-Men escaped Knife's henchmen and were joined by the young Cyclops and his father, Corsair. Receiving multiple distress signals, they split into three groups. Cyclops, Iceman, and Groot stayed behind to delay the Slaughter Lords, but were quickly overpowered and are now prisoners of Mister Knife!

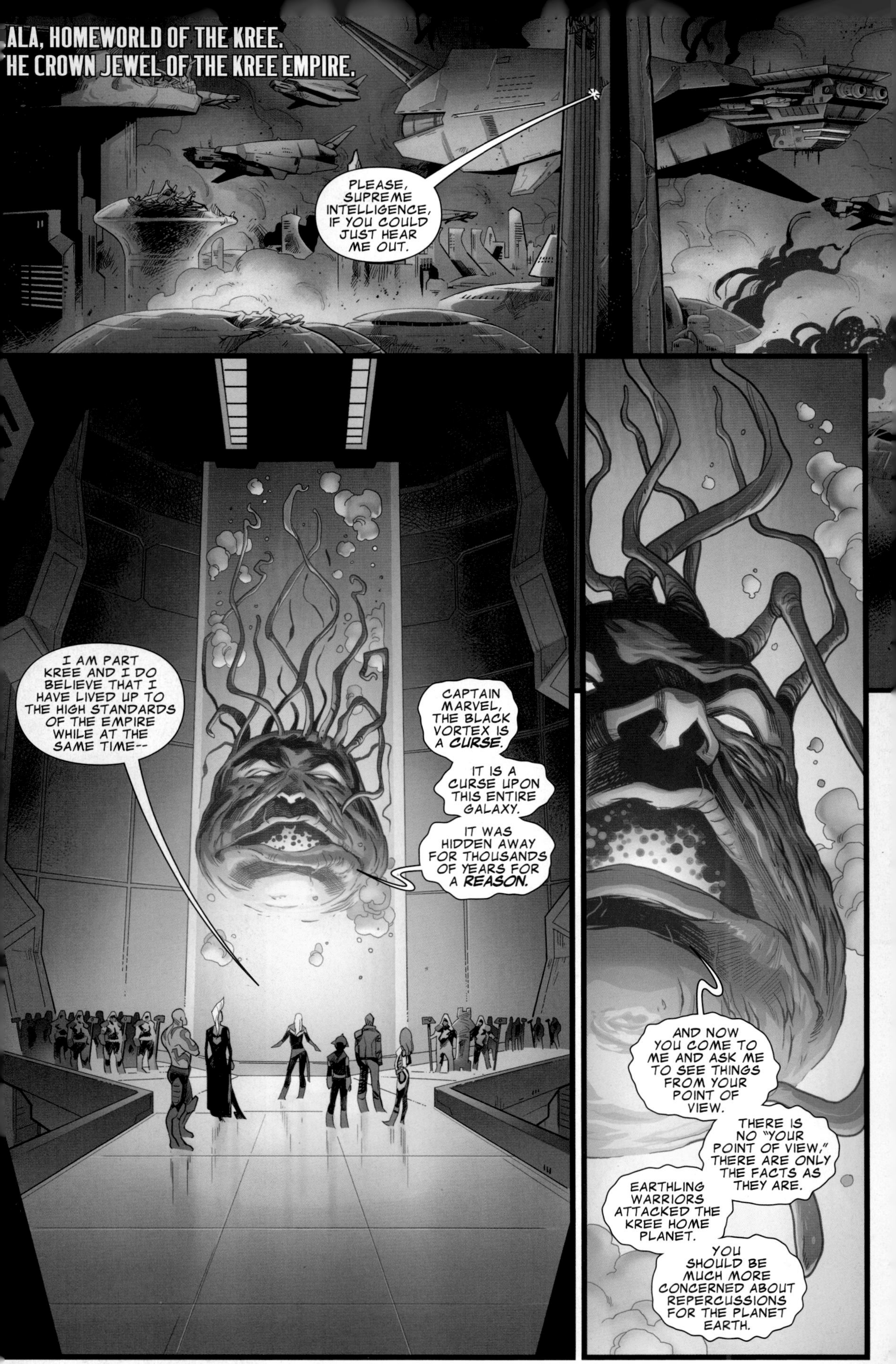

.ALA, HOMEWORLD OF THE KREE.
.HE CROWN JEWEL OF THE KREE EMPIRE.
PLEASE, SUPREME INTELLIGENCE, IF YOU COULD JUST HEAR ME OUT.
I AM PART KREE AND I DO BELIEVE THAT I HAVE LIVED UP TO THE HIGH STANDARDS OF THE EMPIRE WHILE AT THE SAME TIME--
CAPTAIN MARVEL, THE BLACK VORTEX IS A CURSE.
IT IS A CURSE UPON THIS ENTIRE GALAXY.
IT WAS HIDDEN AWAY FOR THOUSANDS OF YEARS FOR A REASON.
AND NOW YOU COME TO ME AND ASK ME TO SEE THINGS FROM YOUR POINT OF VIEW.
THERE IS NO "YOUR POINT OF VIEW," THERE ARE ONLY THE FACTS AS THEY ARE.
EARTHLING WARRIORS ATTACKED THE KREE HOME PLANET.
YOU SHOULD BE MUCH MORE CONCERNED ABOUT REPERCUSSIONS FOR THE PLANET EARTH.

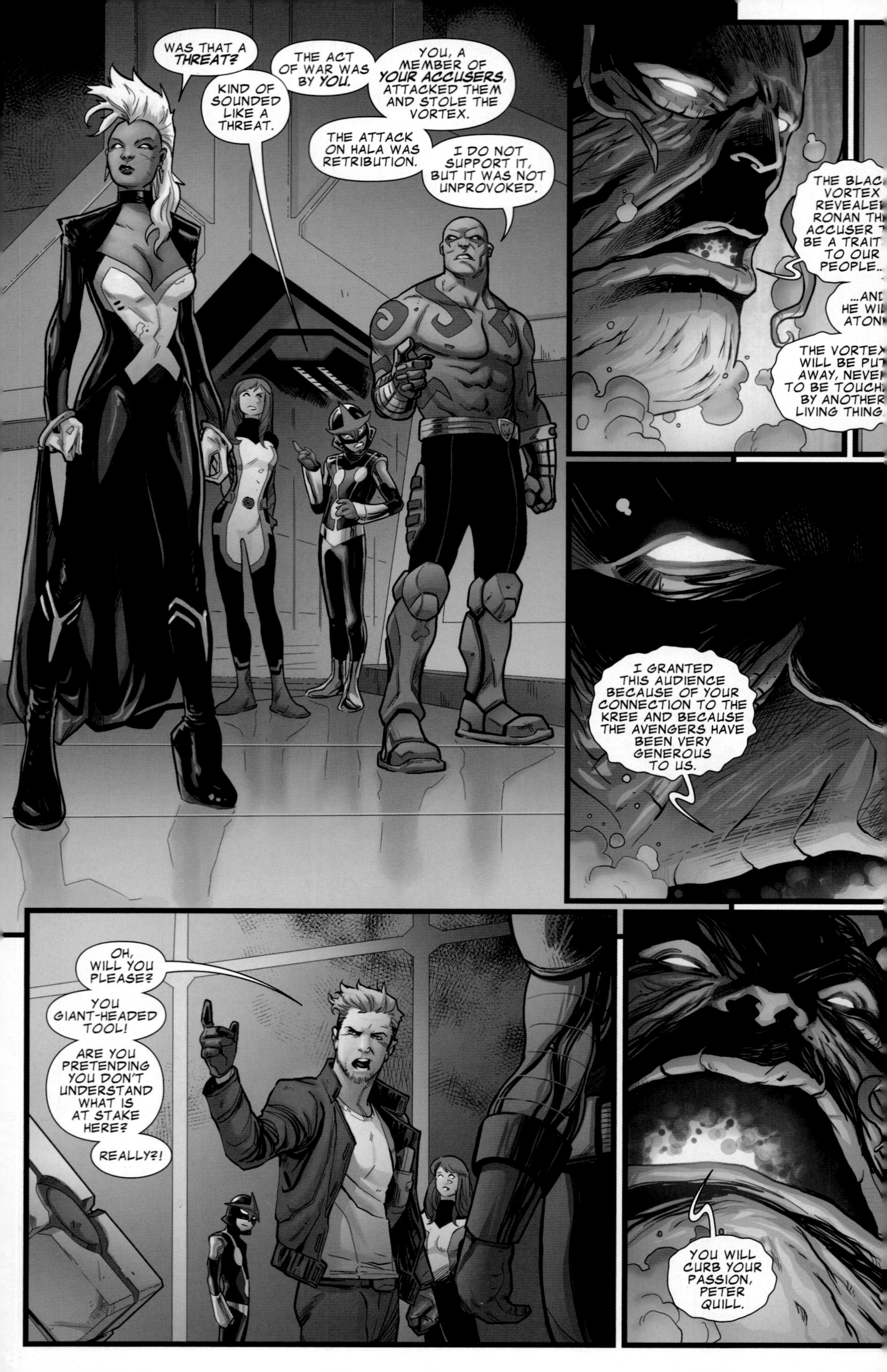
WAS THAT A THREAT?
KIND OF SOUNDED LIKE A THREAT.
THE ACT OF WAR WAS BY YOU.
YOU, A MEMBER OF YOUR ACCUSERS, ATTACKED THEM AND STOLE THE VORTEX.
THE ATTACK ON HALA WAS RETRIBUTION.
I DO NOT SUPPORT IT, BUT IT WAS NOT UNPROVOKED.
THE BLAC VORTEX REVEALE RONAN TH ACCUSER T BE A TRAIT TO OUR PEOPLE..
...AND HE WI ATON
THE VORTEX WILL BE PUT AWAY, NEVE TO BE TOUCH BY ANOTHER LIVING THING.
I GRANTED THIS AUDIENCE BECAUSE OF YOUR CONNECTION TO THE KREE AND BECAUSE THE AVENGERS HAVE BEEN VERY GENEROUS TO US.
OH, WILL YOU PLEASE?
YOU GIANT-HEADED TOOL!
ARE YOU PRETENDING YOU DON'T UNDERSTAND WHAT IS AT STAKE HERE?
REALLY?!
YOU WILL CURB YOUR PASSION, PETER QUILL.

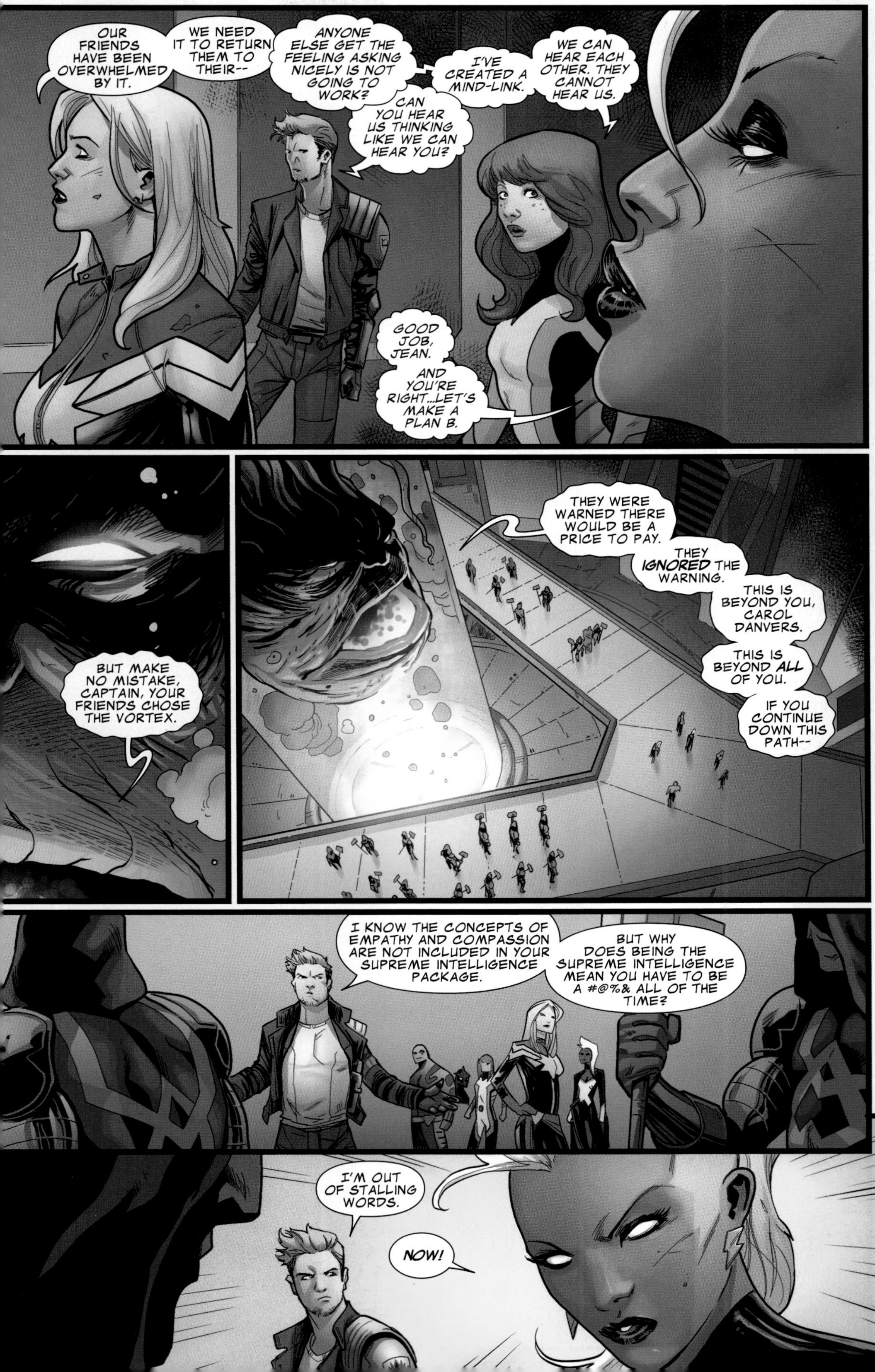
OUR FRIENDS HAVE BEEN OVERWHELMED BY IT.
WE NEED IT TO RETURN THEM TO THEIR--
ANYONE ELSE GET THE FEELING ASKING NICELY IS NOT GOING TO WORK?
I'VE CREATED A MIND-LINK.
WE CAN HEAR EACH OTHER. THEY CANNOT HEAR US.
CAN YOU HEAR US THINKING LIKE WE CAN HEAR YOU?
GOOD JOB, JEAN.
AND YOU'RE RIGHT...LET'S MAKE A PLAN B.
BUT MAKE NO MISTAKE, CAPTAIN. YOUR FRIENDS CHOSE THE VORTEX.
THEY WERE WARNED THERE WOULD BE A PRICE TO PAY.
THEY IGNORED THE WARNING.
THIS IS BEYOND YOU, CAROL DANVERS.
THIS IS BEYOND ALL OF YOU.
IF YOU CONTINUE DOWN THIS PATH--
I KNOW THE CONCEPTS OF EMPATHY AND COMPASSION ARE NOT INCLUDED IN YOUR SUPREME INTELLIGENCE PACKAGE.
BUT WHY DOES BEING THE SUPREME INTELLIGENCE MEAN YOU HAVE TO BE A #@%& ALL OF THE TIME?
I'M OUT OF STALLING WORDS.
NOW!

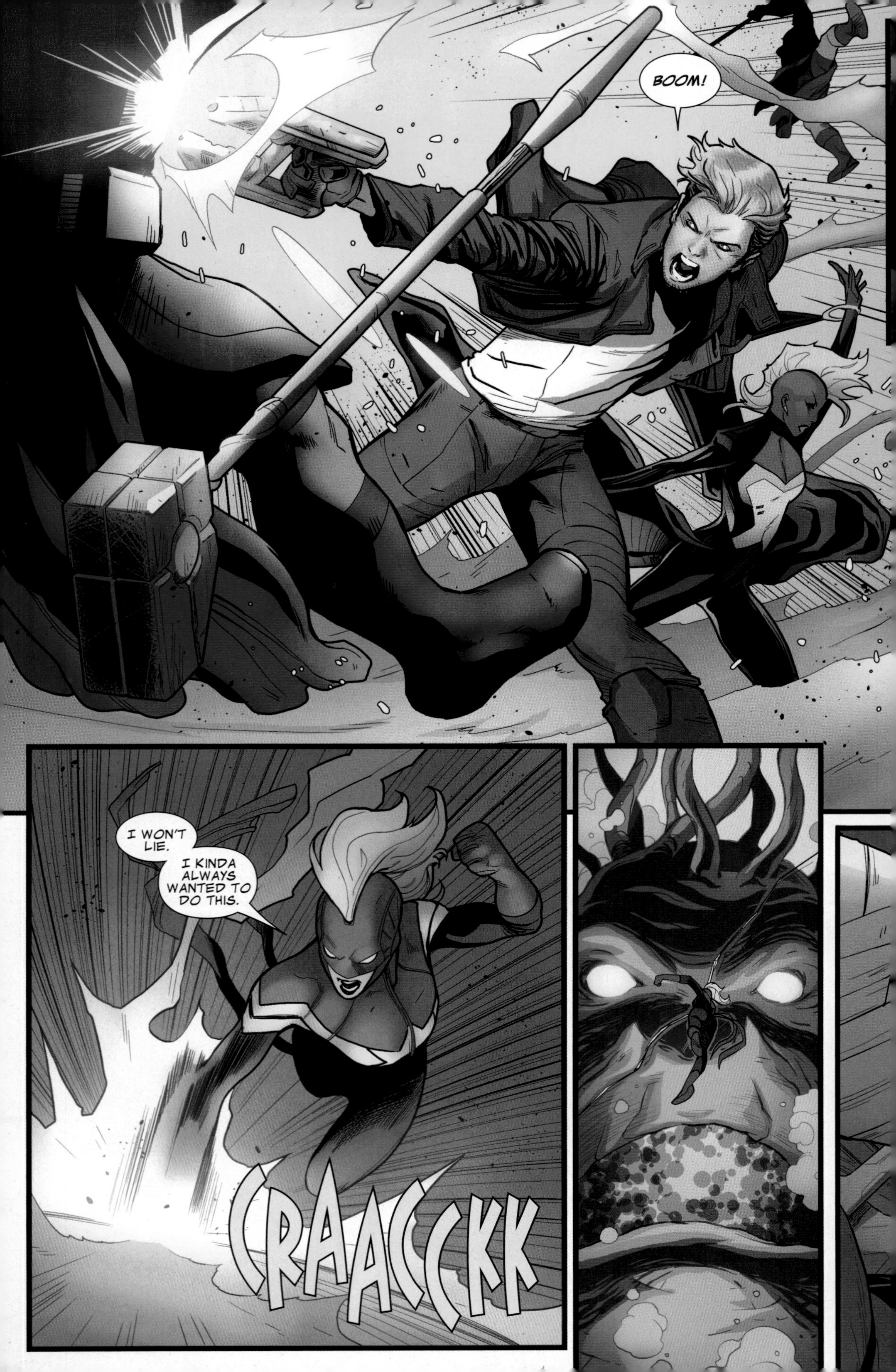
BOOM!
I WON'T LIE.
I KINDA ALWAYS WANTED TO DO THIS.
CRAACCKK

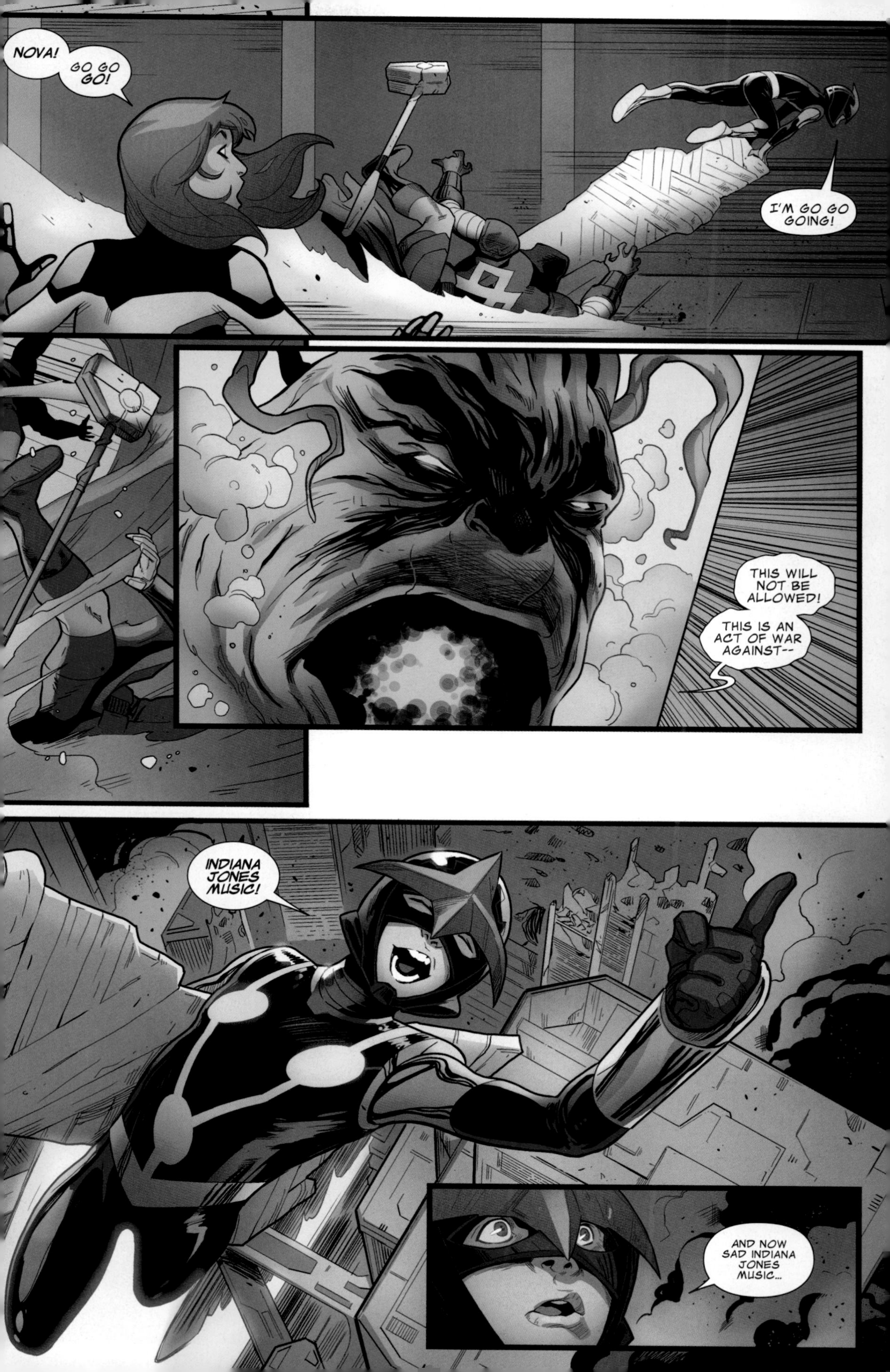
NOVA!
GO GO GO!
I'M GO GO GOING!
THIS WILL NOT BE ALLOWED!
THIS IS AN ACT OF WAR AGAINST--
INDIANA JONES MUSIC!
AND NOW SAD INDIANA JONES MUSIC...

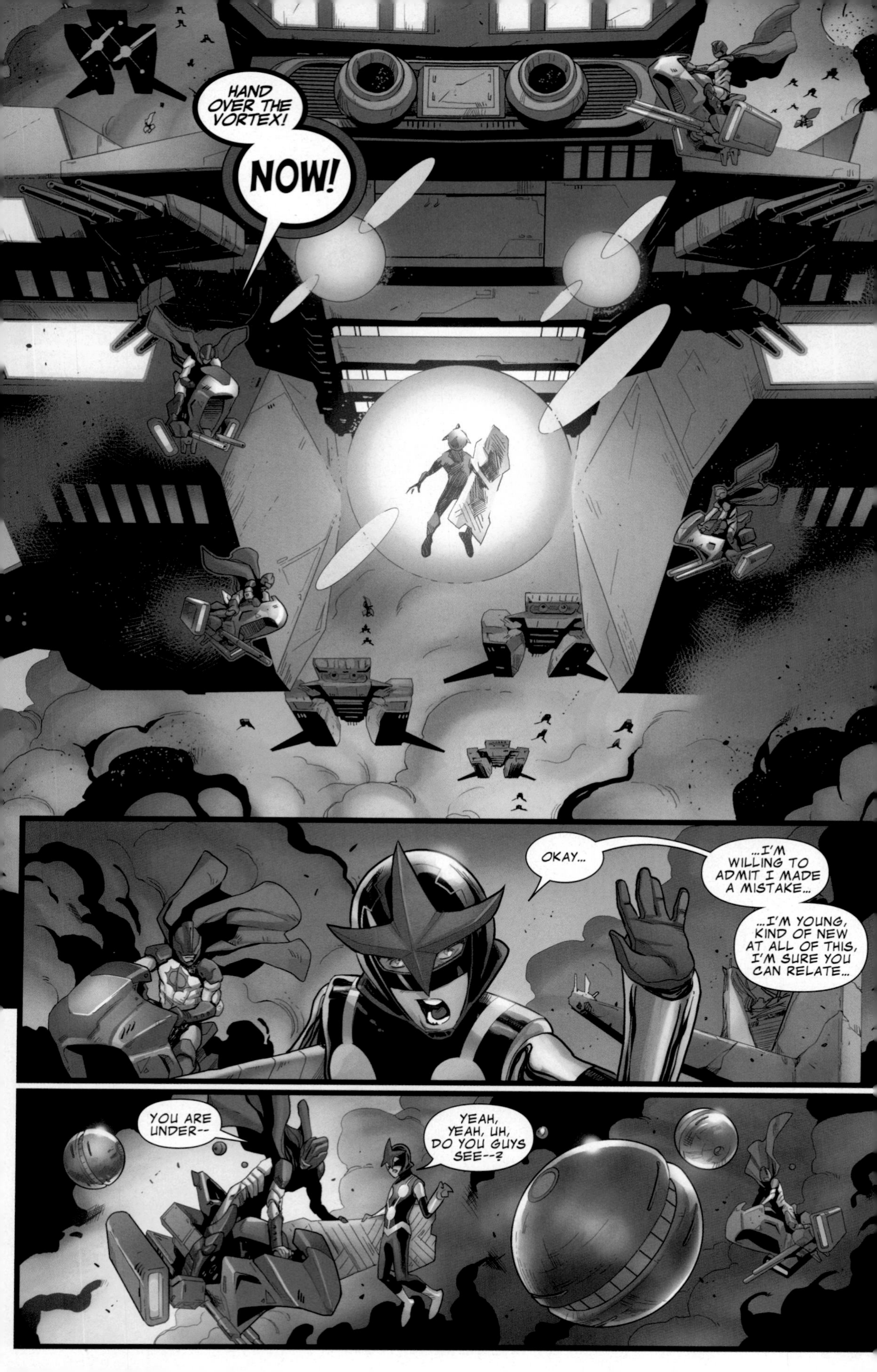
HAND OVER THE VORTEX!
NOW!
OKAY...
...I'M WILLING TO ADMIT I MADE A MISTAKE...
...I'M YOUNG, KIND OF NEW AT ALL OF THIS, I'M SURE YOU CAN RELATE...
YOU ARE UNDER--
YEAH, YEAH, UH, DO YOU GUYS SEE--?

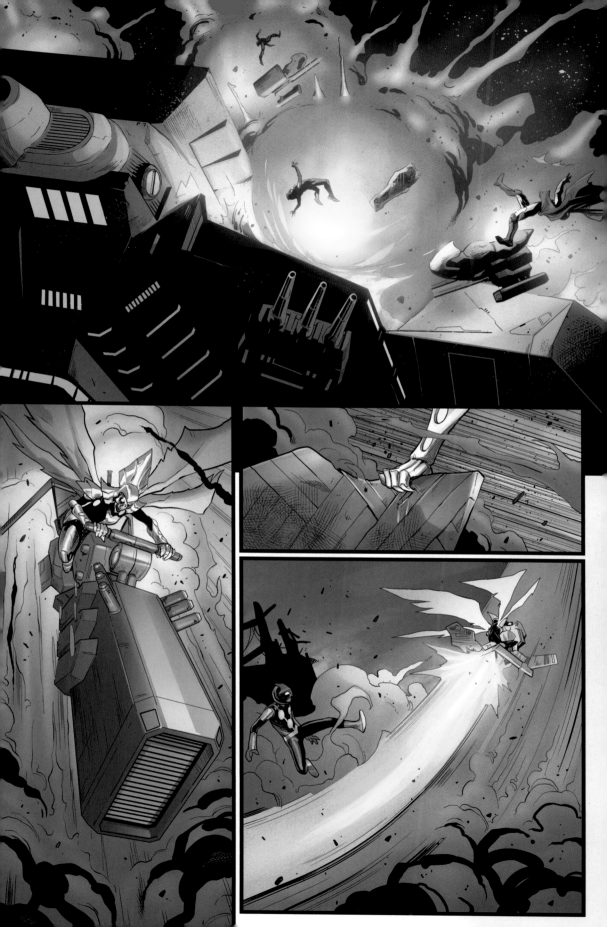

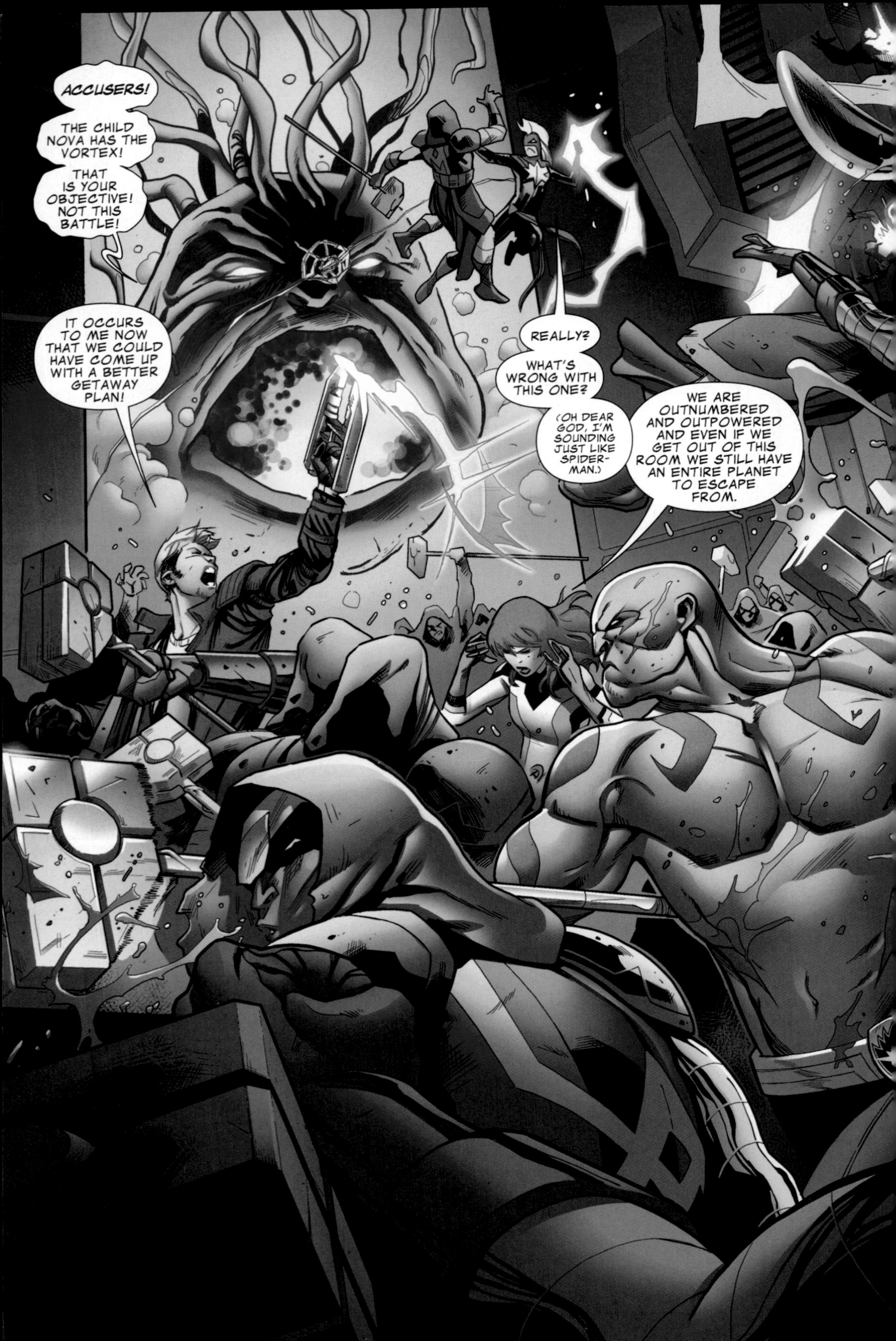
ACCUSERS!
THE CHILD NOVA HAS THE VORTEX!
THAT IS YOUR OBJECTIVE! NOT THIS BATTLE!
IT OCCURS TO ME NOW THAT WE COULD HAVE COME UP WITH A BETTER GETAWAY PLAN!
REALLY?
WHAT'S WRONG WITH THIS ONE?
(OH DEAR GOD, I'M SOUNDING JUST LIKE SPIDER-MAN.)
WE ARE OUTNUMBERED AND OUTPOWERED AND EVEN IF WE GET OUT OF THIS ROOM WE STILL HAVE AN ENTIRE PLANET TO ESCAPE FROM.

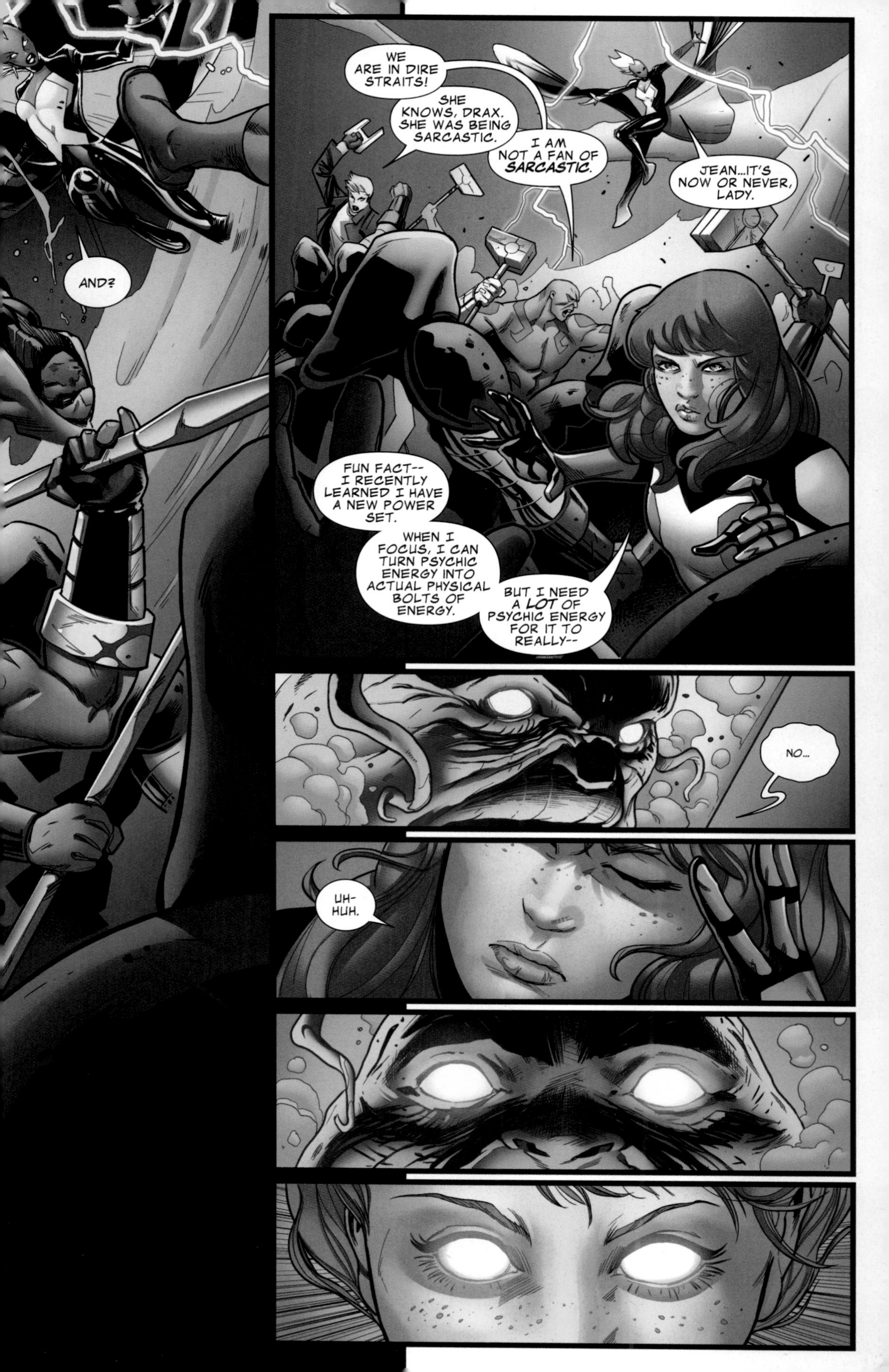
AND?
WE ARE IN DIRE STRAITS!
SHE KNOWS, DRAX. SHE WAS BEING SARCASTIC.
I AM NOT A FAN OF SARCASTIC.
JEAN...IT'S NOW OR NEVER, LADY.
FUN FACT-- I RECENTLY LEARNED I HAVE A NEW POWER SET.
WHEN I FOCUS, I CAN TURN PSYCHIC ENERGY INTO ACTUAL PHYSICAL BOLTS OF ENERGY.
BUT I NEED A LOT OF PSYCHIC ENERGY FOR IT TO REALLY--
NO...
UH-HUH.

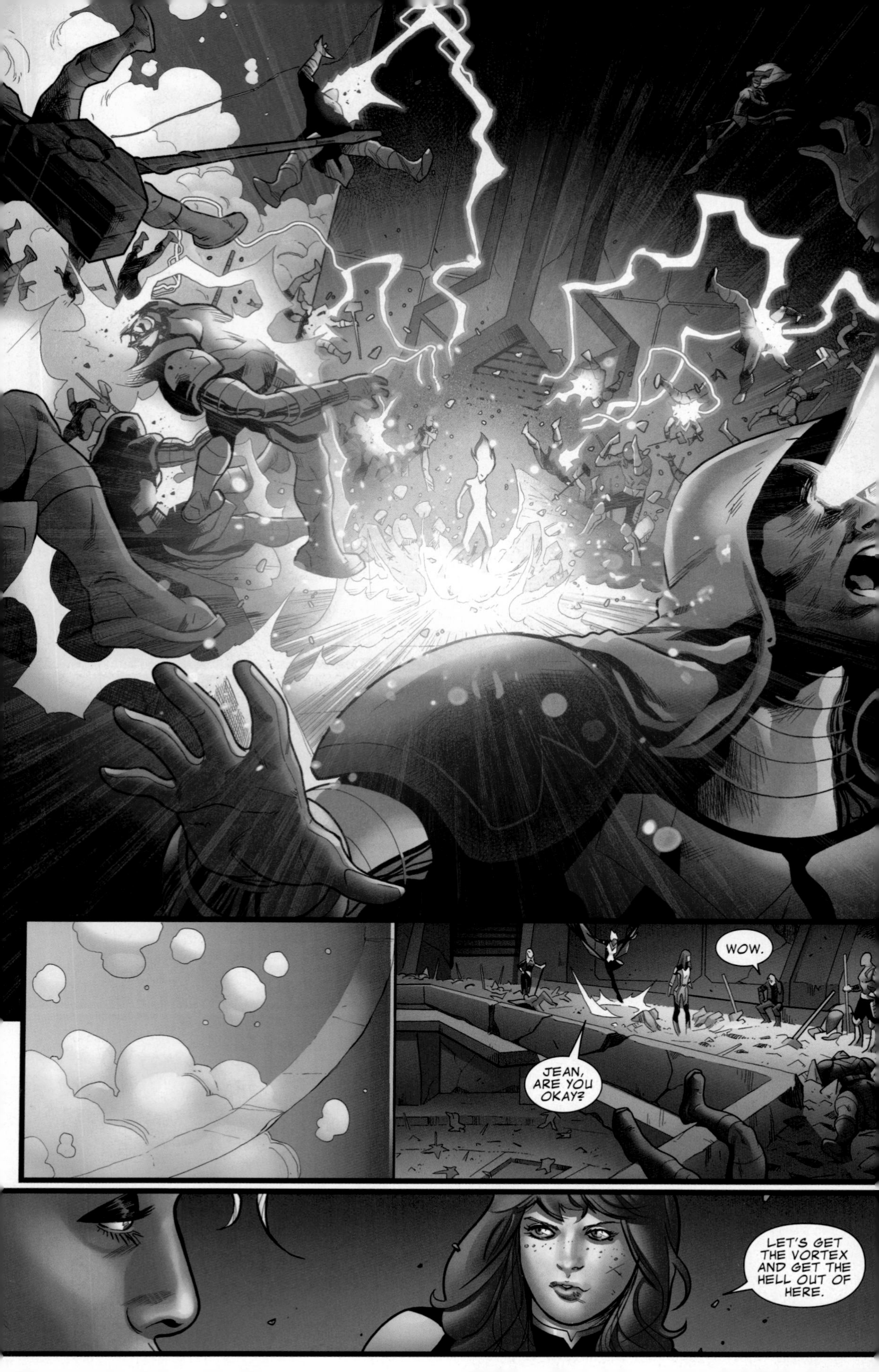
WOW.
JEAN, ARE YOU OKAY?
LET'S GET THE VORTEX AND GET THE HELL OUT OF HERE.

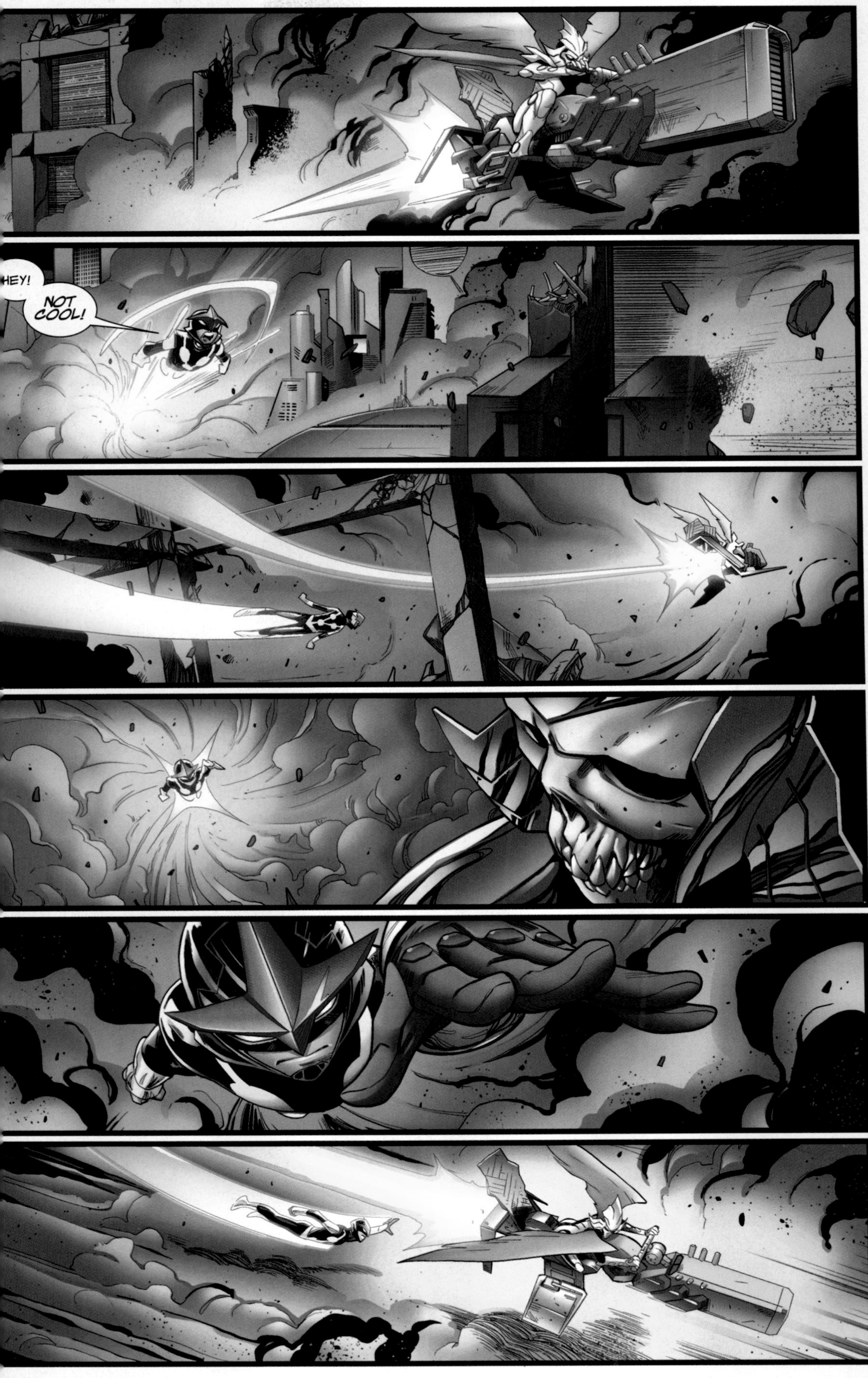
HEY! NOT COOL!

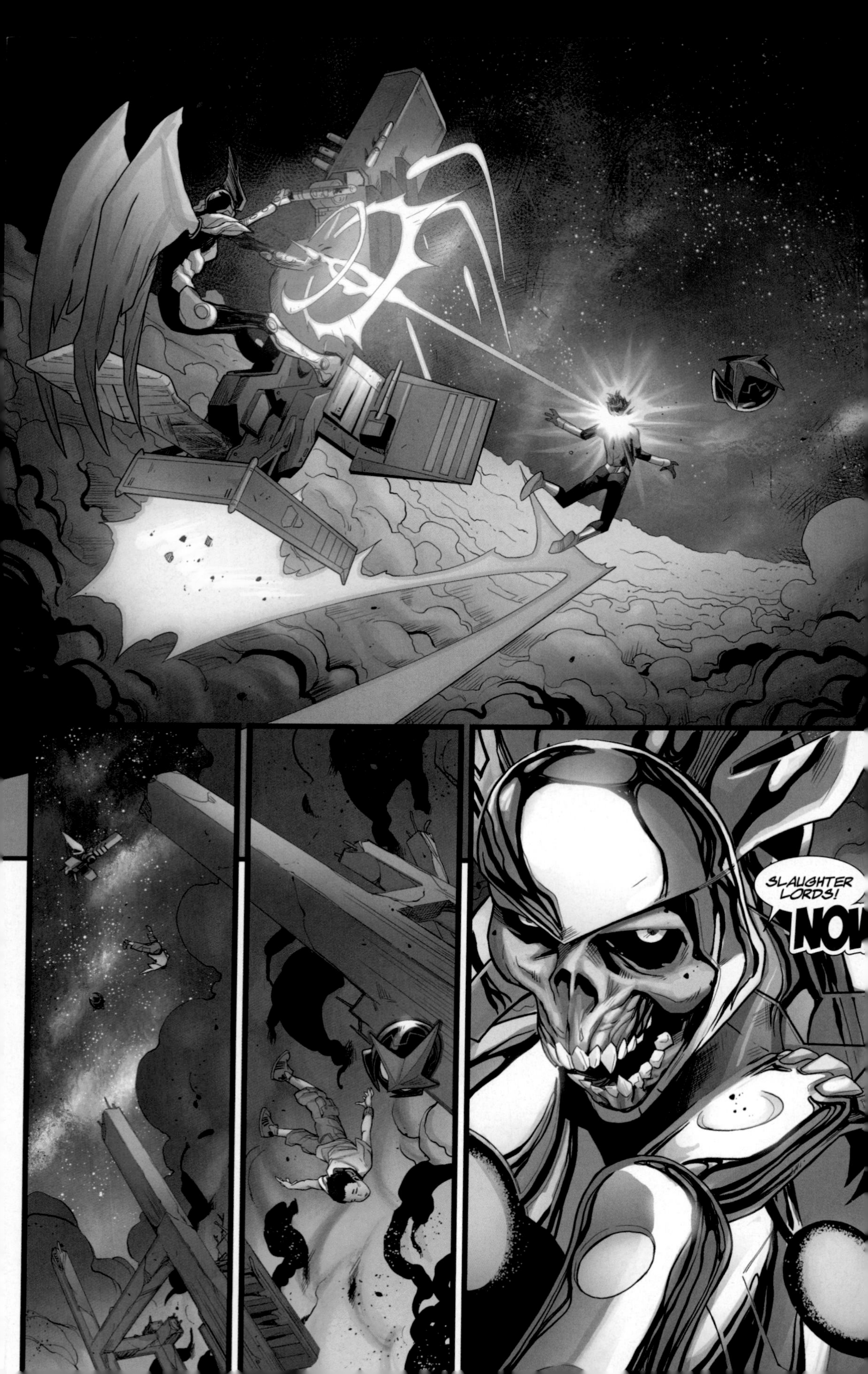
SLAUGHTER LORDS!
NOW

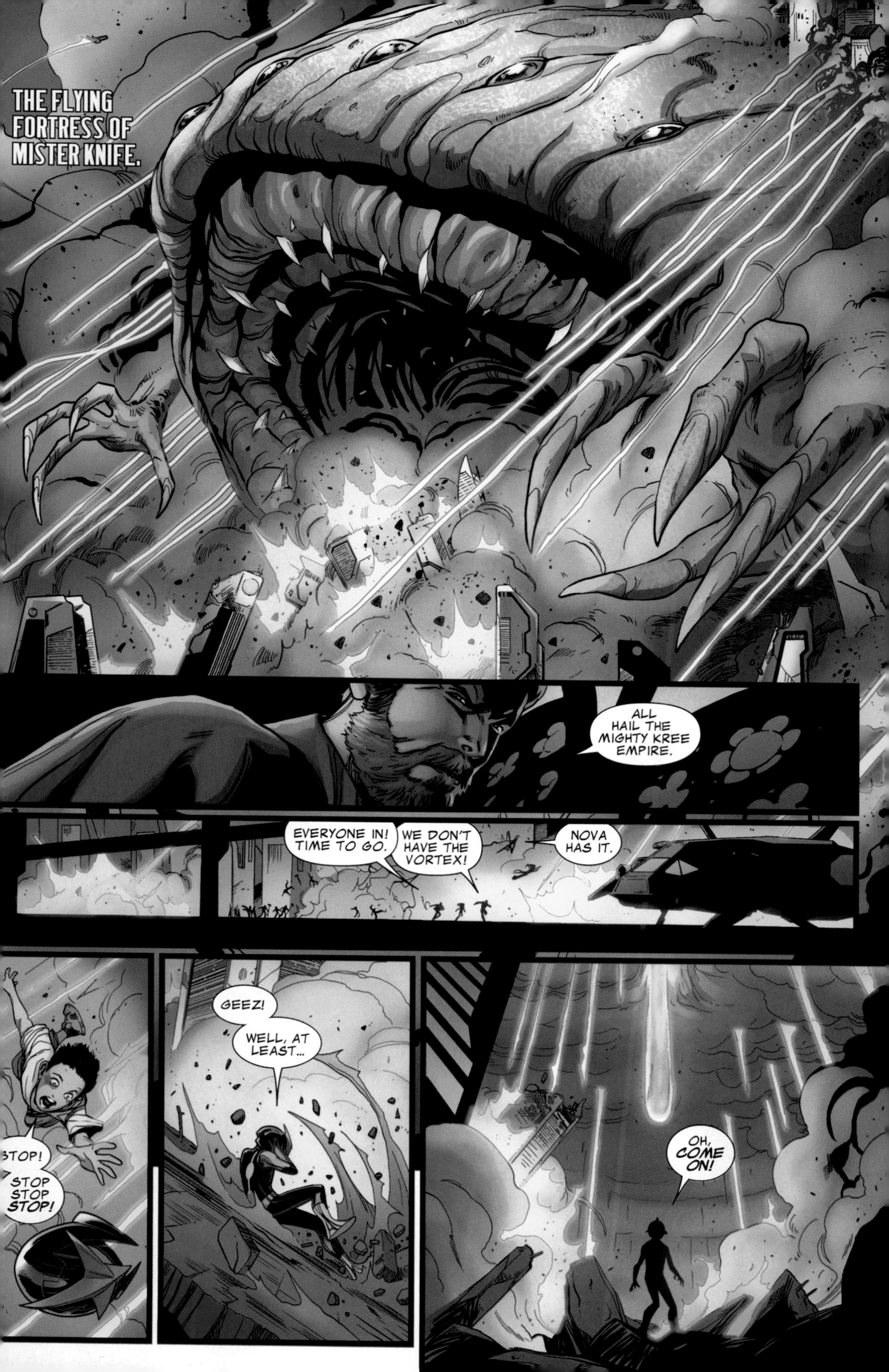
THE FLYING FORTRESS OF MISTER KNIFE.
ALL HAIL THE MIGHTY KREE EMPIRE.
EVERYONE IN! TIME TO GO.
WE DON'T HAVE THE VORTEX!
NOVA HAS IT.
STOP! STOP STOP STOP!
GEEZ!
WELL, AT LEAST...
OH, COME ON!

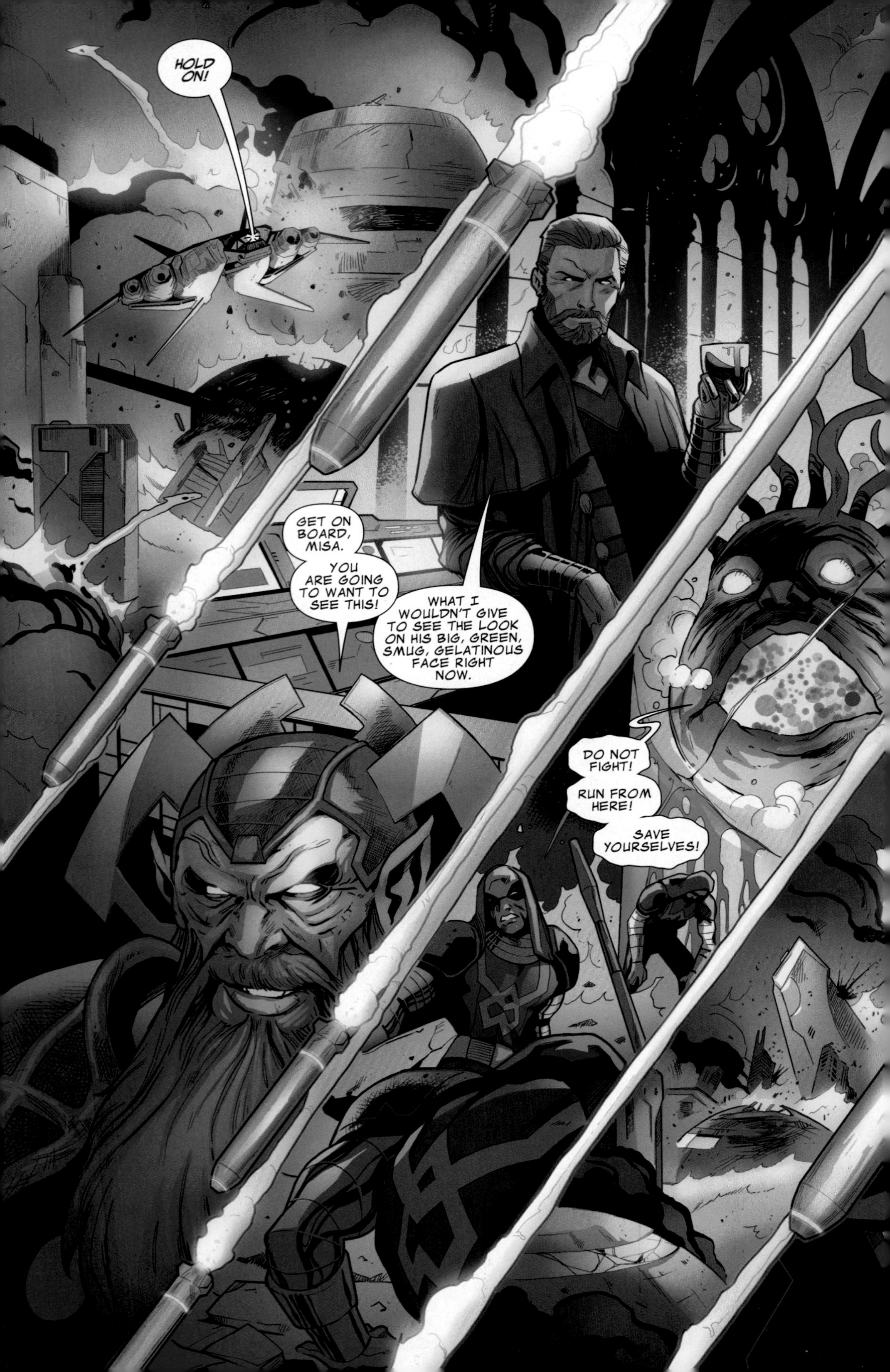
HOLD ON!
GET ON BOARD, MISA.
YOU ARE GOING TO WANT TO SEE THIS!
WHAT I WOULDN'T GIVE TO SEE THE LOOK ON HIS BIG, GREEN, SMUG, GELATINOUS FACE RIGHT NOW.
DO NOT FIGHT!
RUN FROM HERE!
SAVE YOURSELVES!

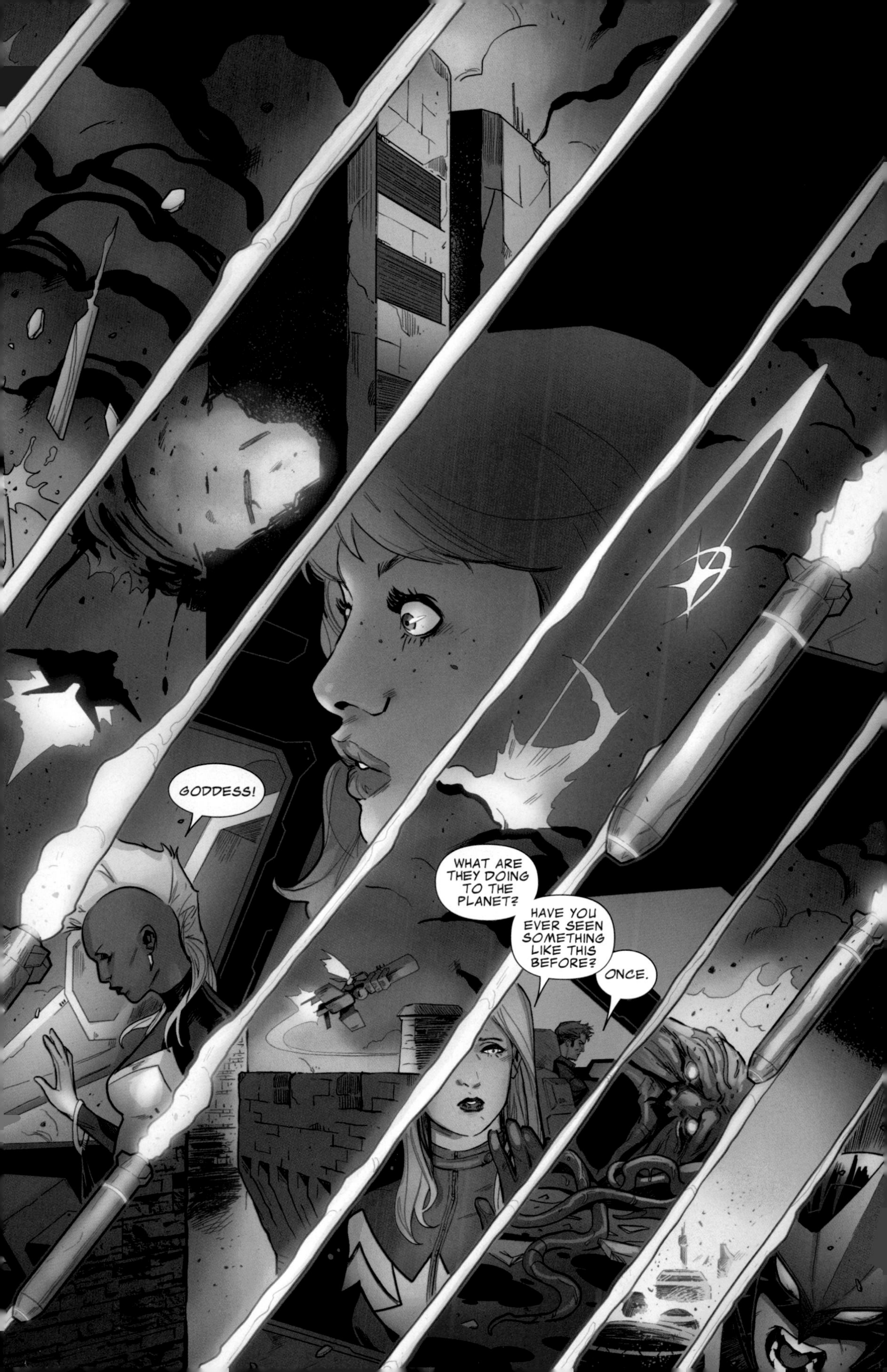
GODDESS!
WHAT ARE THEY DOING TO THE PLANET?
HAVE YOU EVER SEEN SOMETHING LIKE THIS BEFORE?
ONCE.

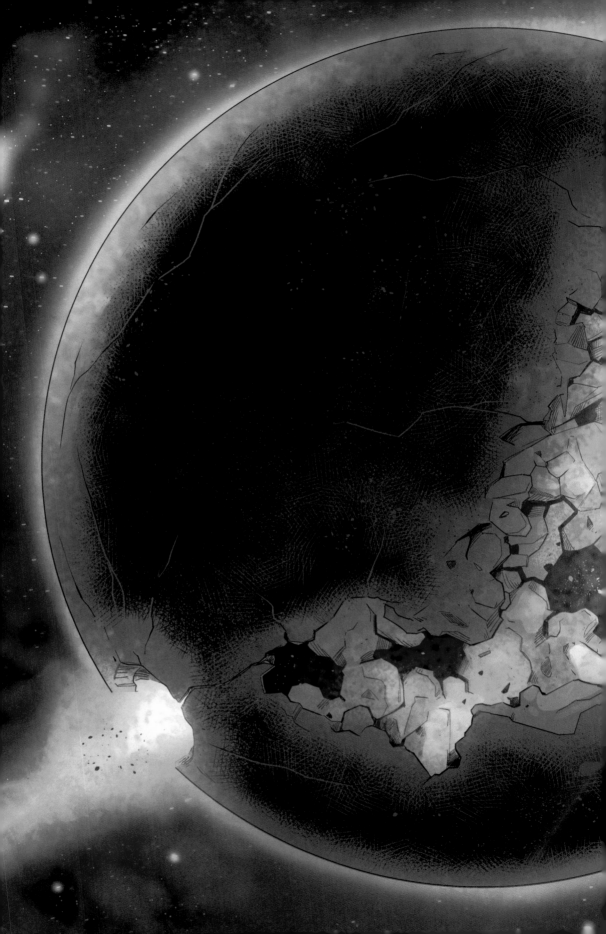

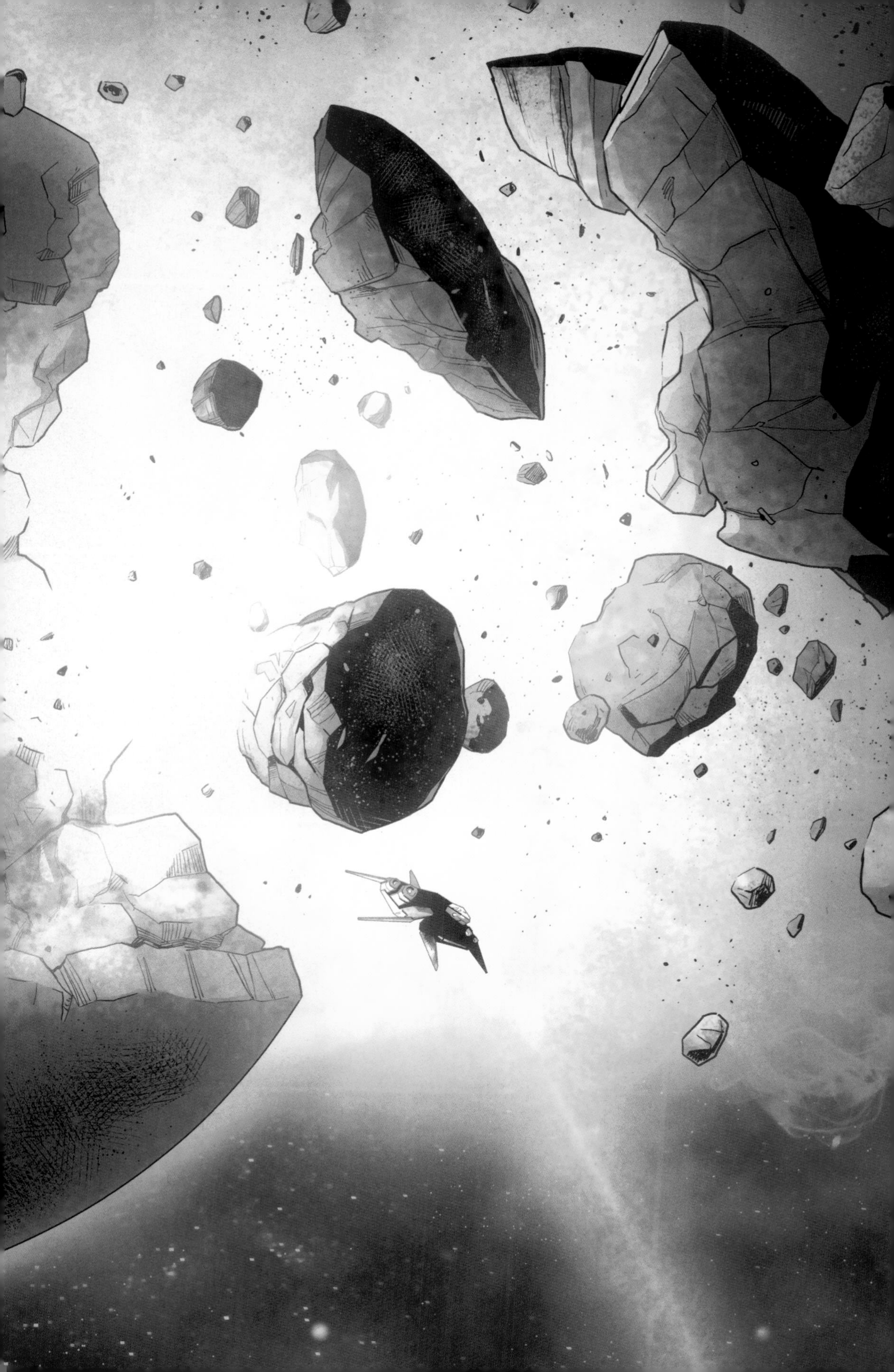

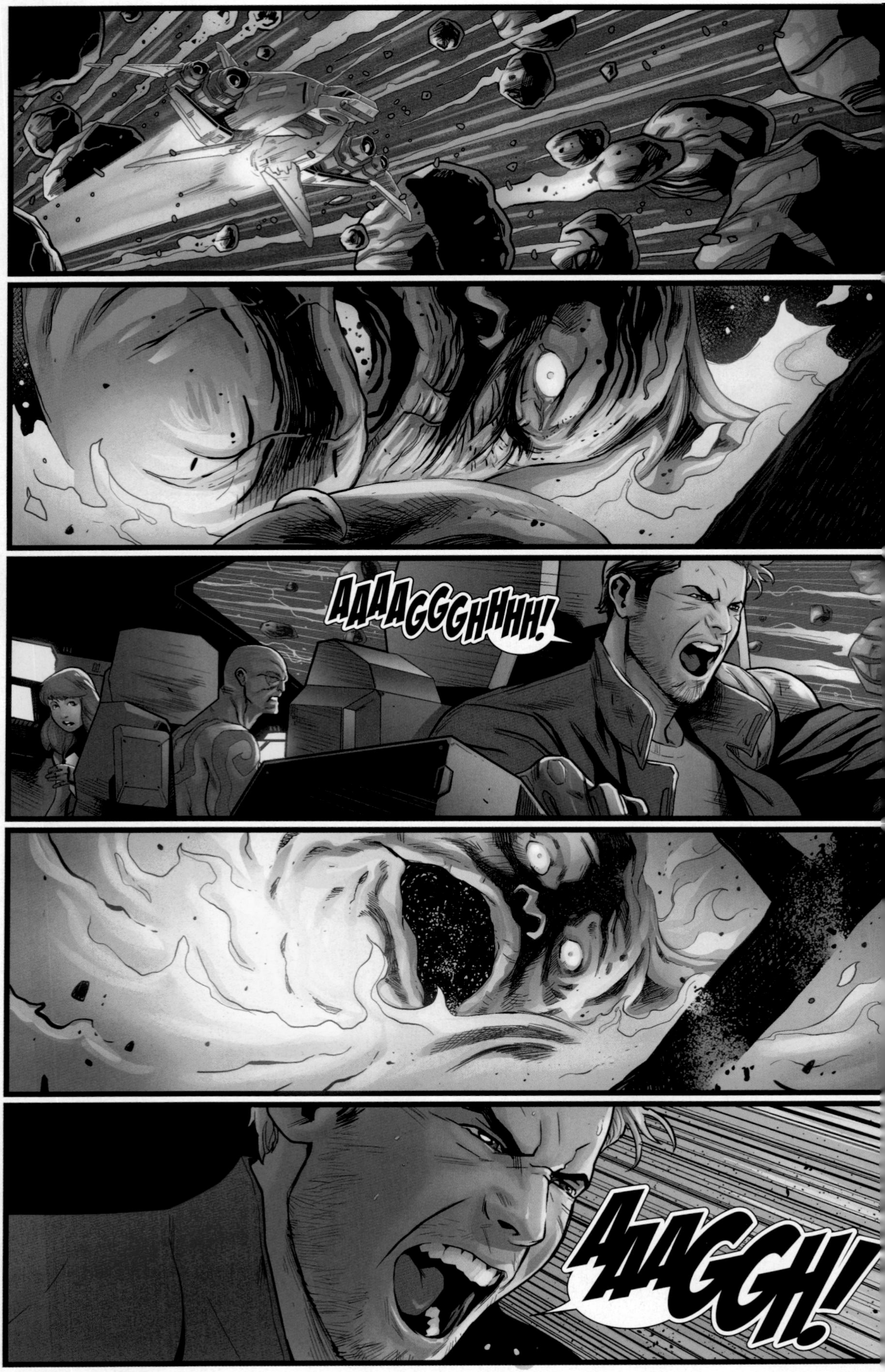
AAAAGGGHHHH!
AAAGGH!

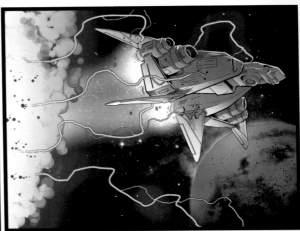

$@*%&#$!

THAT-- THAT **ENTIRE** PLANET JUST **DIED?**

YEAH...

THE ONE WE WERE JUST ON?

IT WAS ATTACKED.

BY WHO?

WHO HAS THAT KIND OF--?

WAS IT THE BLACK **VORTEX?**

IT CAN TAKE OUT A **WHOLE** PLANET?

AND **NOVA?**

WHAT ABOUT NOVA?

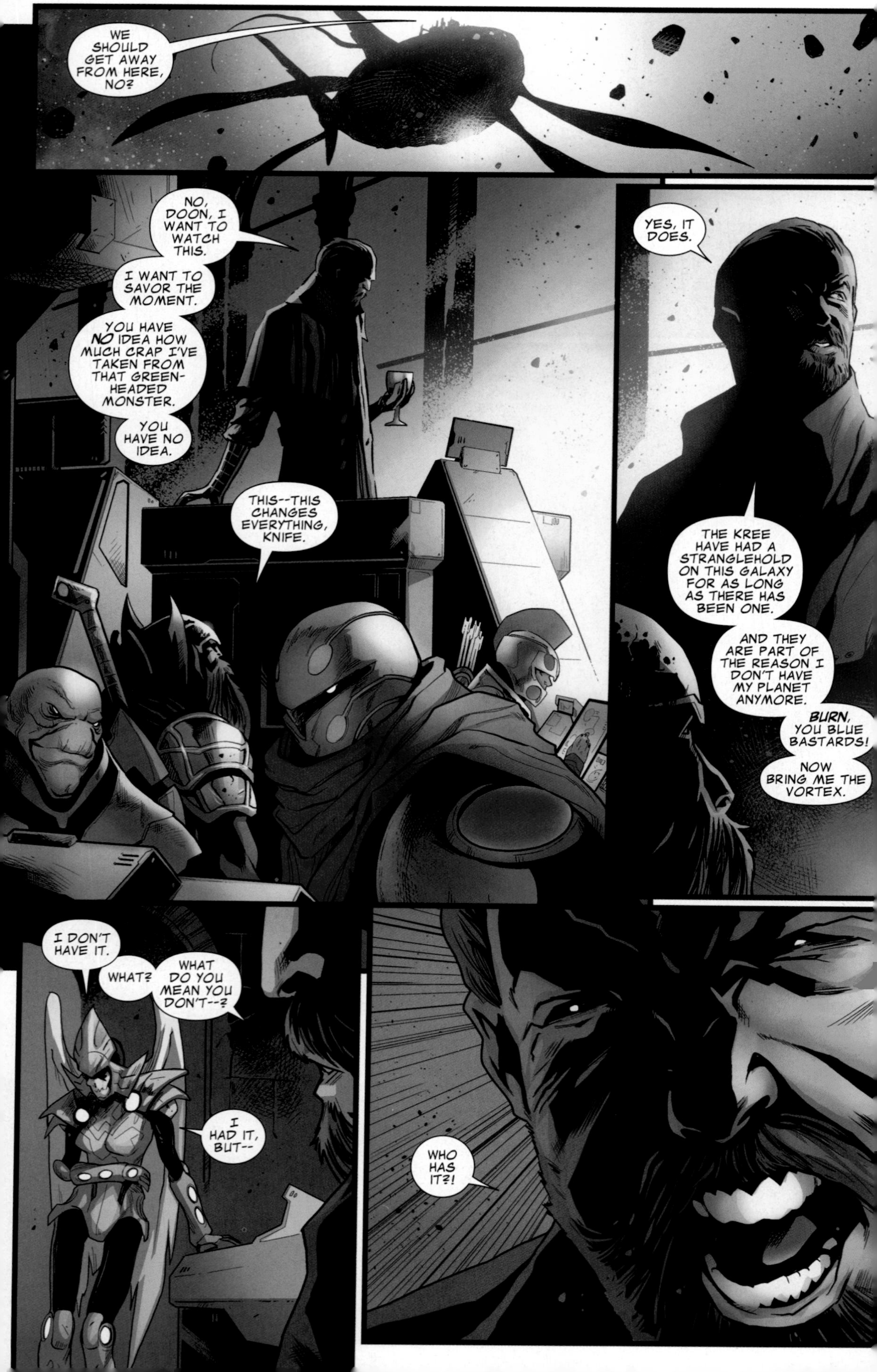
WE SHOULD GET AWAY FROM HERE, NO?
NO, DOON, I WANT TO WATCH THIS.
I WANT TO SAVOR THE MOMENT.
YOU HAVE NO IDEA HOW MUCH CRAP I'VE TAKEN FROM THAT GREEN-HEADED MONSTER.
YOU HAVE NO IDEA.
THIS--THIS CHANGES EVERYTHING, KNIFE.
YES, IT DOES.
THE KREE HAVE HAD A STRANGLEHOLD ON THIS GALAXY FOR AS LONG AS THERE HAS BEEN ONE.
AND THEY ARE PART OF THE REASON I DON'T HAVE MY PLANET ANYMORE.
BURN, YOU BLUE BASTARDS!
NOW BRING ME THE VORTEX.
I DON'T HAVE IT.
WHAT?
WHAT DO YOU MEAN YOU DON'T--?
I HAD IT, BUT--
WHO HAS IT?!

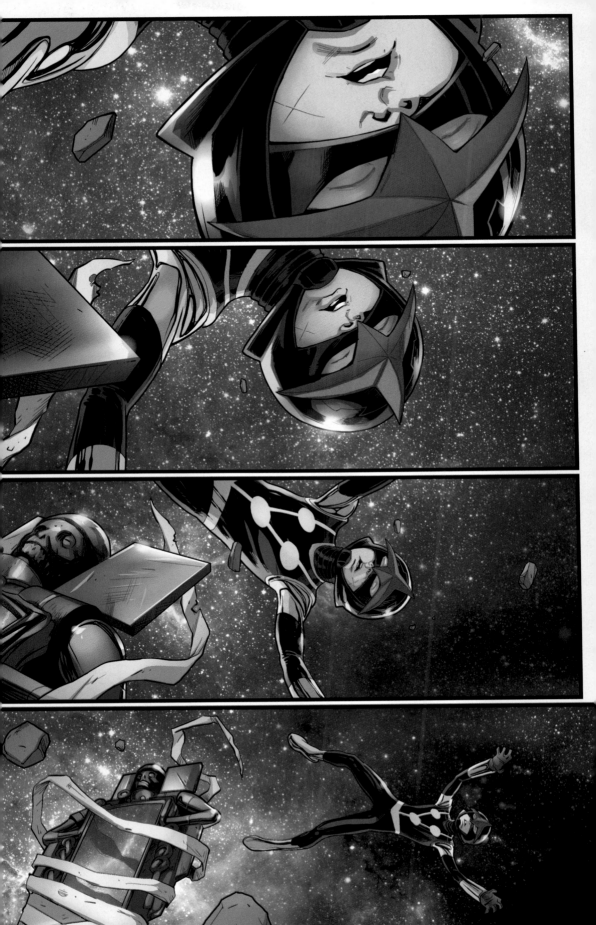

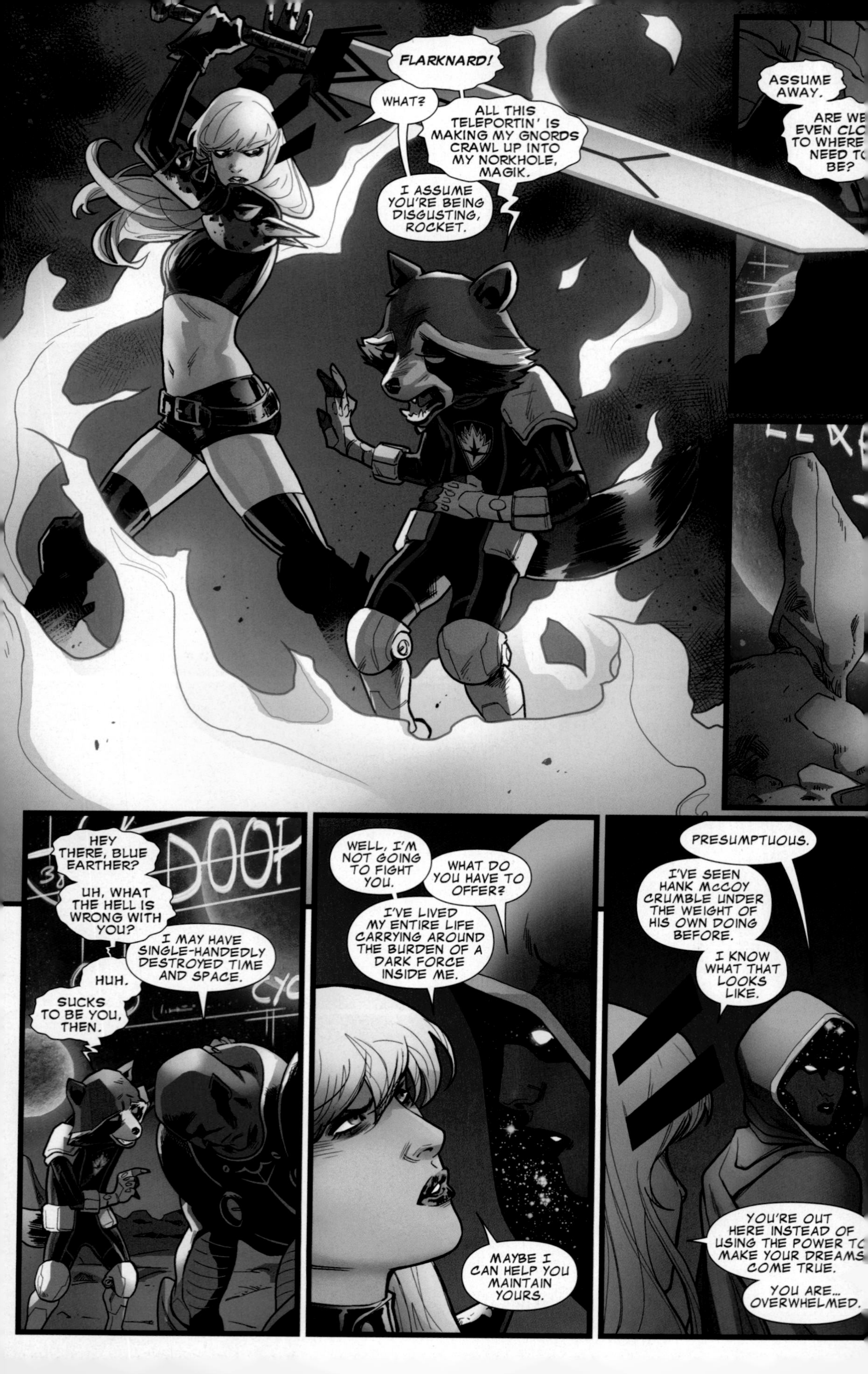
FLARKNARD!
WHAT?
ALL THIS TELEPORTIN' IS MAKING MY GNORDS CRAWL UP INTO MY NORKHOLE, MAGIK.
I ASSUME YOU'RE BEING DISGUSTING, ROCKET.
ASSUME AWAY.
ARE WE EVEN CLO TO WHERE NEED TO BE?
HEY THERE, BLUE EARTHER?
UH, WHAT THE HELL IS WRONG WITH YOU?
I MAY HAVE SINGLE-HANDEDLY DESTROYED TIME AND SPACE.
HUH.
SUCKS TO BE YOU, THEN.
WELL, I'M NOT GOING TO FIGHT YOU.
WHAT DO YOU HAVE TO OFFER?
I'VE LIVED MY ENTIRE LIFE CARRYING AROUND THE BURDEN OF A DARK FORCE INSIDE ME.
MAYBE I CAN HELP YOU MAINTAIN YOURS.
PRESUMPTUOUS.
I'VE SEEN HANK McCOY CRUMBLE UNDER THE WEIGHT OF HIS OWN DOING BEFORE.
I KNOW WHAT THAT LOOKS LIKE.
YOU'RE OUT HERE INSTEAD OF USING THE POWER TO MAKE YOUR DREAMS COME TRUE.
YOU ARE... OVERWHELMED.

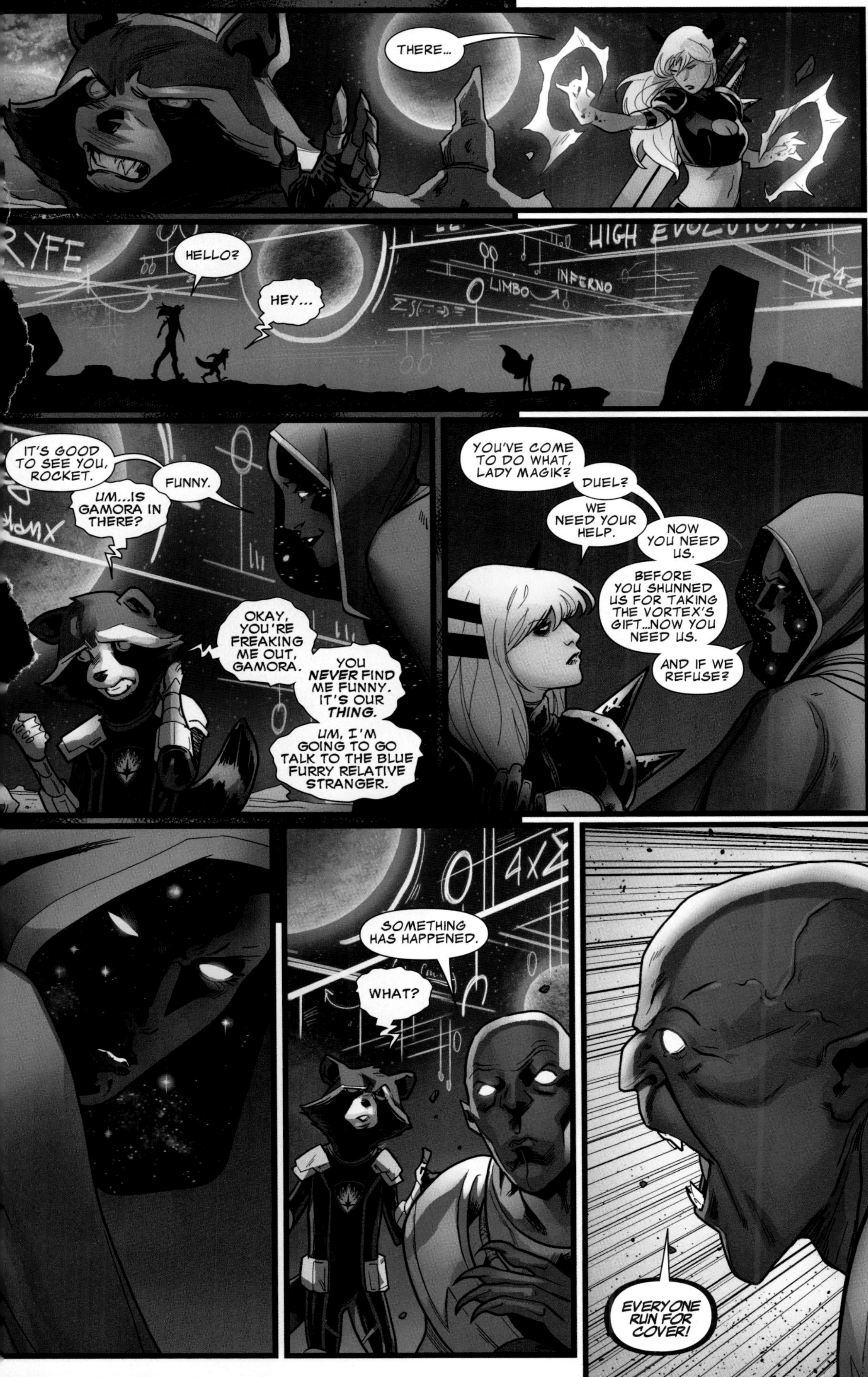
THERE...
RYFE
HIGH EVOLUTION
LIMBO
INFERNO
HELLO?
HEY...
IT'S GOOD TO SEE YOU, ROCKET.
FUNNY.
UM...IS GAMORA IN THERE?
OKAY, YOU'RE FREAKING ME OUT, GAMORA.
YOU NEVER FIND ME FUNNY. IT'S OUR THING.
UM, I'M GOING TO GO TALK TO THE BLUE FURRY RELATIVE STRANGER.
YOU'VE COME TO DO WHAT, LADY MAGIK?
DUEL?
WE NEED YOUR HELP.
NOW YOU NEED US.
BEFORE YOU SHUNNED US FOR TAKING THE VORTEX'S GIFT...NOW YOU NEED US.
AND IF WE REFUSE?
4x∑
SOMETHING HAS HAPPENED.
WHAT?
EVERYONE RUN FOR COVER!

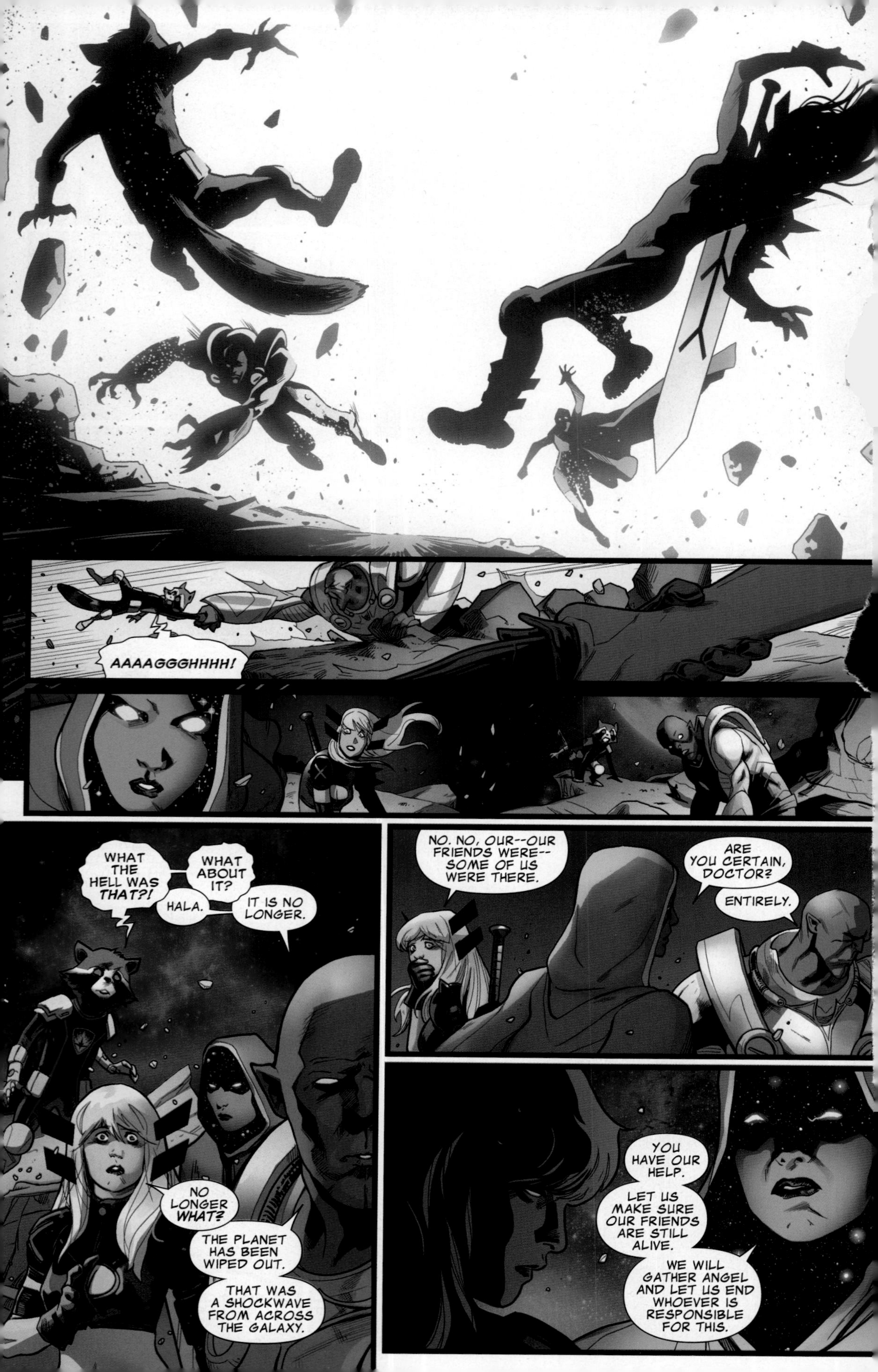
AAAAGGGHHHH!
WHAT THE HELL WAS THAT?!
WHAT ABOUT IT?
HALA.
IT IS NO LONGER.
NO LONGER WHAT?
THE PLANET HAS BEEN WIPED OUT.
THAT WAS A SHOCKWAVE FROM ACROSS THE GALAXY.
NO. NO, OUR--OUR FRIENDS WERE-- SOME OF US WERE THERE.
ARE YOU CERTAIN, DOCTOR?
ENTIRELY.
YOU HAVE OUR HELP.
LET US MAKE SURE OUR FRIENDS ARE STILL ALIVE.
WE WILL GATHER ANGEL AND LET US END WHOEVER IS RESPONSIBLE FOR THIS.

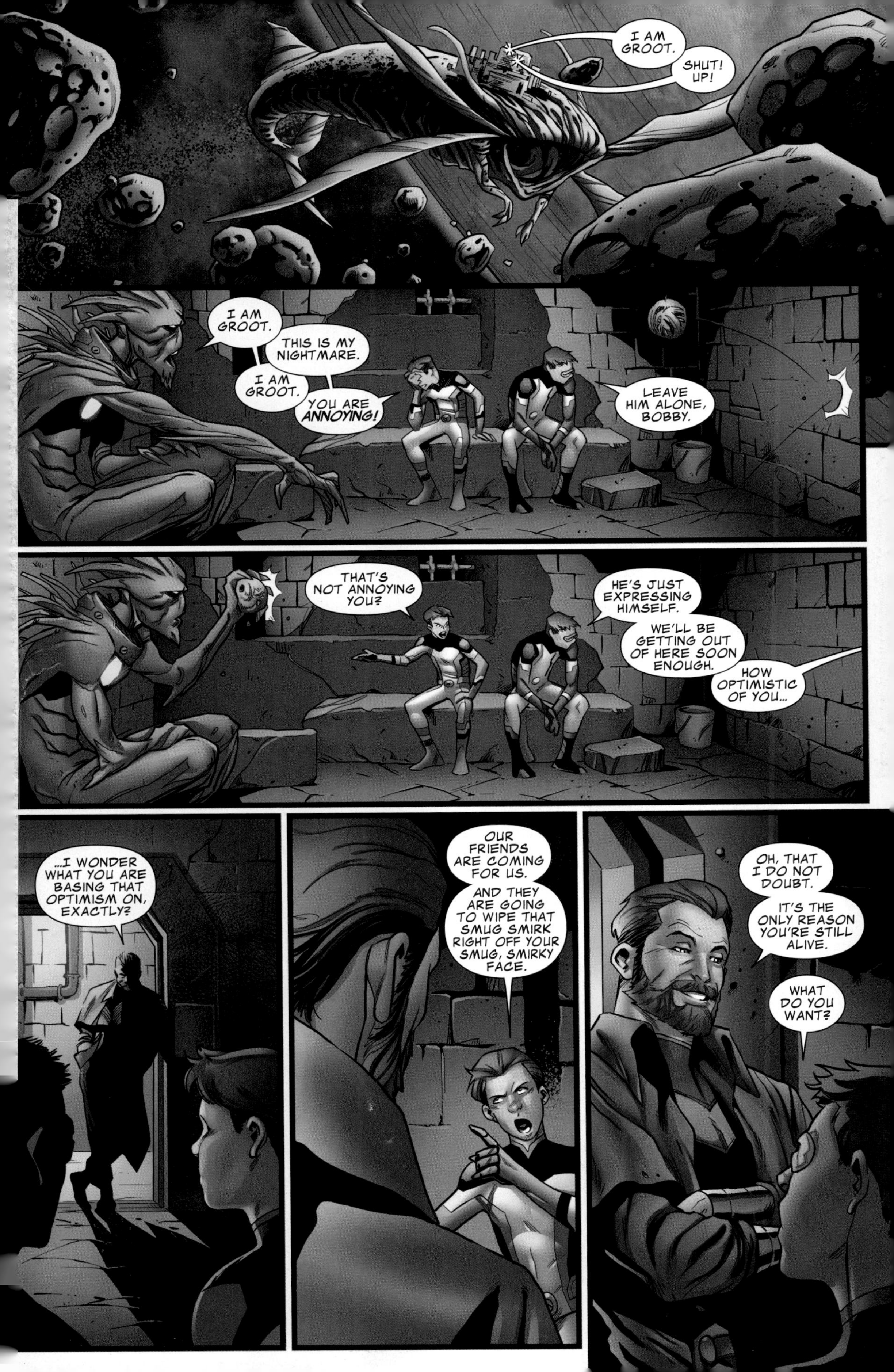

I AM GROOT.
SHUT! UP!
I AM GROOT.
THIS IS MY NIGHTMARE.
I AM GROOT.
YOU ARE ANNOYING!
LEAVE HIM ALONE, BOBBY.
THAT'S NOT ANNOYING YOU?
HE'S JUST EXPRESSING HIMSELF.
WE'LL BE GETTING OUT OF HERE SOON ENOUGH.
HOW OPTIMISTIC OF YOU...
...I WONDER WHAT YOU ARE BASING THAT OPTIMISM ON, EXACTLY?
OUR FRIENDS ARE COMING FOR US.
AND THEY ARE GOING TO WIPE THAT SMUG SMIRK RIGHT OFF YOUR SMUG, SMIRKY FACE.
OH, THAT I DO NOT DOUBT.
IT'S THE ONLY REASON YOU'RE STILL ALIVE.
WHAT DO YOU WANT?

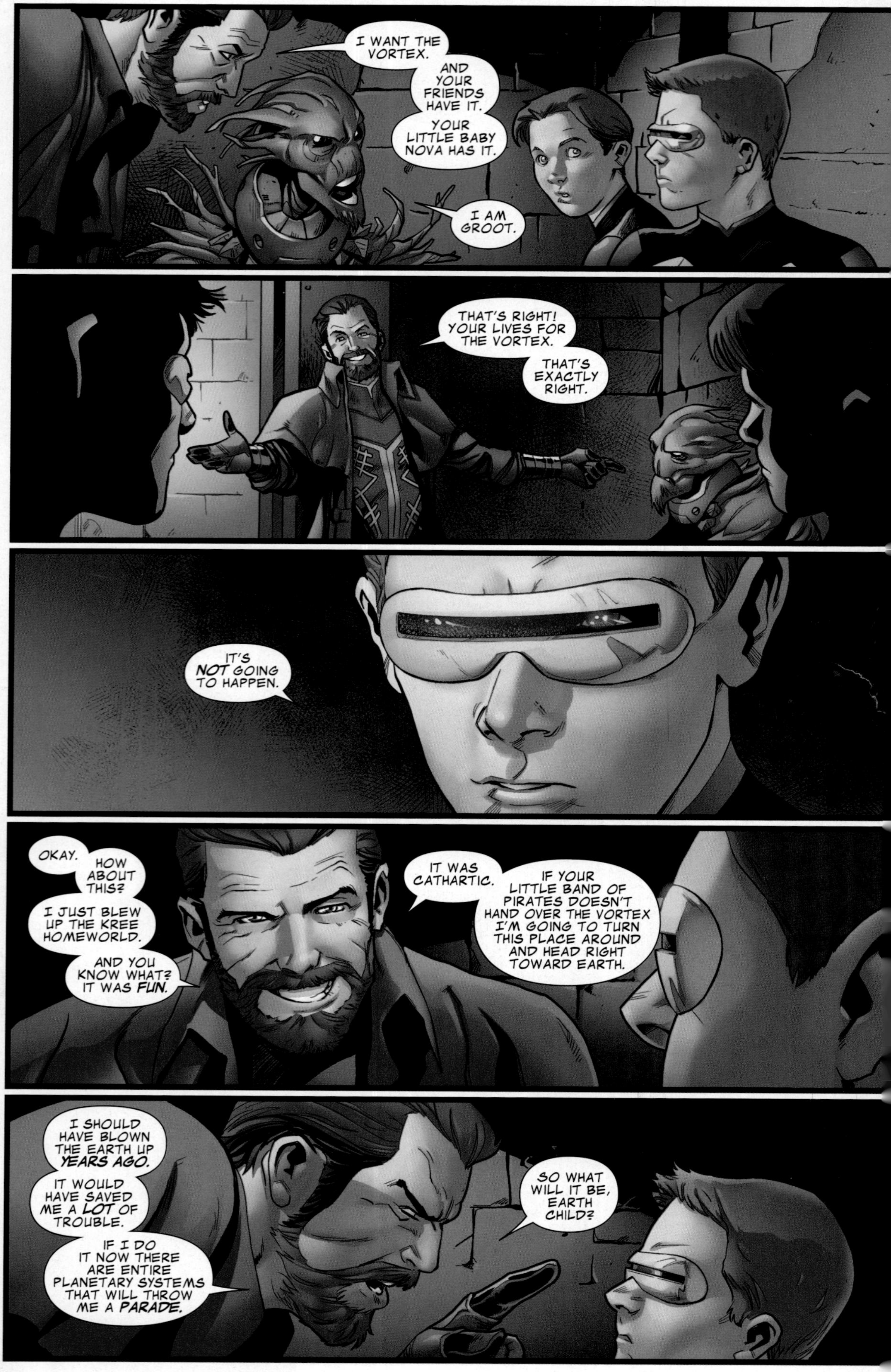
I WANT THE VORTEX.
AND YOUR FRIENDS HAVE IT.
YOUR LITTLE BABY NOVA HAS IT.
I AM GROOT.
THAT'S RIGHT! YOUR LIVES FOR THE VORTEX.
THAT'S EXACTLY RIGHT.
IT'S NOT GOING TO HAPPEN.
OKAY.
HOW ABOUT THIS?
I JUST BLEW UP THE KREE HOMEWORLD.
AND YOU KNOW WHAT? IT WAS FUN.
IT WAS CATHARTIC.
IF YOUR LITTLE BAND OF PIRATES DOESN'T HAND OVER THE VORTEX I'M GOING TO TURN THIS PLACE AROUND AND HEAD RIGHT TOWARD EARTH.
I SHOULD HAVE BLOWN THE EARTH UP YEARS AGO.
IT WOULD HAVE SAVED ME A LOT OF TROUBLE.
IF I DO IT NOW THERE ARE ENTIRE PLANETARY SYSTEMS THAT WILL THROW ME A PARADE.
SO WHAT WILL IT BE, EARTH CHILD?

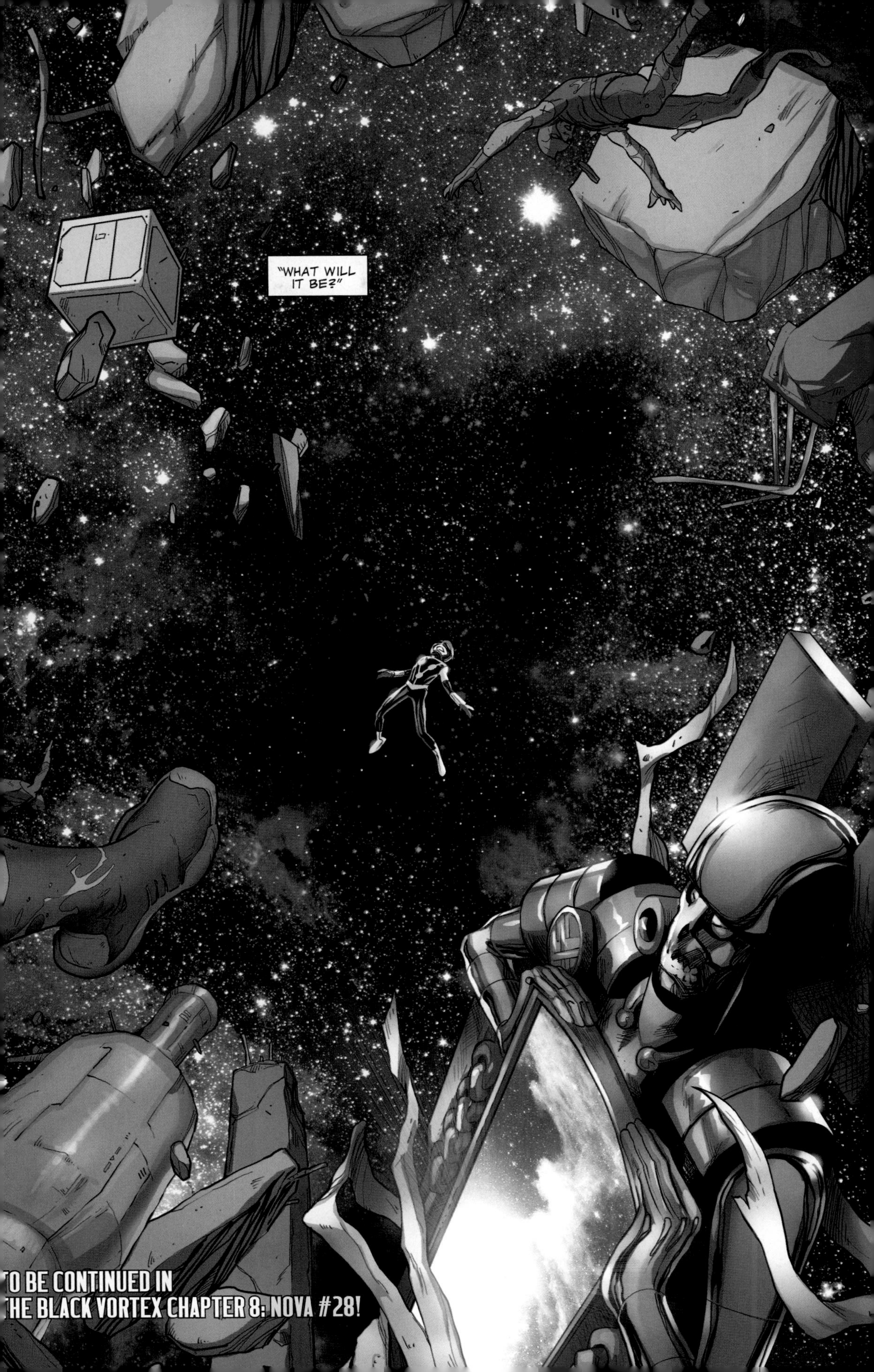
"WHAT WILL IT BE?"
TO BE CONTINUED IN THE BLACK VORTEX CHAPTER 8: NOVA #28!

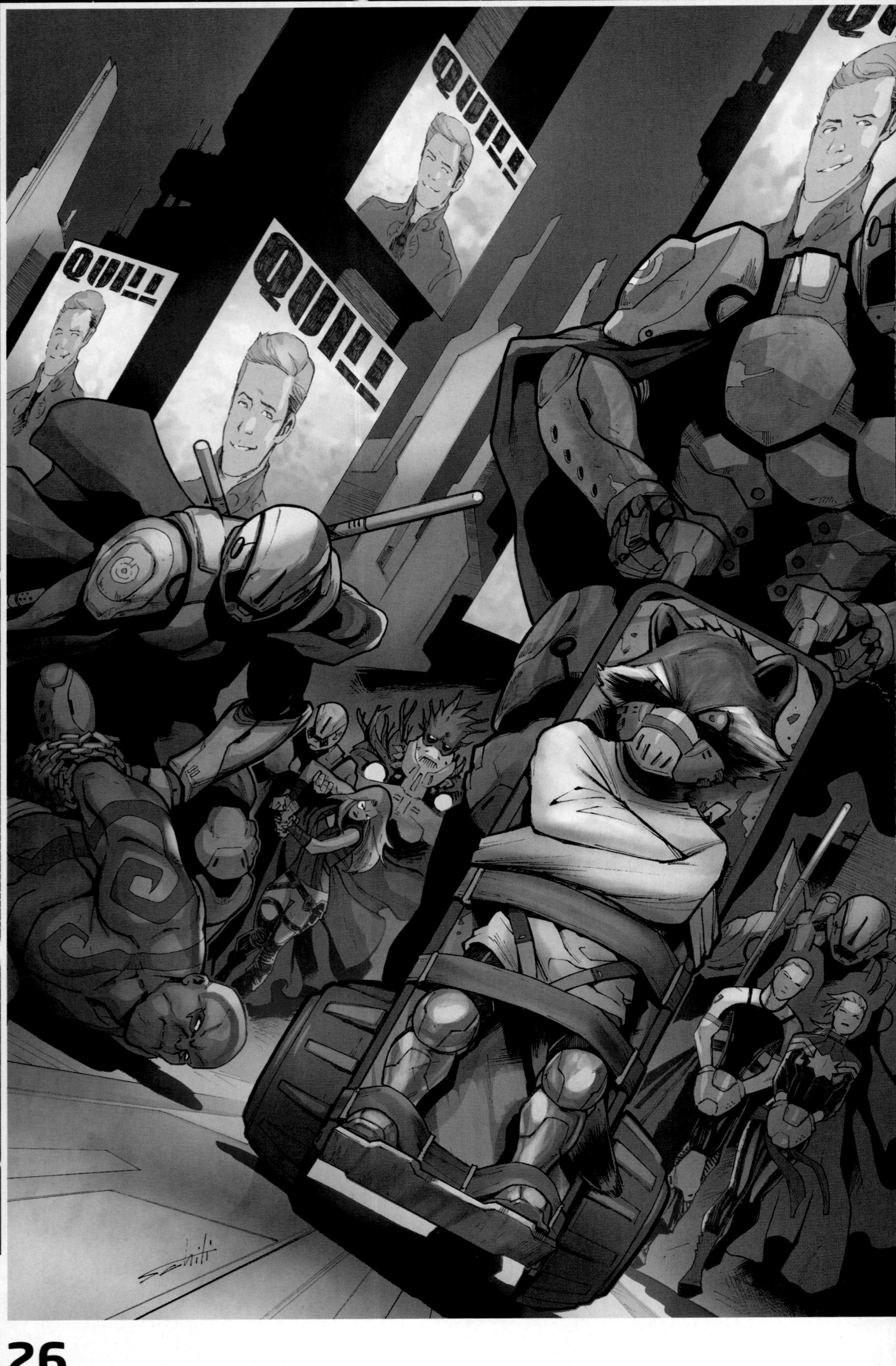
QUILL
QUILL
QUILL

PREVIOUSLY...

RECENTLY, PETER QUILL'S FATHER, J'SON, ACQUIRED AN ANCIENT AND POWERFUL ARTIFACT, THE BLACK VORTEX. USING THE VORTEX TO IMBUE THANOS' SON THANE WITH COSMIC POWER, J'SON HAD THANE SEAL THE PLANET SPARTAX IN AMBER. J'SON INTENDED TO GIFT THE PLANET TO THE BROOD SO THAT THEY MIGHT USE THE CITIZENS TO INCUBATE THEIR EGGS. FACED WITH THE PROSPECT OF A PLANET-WIDE EXTINCTION, AND NOT TO MENTION AN OVERWHELMING ARMY OF BROOD SOLDIERS, KITTY PRYDE CHOSE TO SUBMIT TO THE BLACK VORTEX. SHE THEN USED HER ENHANCED POWERS TO PHASE THE PLANET OUT OF ITS AMBER PRISON, SAVING THE PEOPLE OF SPARTAX.

WITH THE BATTLE OVER CONTROL OF THE COSMICALLY POWERED BLACK VORTEX NOW FINISHED, THINGS SEEM TO HAVE SETTLED DOWN A LITTLE BIT FOR THE GUARDIANS. ALTHOUGH THERE IS ONE SLIGHT CHANGE, WHAT WITH PETER GETTING ENGAGED TO THE NOW COSMICALLY ENHANCED KITTY PRYDE. BUT IN ALL THE MESS CAUSED BY THE BLACK VORTEX, PETER HAS CONVENIENTLY FORGOTTEN THE OTHER RECENT EVENTS ON HIS HOME PLANET OF SPARTAX...

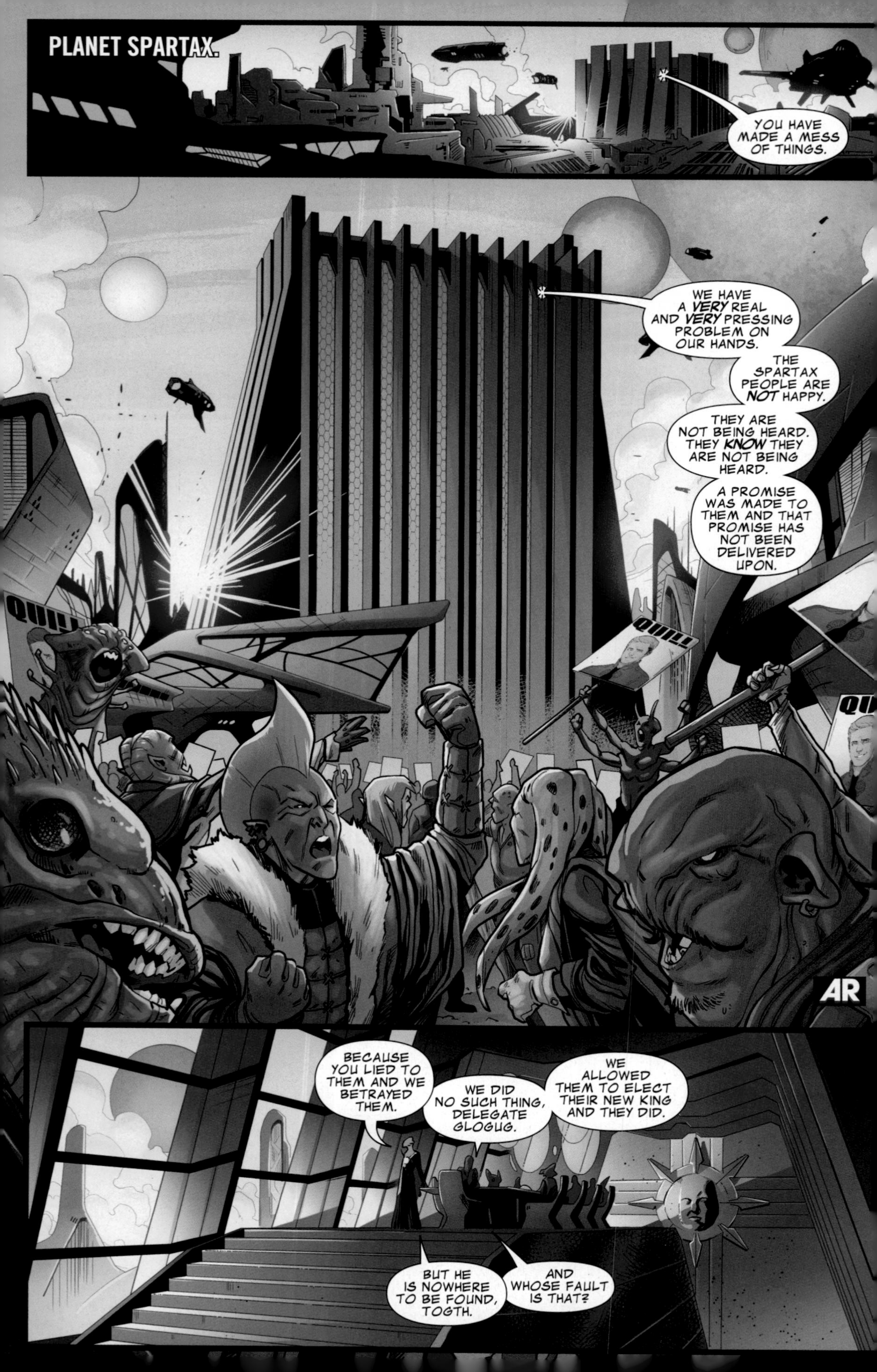
PLANET SPARTAX.
YOU HAVE MADE A MESS OF THINGS.
WE HAVE A VERY REAL AND VERY PRESSING PROBLEM ON OUR HANDS.
THE SPARTAX PEOPLE ARE NOT HAPPY.
THEY ARE NOT BEING HEARD. THEY KNOW THEY ARE NOT BEING HEARD.
A PROMISE WAS MADE TO THEM AND THAT PROMISE HAS NOT BEEN DELIVERED UPON.
QUILL
AR
BECAUSE YOU LIED TO THEM AND WE BETRAYED THEM.
WE DID NO SUCH THING, DELEGATE GLOGUG.
WE ALLOWED THEM TO ELECT THEIR NEW KING AND THEY DID.
BUT HE IS NOWHERE TO BE FOUND, TOGTH.
AND WHOSE FAULT IS THAT?

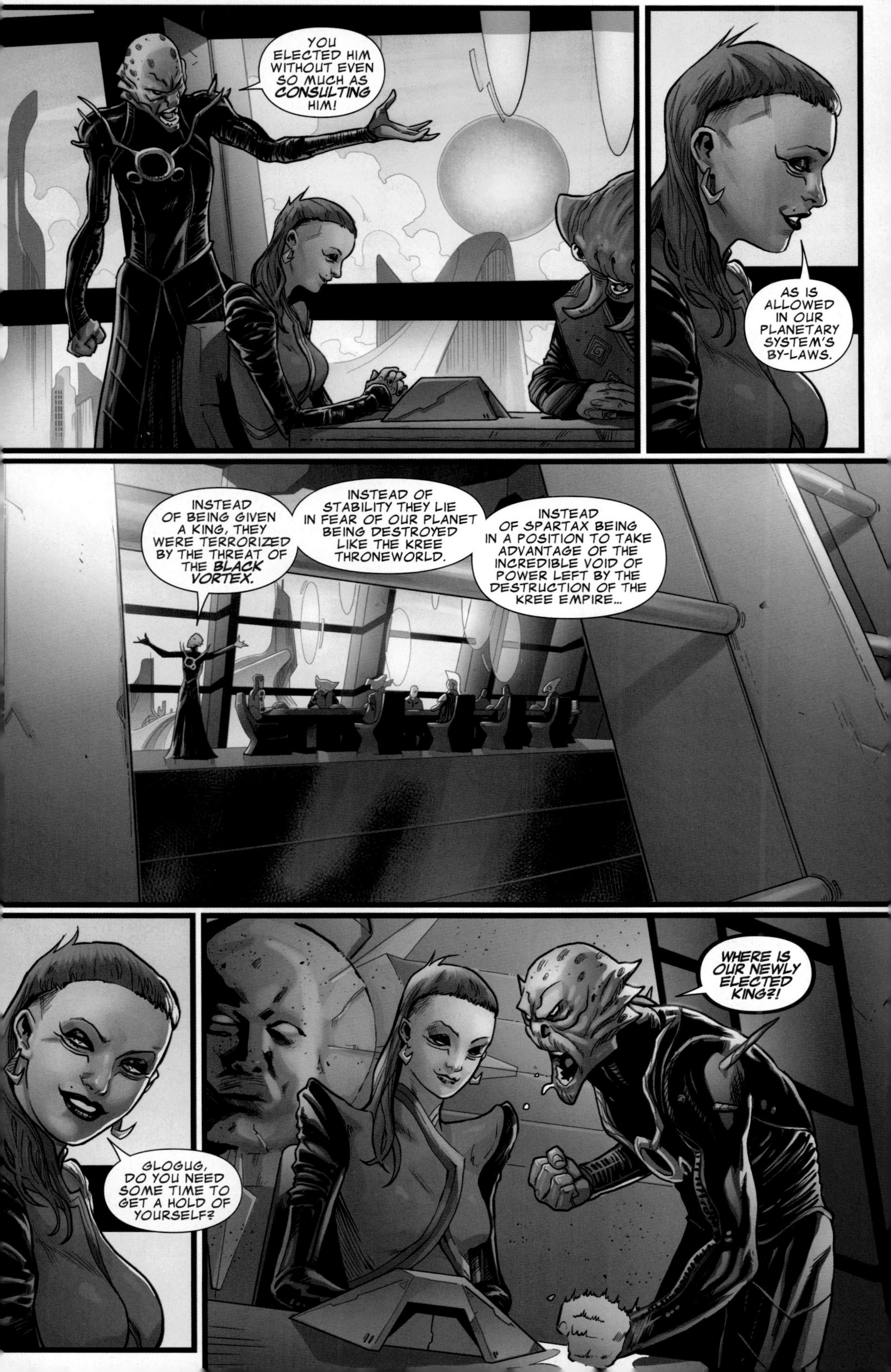
YOU ELECTED HIM WITHOUT EVEN SO MUCH AS CONSULTING HIM!
AS IS ALLOWED IN OUR PLANETARY SYSTEM'S BY-LAWS.
INSTEAD OF BEING GIVEN A KING, THEY WERE TERRORIZED BY THE THREAT OF THE BLACK VORTEX.
INSTEAD OF STABILITY THEY LIE IN FEAR OF OUR PLANET BEING DESTROYED LIKE THE KREE THRONEWORLD.
INSTEAD OF SPARTAX BEING IN A POSITION TO TAKE ADVANTAGE OF THE INCREDIBLE VOID OF POWER LEFT BY THE DESTRUCTION OF THE KREE EMPIRE...
WHERE IS OUR NEWLY ELECTED KING?!
GLOGUG, DO YOU NEED SOME TIME TO GET A HOLD OF YOURSELF?

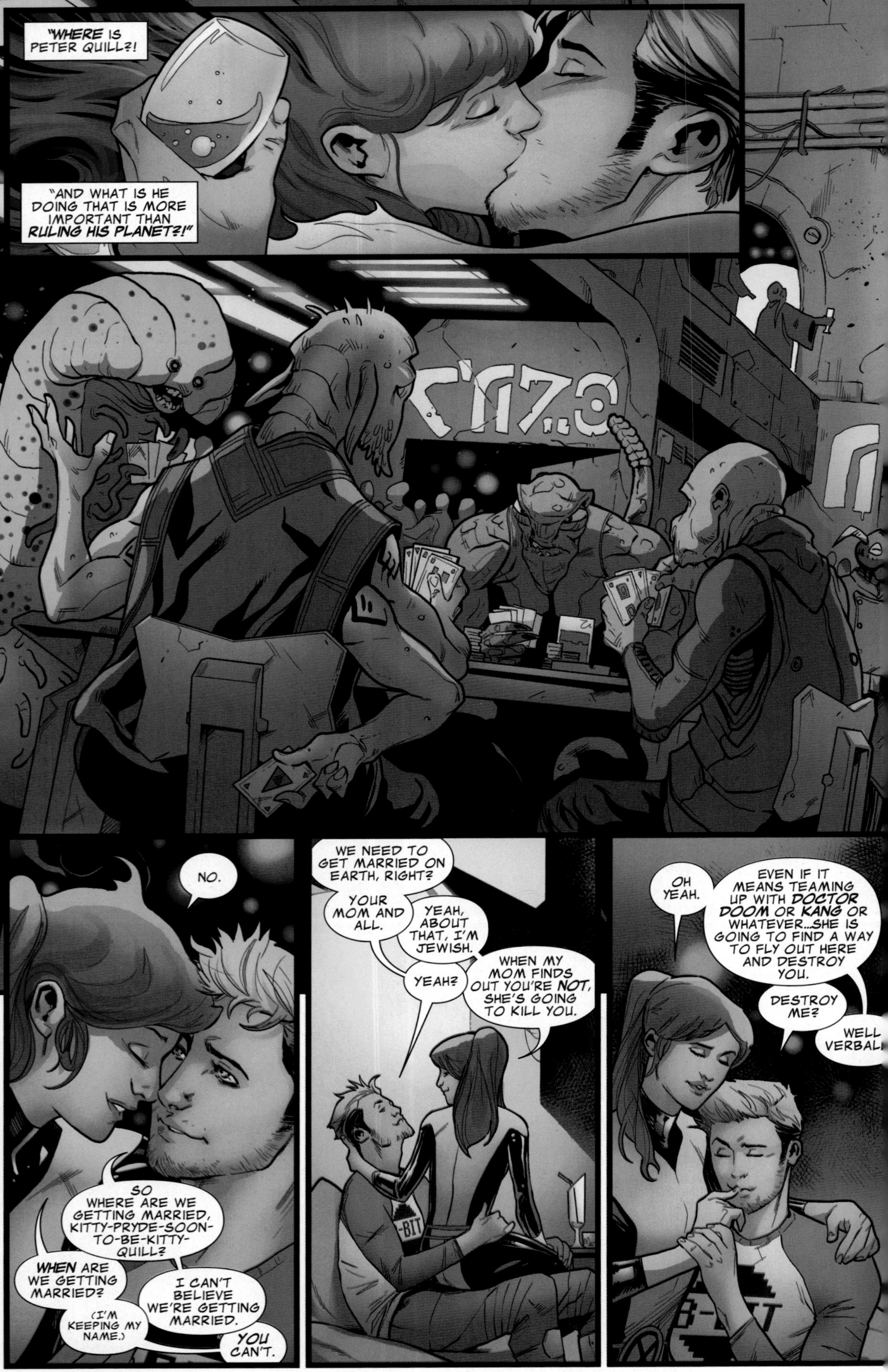
"WHERE IS PETER QUILL?!
"AND WHAT IS HE DOING THAT IS MORE IMPORTANT THAN RULING HIS PLANET?!"
NO.
SO WHERE ARE WE GETTING MARRIED, KITTY-PRYDE-SOON-TO-BE-KITTY-QUILL?
WHEN ARE WE GETTING MARRIED?
I CAN'T BELIEVE WE'RE GETTING MARRIED.
(I'M KEEPING MY NAME.)
YOU CAN'T.
WE NEED TO GET MARRIED ON EARTH, RIGHT?
YOUR MOM AND ALL.
YEAH, ABOUT THAT, I'M JEWISH.
YEAH?
WHEN MY MOM FINDS OUT YOU'RE NOT, SHE'S GOING TO KILL YOU.
OH YEAH.
EVEN IF IT MEANS TEAMING UP WITH DOCTOR DOOM OR KANG OR WHATEVER...SHE IS GOING TO FIND A WAY TO FLY OUT HERE AND DESTROY YOU.
DESTROY ME?
WELL VERBAL

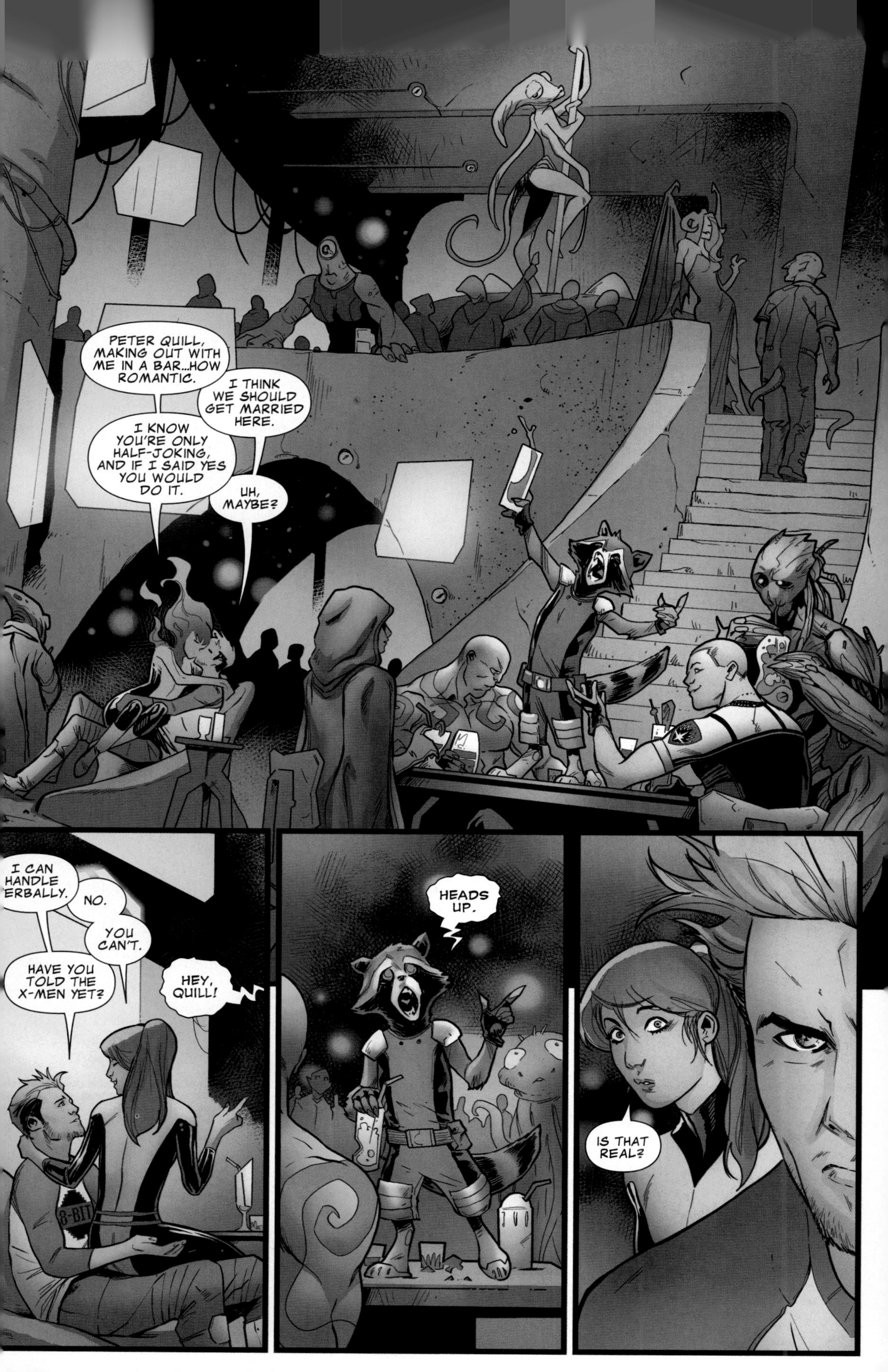

PETER QUILL, MAKING OUT WITH ME IN A BAR...HOW ROMANTIC.
I THINK WE SHOULD GET MARRIED HERE.
I KNOW YOU'RE ONLY HALF-JOKING, AND IF I SAID YES YOU WOULD DO IT.
UH, MAYBE?
I CAN HANDLE ERBALLY.
NO.
YOU CAN'T.
HAVE YOU TOLD THE X-MEN YET?
HEY, QUILL!
HEADS UP.
IS THAT REAL?

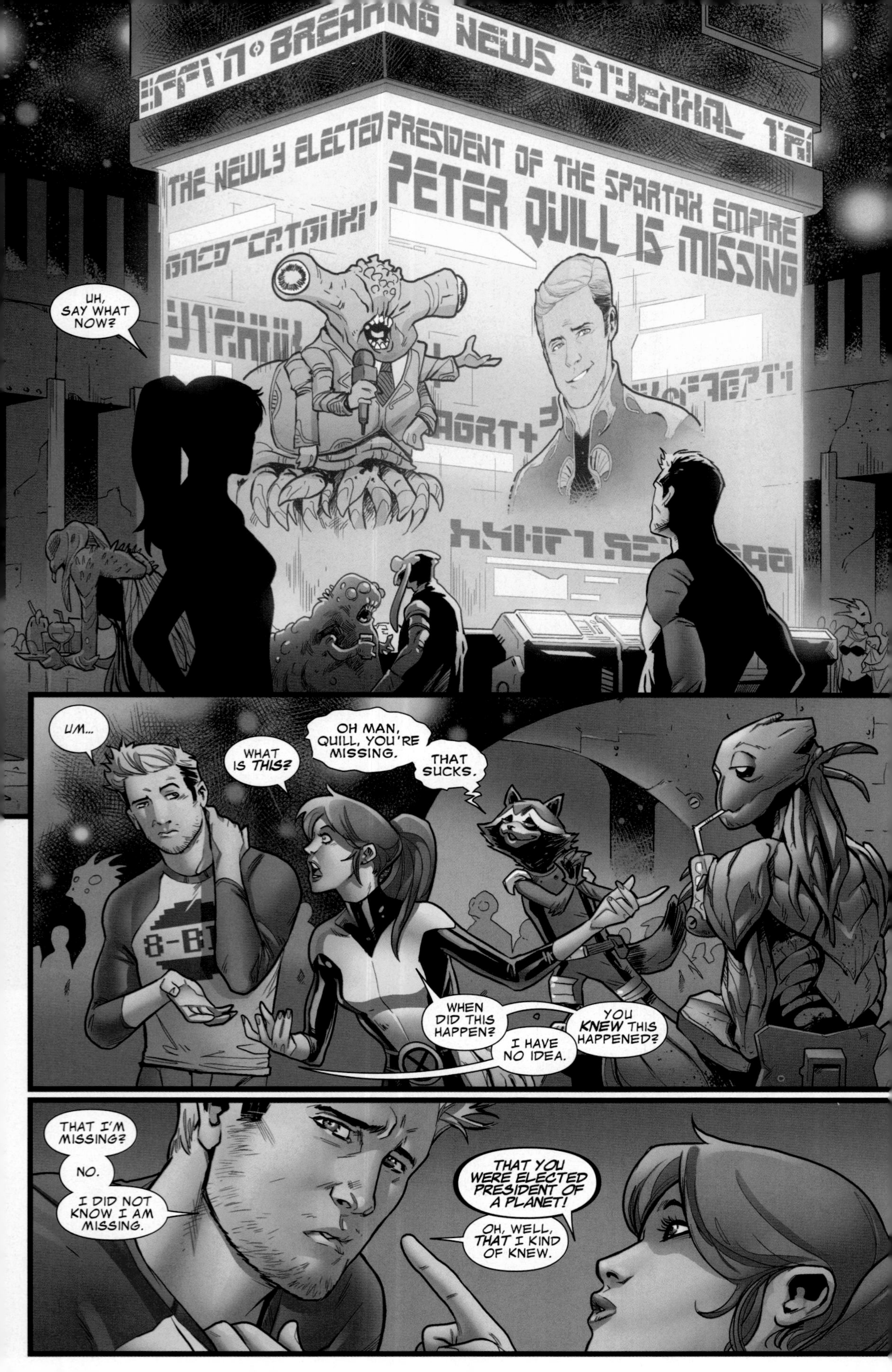
BREAKING NEWS
THE NEWLY ELECTED PRESIDENT OF THE SPARTAX EMPIRE
PETER QUILL IS MISSING
UH, SAY WHAT NOW?
UM...
WHAT IS THIS?
OH MAN, QUILL, YOU'RE MISSING.
THAT SUCKS.
WHEN DID THIS HAPPEN?
I HAVE NO IDEA.
YOU KNEW THIS HAPPENED?
8-BI
THAT I'M MISSING?
NO.
I DID NOT KNOW I AM MISSING.
THAT YOU WERE ELECTED PRESIDENT OF A PLANET!
OH, WELL, THAT I KIND OF KNEW.

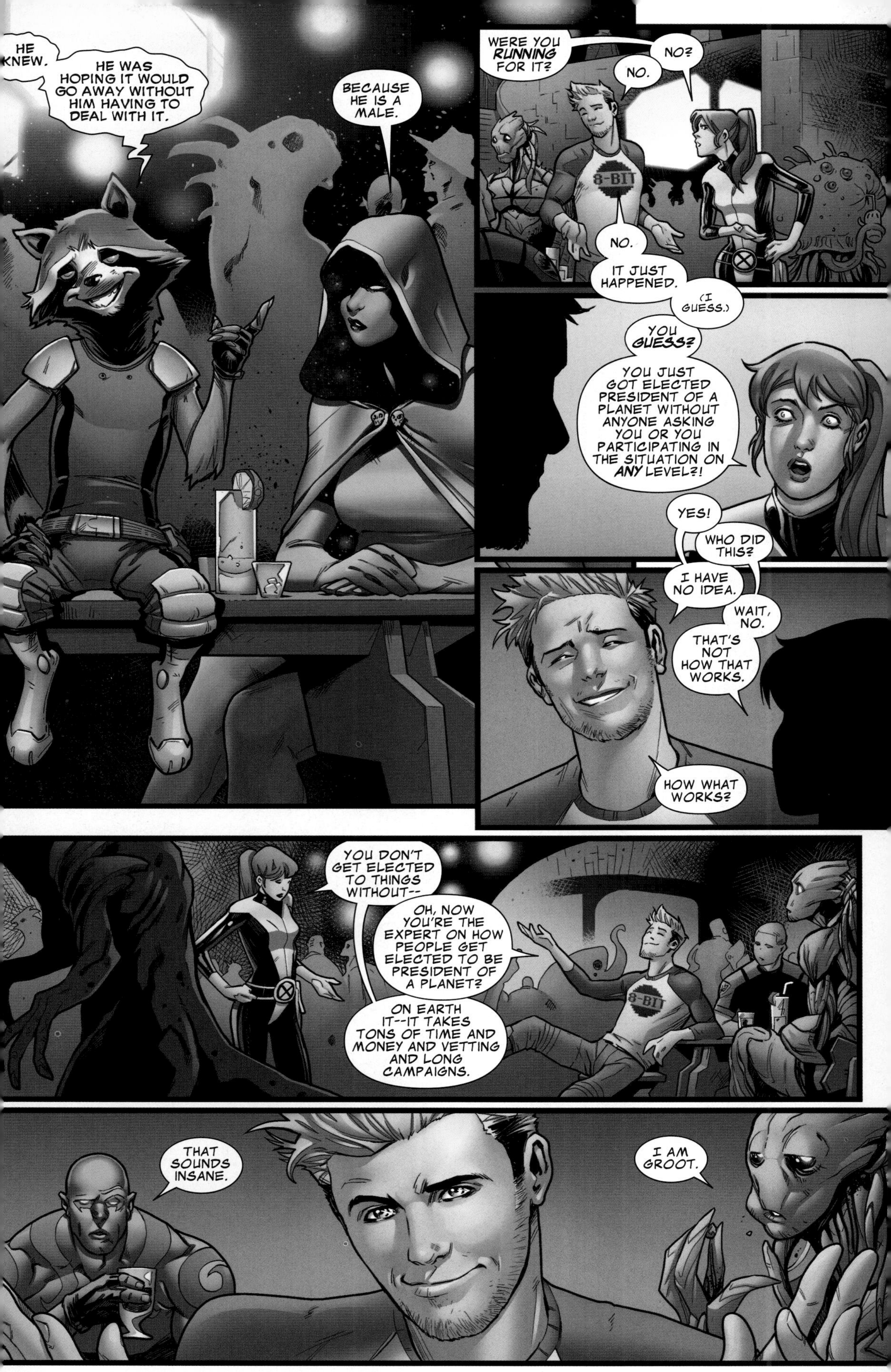
HE KNEW.
HE WAS HOPING IT WOULD GO AWAY WITHOUT HIM HAVING TO DEAL WITH IT.
BECAUSE HE IS A MALE.
WERE YOU RUNNING FOR IT?
NO?
NO.
NO.
IT JUST HAPPENED.
(I GUESS.)
YOU GUESS?
YOU JUST GOT ELECTED PRESIDENT OF A PLANET WITHOUT ANYONE ASKING YOU OR YOU PARTICIPATING IN THE SITUATION ON ANY LEVEL?!
YES!
WHO DID THIS?
I HAVE NO IDEA.
WAIT, NO.
THAT'S NOT HOW THAT WORKS.
HOW WHAT WORKS?
YOU DON'T GET ELECTED TO THINGS WITHOUT--
OH, NOW YOU'RE THE EXPERT ON HOW PEOPLE GET ELECTED TO BE PRESIDENT OF A PLANET?
ON EARTH IT--IT TAKES TONS OF TIME AND MONEY AND VETTING AND LONG CAMPAIGNS.
THAT SOUNDS INSANE.
I AM GROOT.

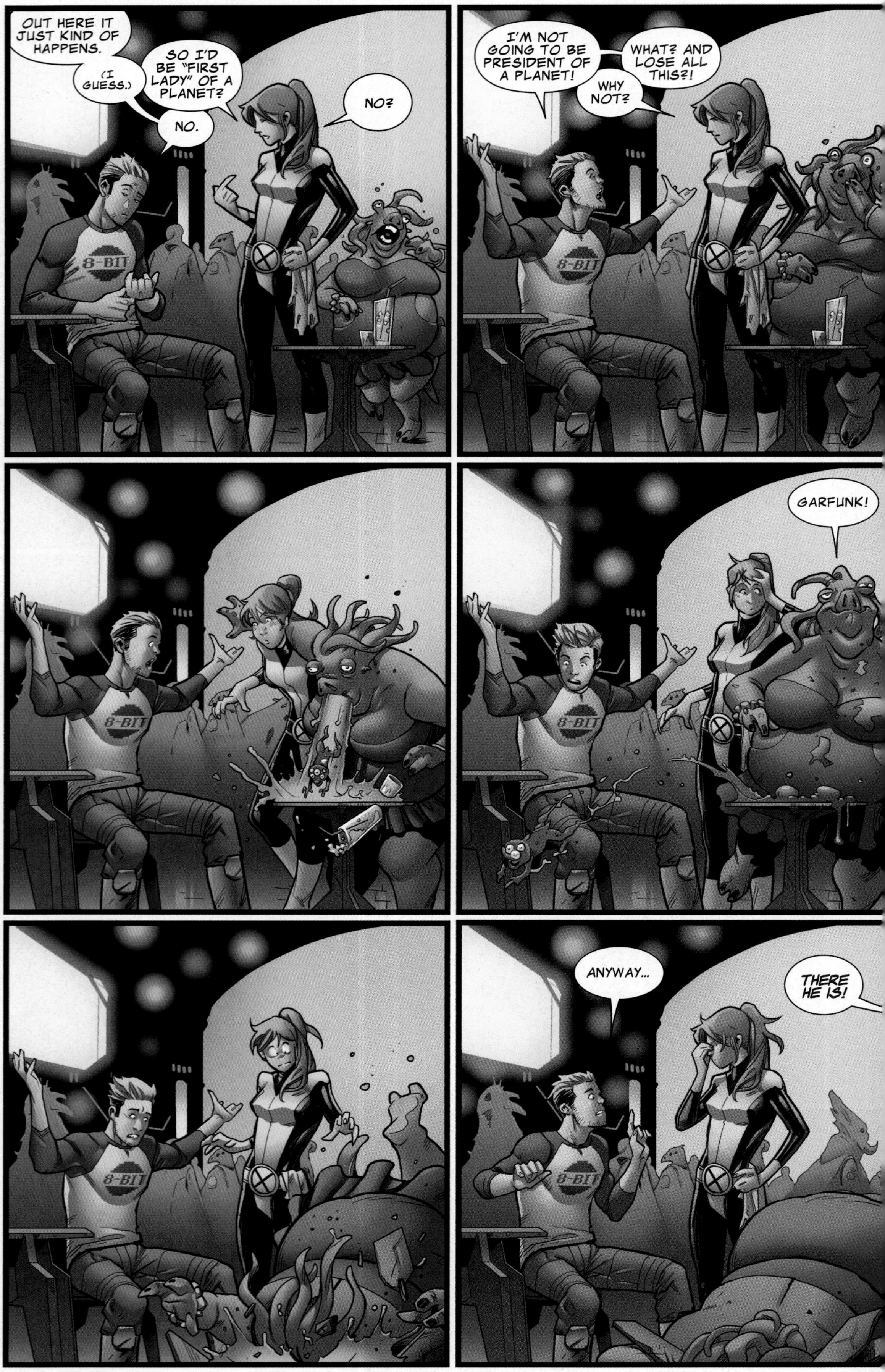
OUT HERE IT JUST KIND OF HAPPENS.
(I GUESS.)
SO I'D BE "FIRST LADY" OF A PLANET?
NO.
NO?
I'M NOT GOING TO BE PRESIDENT OF A PLANET!
WHAT? AND LOSE ALL THIS?!
WHY NOT?
GARFUNK!
ANYWAY...
THERE HE IS!

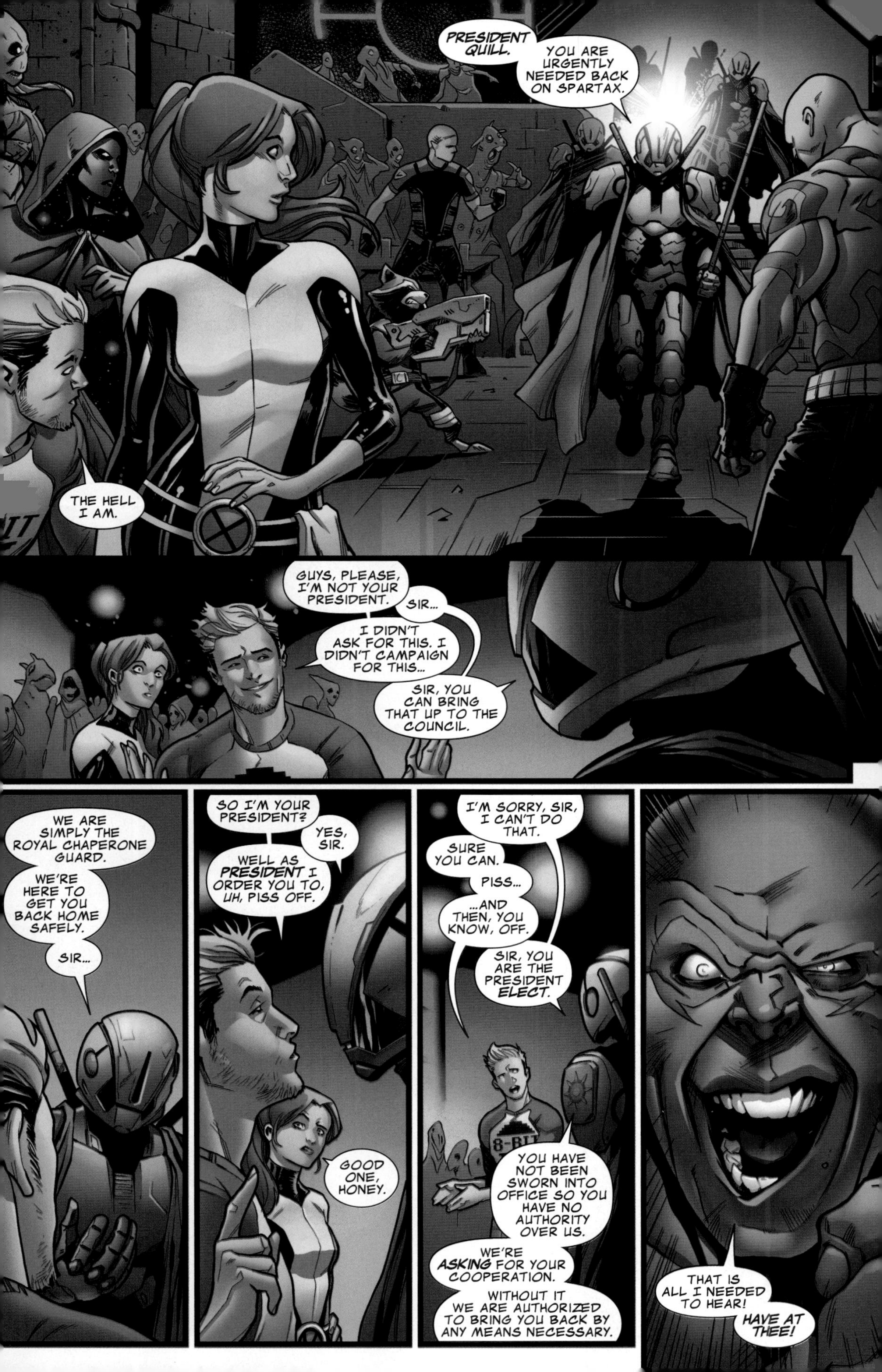
PRESIDENT QUILL.
YOU ARE URGENTLY NEEDED BACK ON SPARTAX.
THE HELL I AM.
GUYS, PLEASE, I'M NOT YOUR PRESIDENT.
SIR...
I DIDN'T ASK FOR THIS. I DIDN'T CAMPAIGN FOR THIS...
SIR, YOU CAN BRING THAT UP TO THE COUNCIL.
WE ARE SIMPLY THE ROYAL CHAPERONE GUARD.
WE'RE HERE TO GET YOU BACK HOME SAFELY.
SIR...
SO I'M YOUR PRESIDENT?
YES, SIR.
WELL AS PRESIDENT I ORDER YOU TO, UH, PISS OFF.
GOOD ONE, HONEY.
I'M SORRY, SIR, I CAN'T DO THAT.
SURE YOU CAN.
PISS...
...AND THEN, YOU KNOW, OFF.
SIR, YOU ARE THE PRESIDENT ELECT.
YOU HAVE NOT BEEN SWORN INTO OFFICE SO YOU HAVE NO AUTHORITY OVER US.
WE'RE ASKING FOR YOUR COOPERATION.
WITHOUT IT WE ARE AUTHORIZED TO BRING YOU BACK BY ANY MEANS NECESSARY.
THAT IS ALL I NEEDED TO HEAR! HAVE AT THEE!

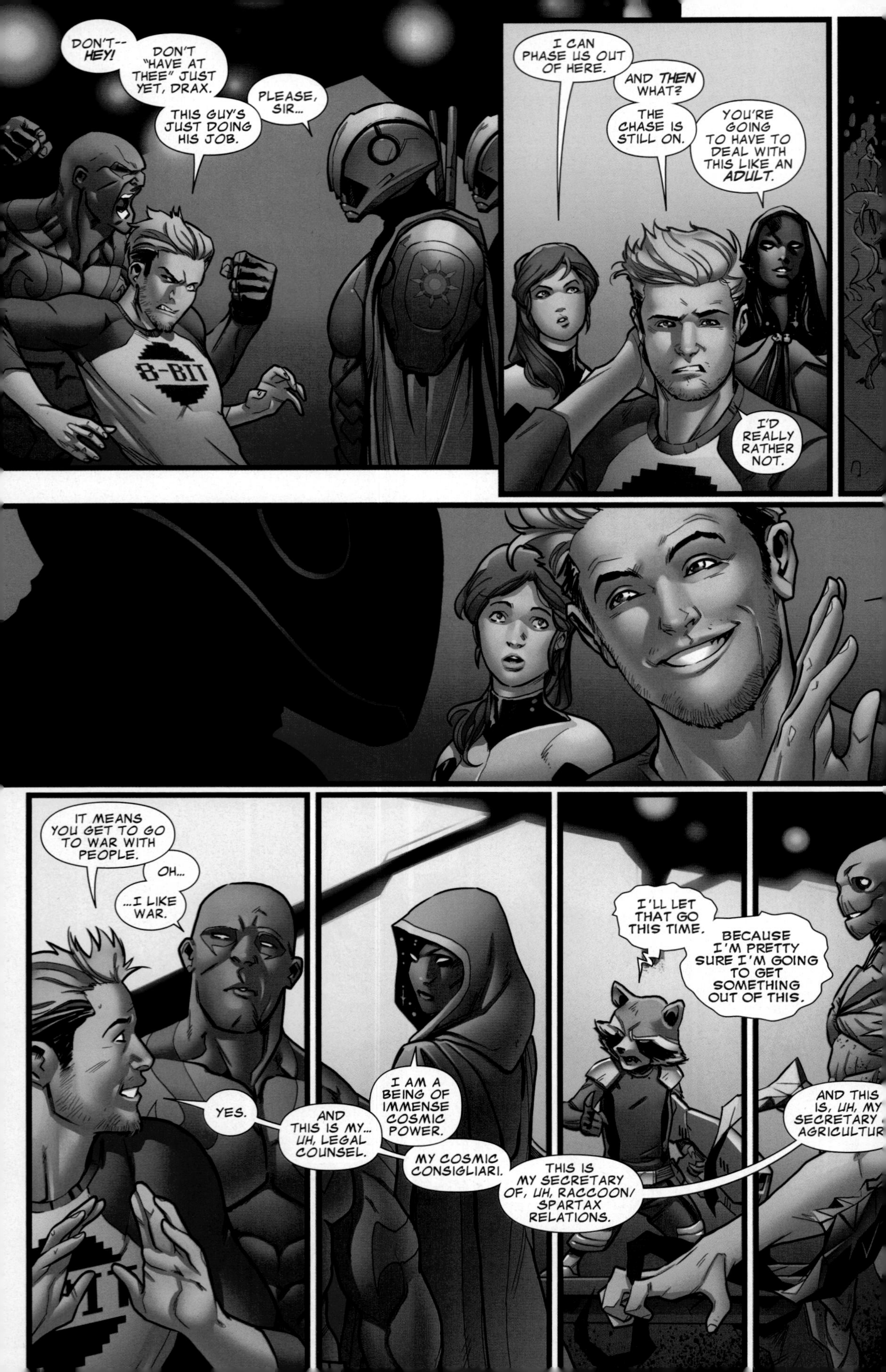
DON'T-- HEY!
DON'T "HAVE AT THEE" JUST YET, DRAX.
THIS GUY'S JUST DOING HIS JOB.
PLEASE, SIR...
I CAN PHASE US OUT OF HERE.
AND THEN WHAT?
THE CHASE IS STILL ON.
YOU'RE GOING TO HAVE TO DEAL WITH THIS LIKE AN ADULT.
I'D REALLY RATHER NOT.
IT MEANS YOU GET TO GO TO WAR WITH PEOPLE.
OH...
...I LIKE WAR.
YES.
AND THIS IS MY... UH, LEGAL COUNSEL.
I AM A BEING OF IMMENSE COSMIC POWER.
MY COSMIC CONSIGLIARI.
I'LL LET THAT GO THIS TIME.
BECAUSE I'M PRETTY SURE I'M GOING TO GET SOMETHING OUT OF THIS.
THIS IS MY SECRETARY OF, UH, RACCOON/SPARTAX RELATIONS.
AND THIS IS, UH, MY SECRETARY AGRICULTUR

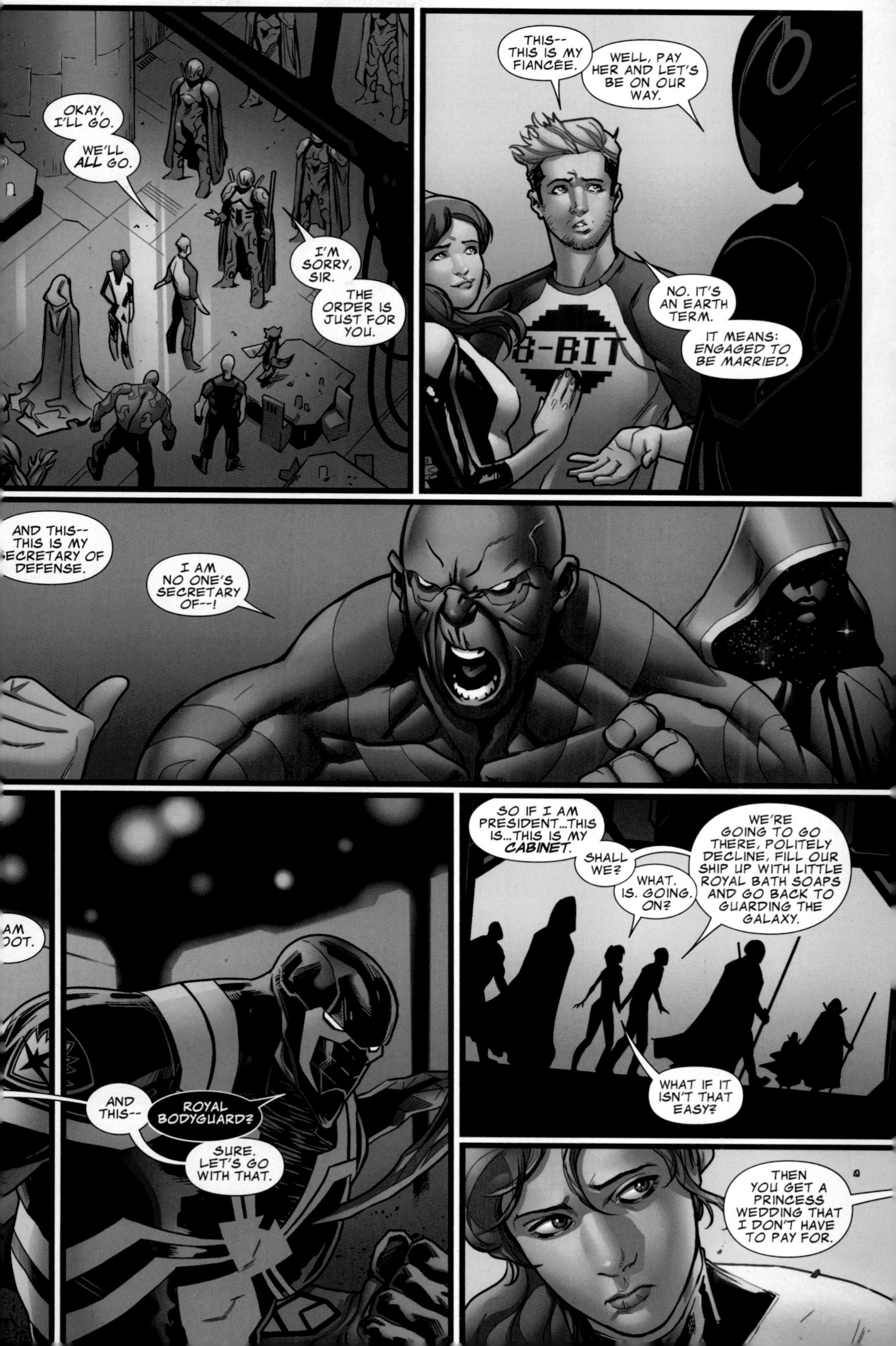
OKAY, I'LL GO.
WE'LL ALL GO.
I'M SORRY, SIR.
THE ORDER IS JUST FOR YOU.
THIS-- THIS IS MY FIANCÉE.
WELL, PAY HER AND LET'S BE ON OUR WAY.
8-BIT
NO. IT'S AN EARTH TERM.
IT MEANS: ENGAGED TO BE MARRIED.
AND THIS-- THIS IS MY SECRETARY OF DEFENSE.
I AM NO ONE'S SECRETARY OF--!
AM OOT.
AND THIS--
ROYAL BODYGUARD?
SURE. LET'S GO WITH THAT.
SO IF I AM PRESIDENT...THIS IS...THIS IS MY CABINET.
SHALL WE?
WHAT. IS. GOING. ON?
WE'RE GOING TO GO THERE, POLITELY DECLINE, FILL OUR SHIP UP WITH LITTLE ROYAL BATH SOAPS AND GO BACK TO GUARDING THE GALAXY.
WHAT IF IT ISN'T THAT EASY?
THEN YOU GET A PRINCESS WEDDING THAT I DON'T HAVE TO PAY FOR.

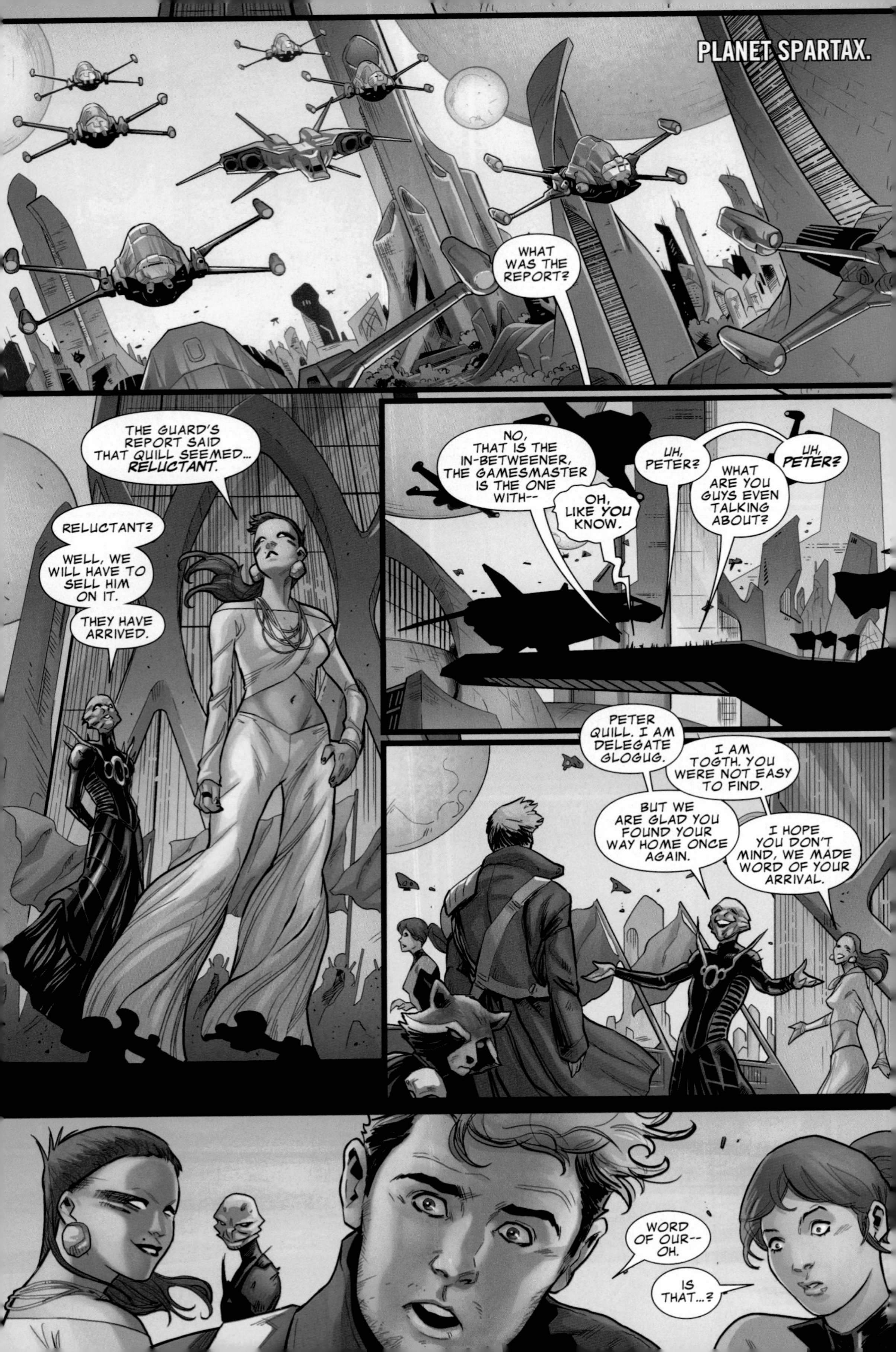
PLANET SPARTAX.
WHAT WAS THE REPORT?
THE GUARD'S REPORT SAID THAT QUILL SEEMED... RELUCTANT.
RELUCTANT?
WELL, WE WILL HAVE TO SELL HIM ON IT.
THEY HAVE ARRIVED.
NO, THAT IS THE IN-BETWEENER, THE GAMESMASTER IS THE ONE WITH--
OH, LIKE YOU KNOW.
UH, PETER?
WHAT ARE YOU GUYS EVEN TALKING ABOUT?
UH, PETER?
PETER QUILL. I AM DELEGATE GLOGUG.
I AM TOGTH. YOU WERE NOT EASY TO FIND.
BUT WE ARE GLAD YOU FOUND YOUR WAY HOME ONCE AGAIN.
I HOPE YOU DON'T MIND, WE MADE WORD OF YOUR ARRIVAL.
WORD OF OUR-- OH.
IS THAT...?

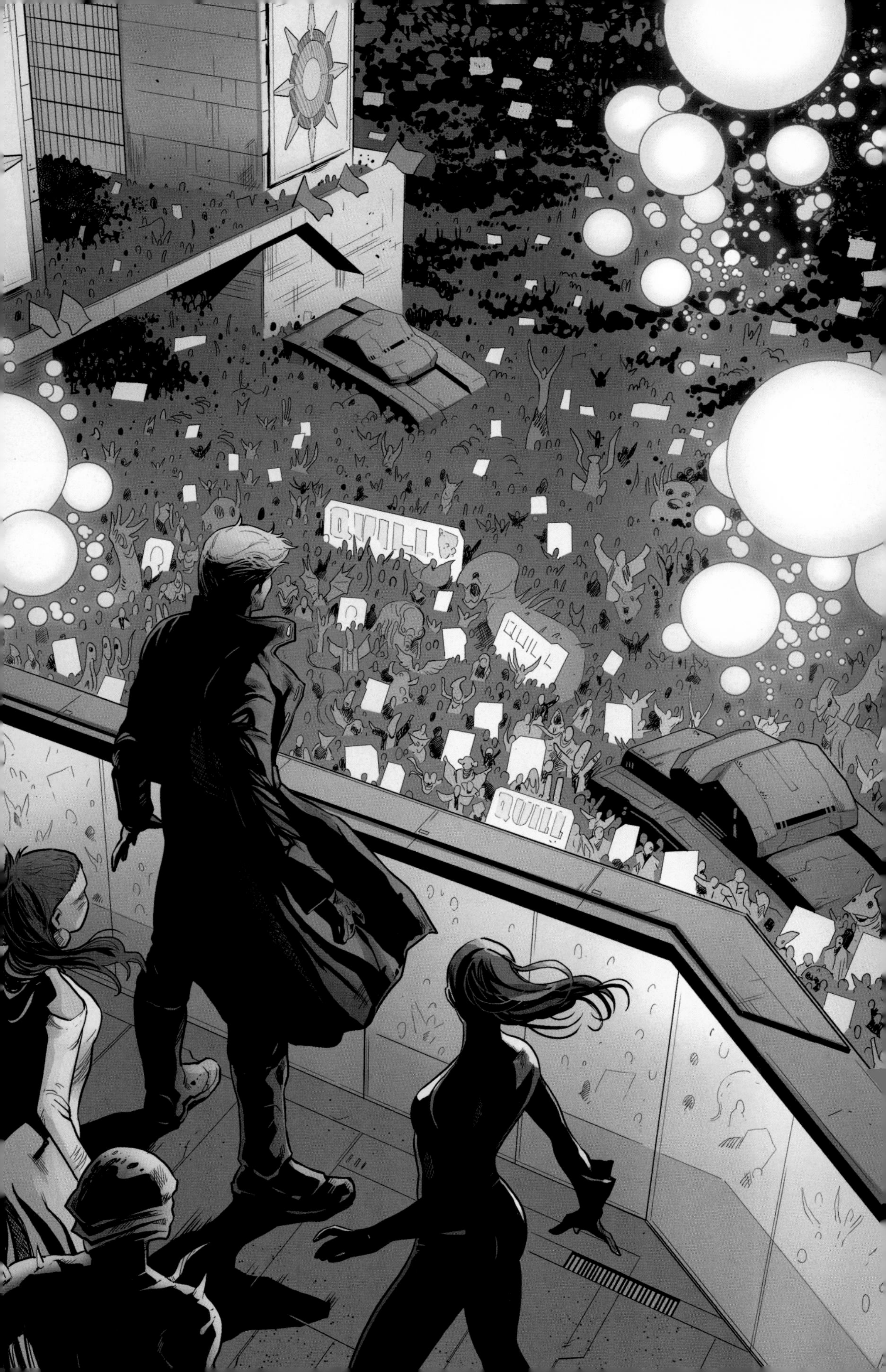
QUILL
QUILL
QUILL

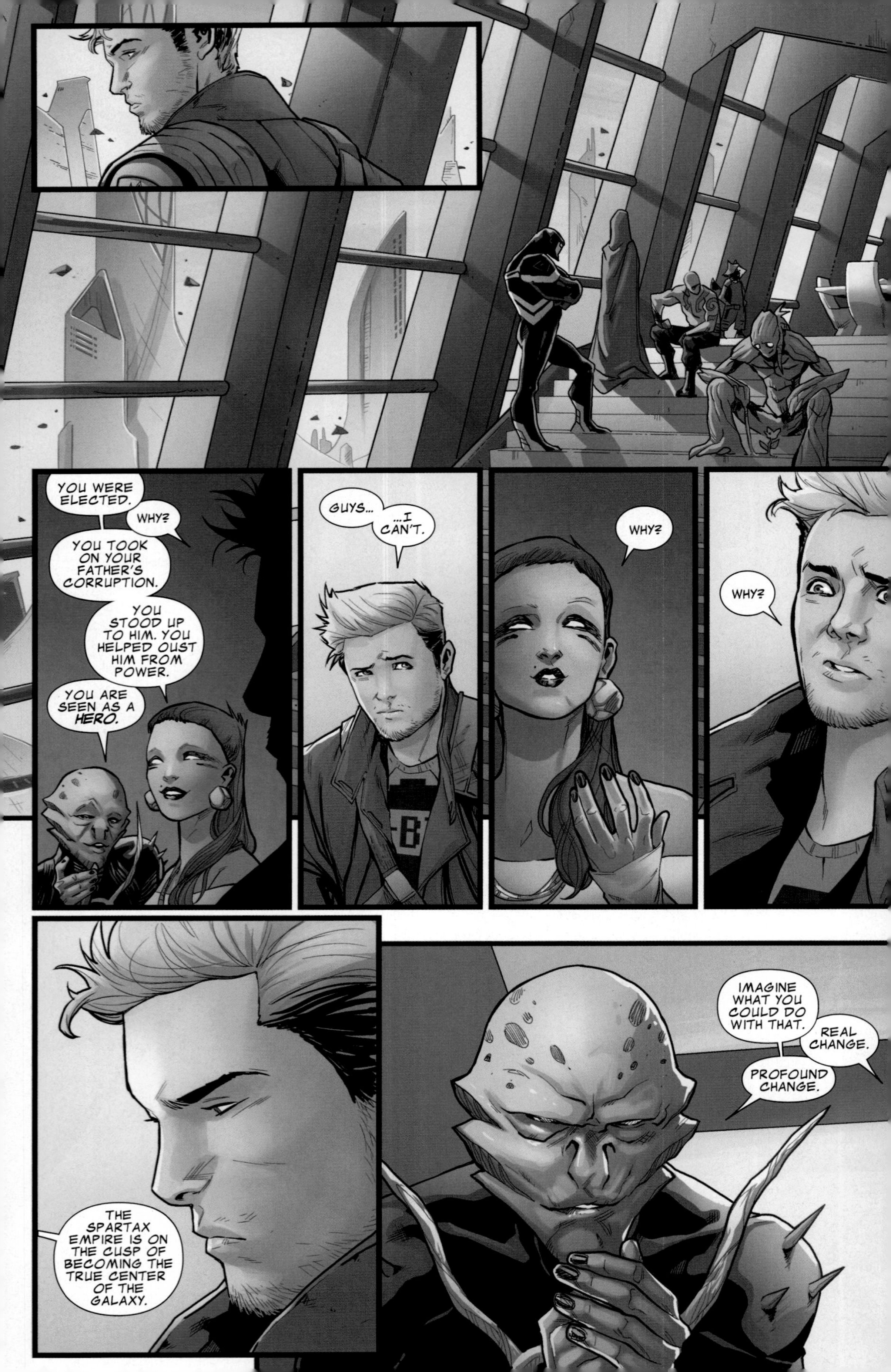
YOU WERE ELECTED.
WHY?
YOU TOOK ON YOUR FATHER'S CORRUPTION.
YOU STOOD UP TO HIM. YOU HELPED OUST HIM FROM POWER.
YOU ARE SEEN AS A **HERO.**
GUYS...
...I CAN'T.
WHY?
WHY?
THE SPARTAX EMPIRE IS ON THE CUSP OF BECOMING THE TRUE CENTER OF THE GALAXY.
IMAGINE WHAT YOU COULD DO WITH THAT.
REAL CHANGE.
PROFOUND CHANGE.

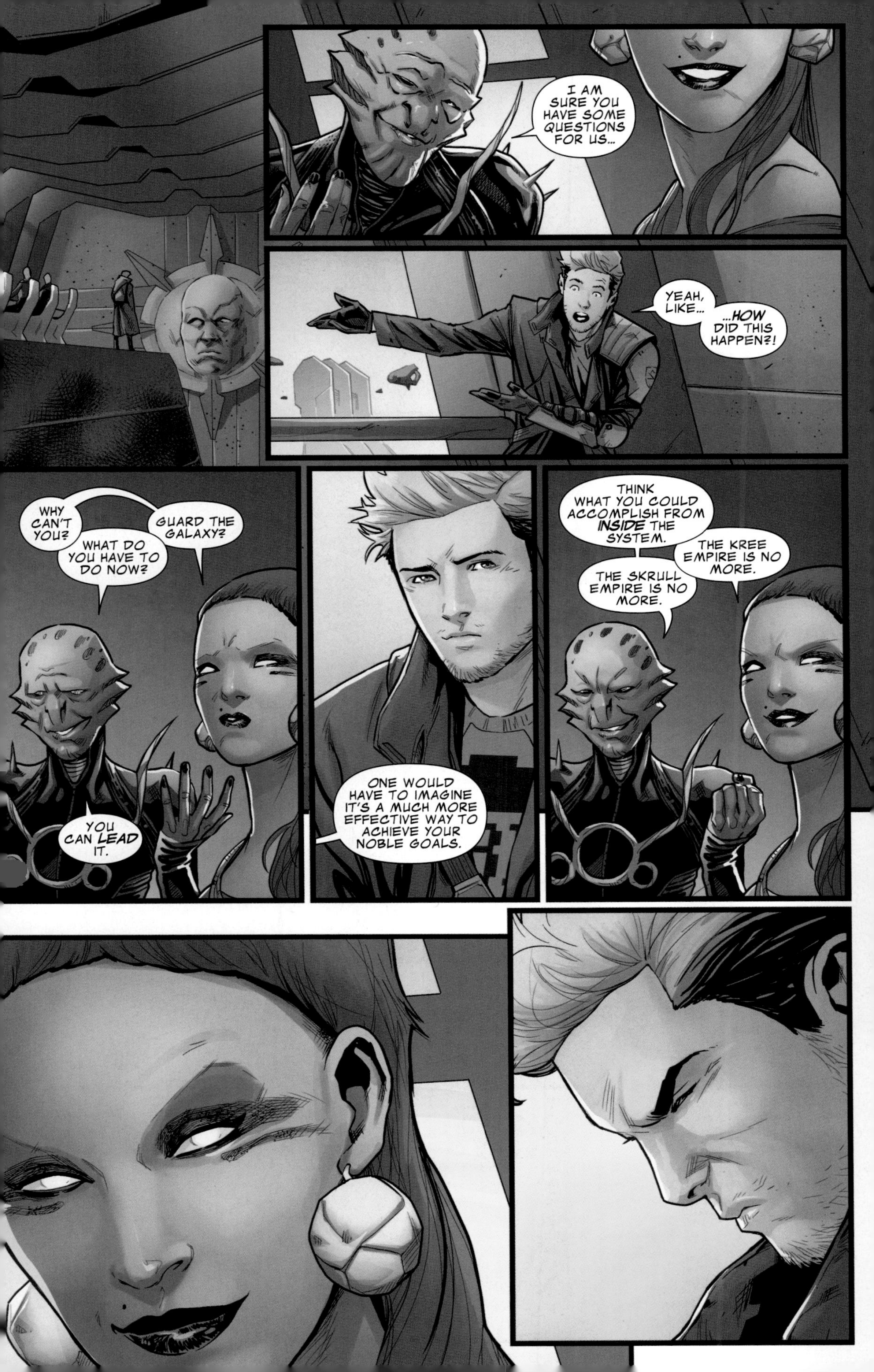
I AM SURE YOU HAVE SOME QUESTIONS FOR US...
YEAH, LIKE...
...HOW DID THIS HAPPEN?!
WHY CAN'T YOU?
GUARD THE GALAXY?
WHAT DO YOU HAVE TO DO NOW?
YOU CAN LEAD IT.
ONE WOULD HAVE TO IMAGINE IT'S A MUCH MORE EFFECTIVE WAY TO ACHIEVE YOUR NOBLE GOALS.
THINK WHAT YOU COULD ACCOMPLISH FROM INSIDE THE SYSTEM.
THE SKRULL EMPIRE IS NO MORE.
THE KREE EMPIRE IS NO MORE.

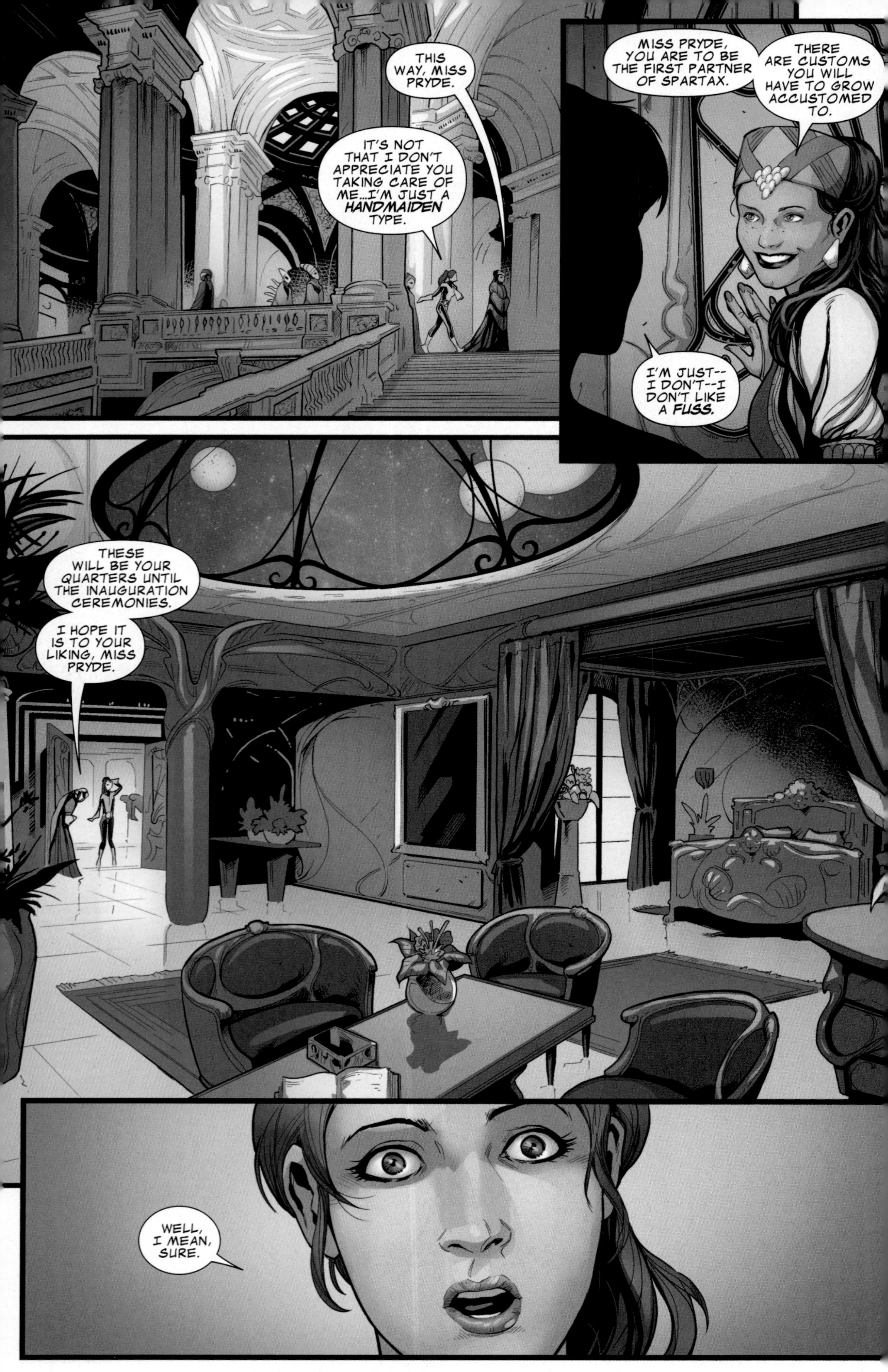
THIS WAY, MISS PRYDE.
IT'S NOT THAT I DON'T APPRECIATE YOU TAKING CARE OF ME...I'M JUST A HANDMAIDEN TYPE.
MISS PRYDE, YOU ARE TO BE THE FIRST PARTNER OF SPARTAX.
THERE ARE CUSTOMS YOU WILL HAVE TO GROW ACCUSTOMED TO.
I'M JUST-- I DON'T--I DON'T LIKE A FUSS.
THESE WILL BE YOUR QUARTERS UNTIL THE INAUGURATION CEREMONIES.
I HOPE IT IS TO YOUR LIKING, MISS PRYDE.
WELL, I MEAN, SURE.

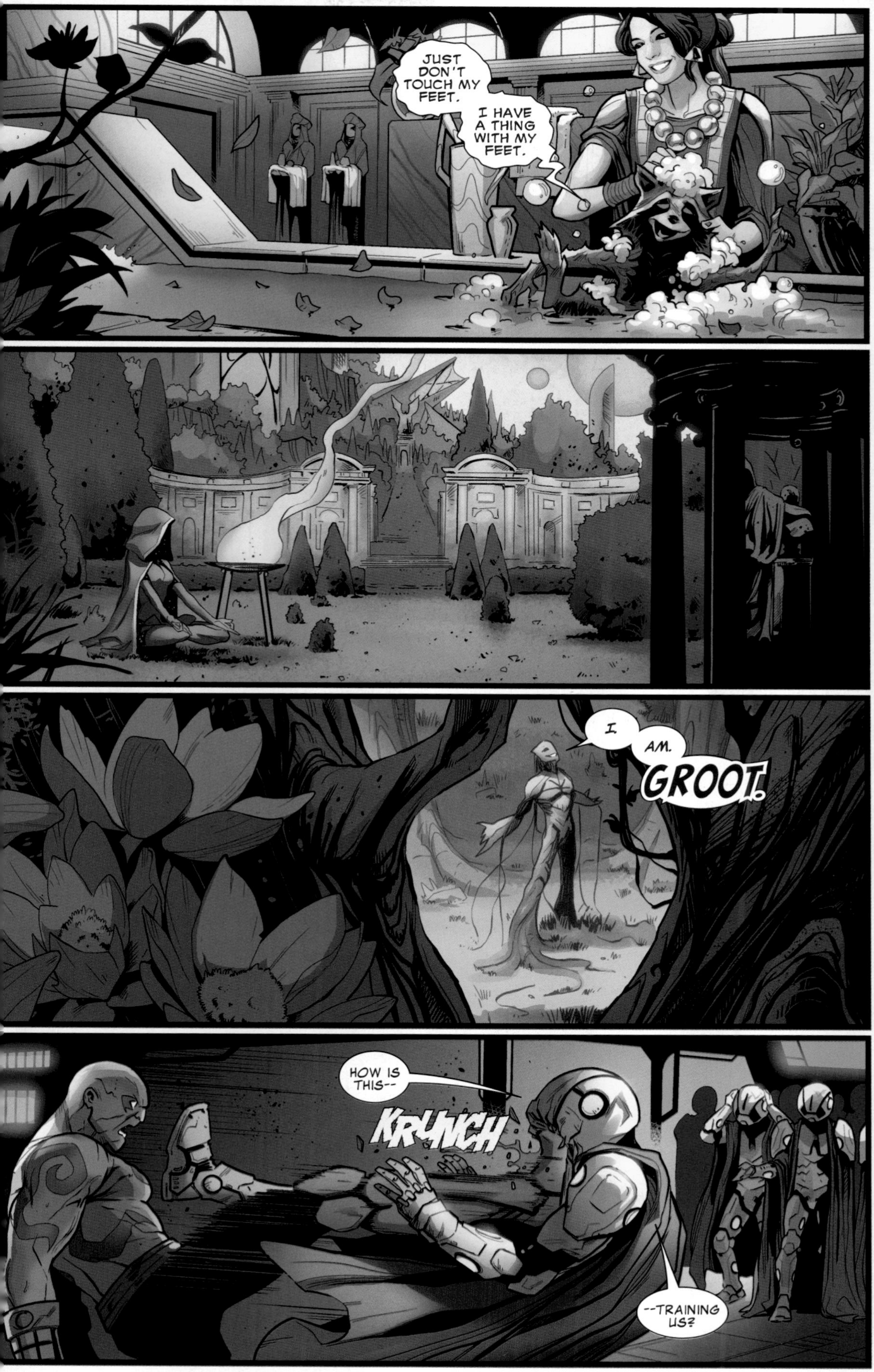
JUST DON'T TOUCH MY FEET.
I HAVE A THING WITH MY FEET.
I
AM.
GROOT.
HOW IS THIS--
KRUNCH
--TRAINING US?

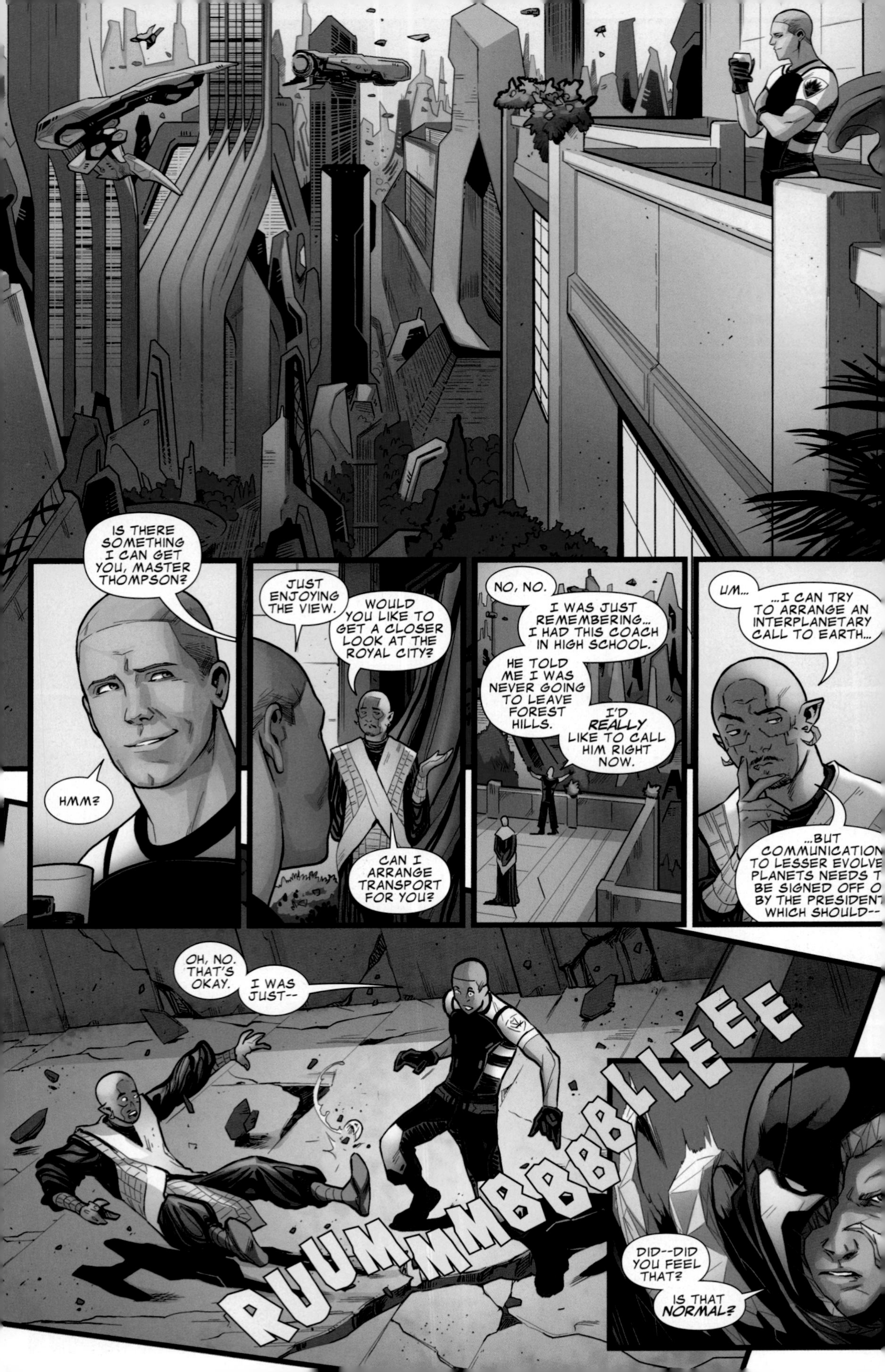
IS THERE SOMETHING I CAN GET YOU, MASTER THOMPSON?
HMM?
JUST ENJOYING THE VIEW.
WOULD YOU LIKE TO GET A CLOSER LOOK AT THE ROYAL CITY?
CAN I ARRANGE TRANSPORT FOR YOU?
NO, NO.
I WAS JUST REMEMBERING... I HAD THIS COACH IN HIGH SCHOOL.
HE TOLD ME I WAS NEVER GOING TO LEAVE FOREST HILLS.
I'D REALLY LIKE TO CALL HIM RIGHT NOW.
UM...
...I CAN TRY TO ARRANGE AN INTERPLANETARY CALL TO EARTH...
OH, NO. THAT'S OKAY.
I WAS JUST--
RUUMMMBBBBLLEEE
DID--DID YOU FEEL THAT?
IS THAT NORMAL?

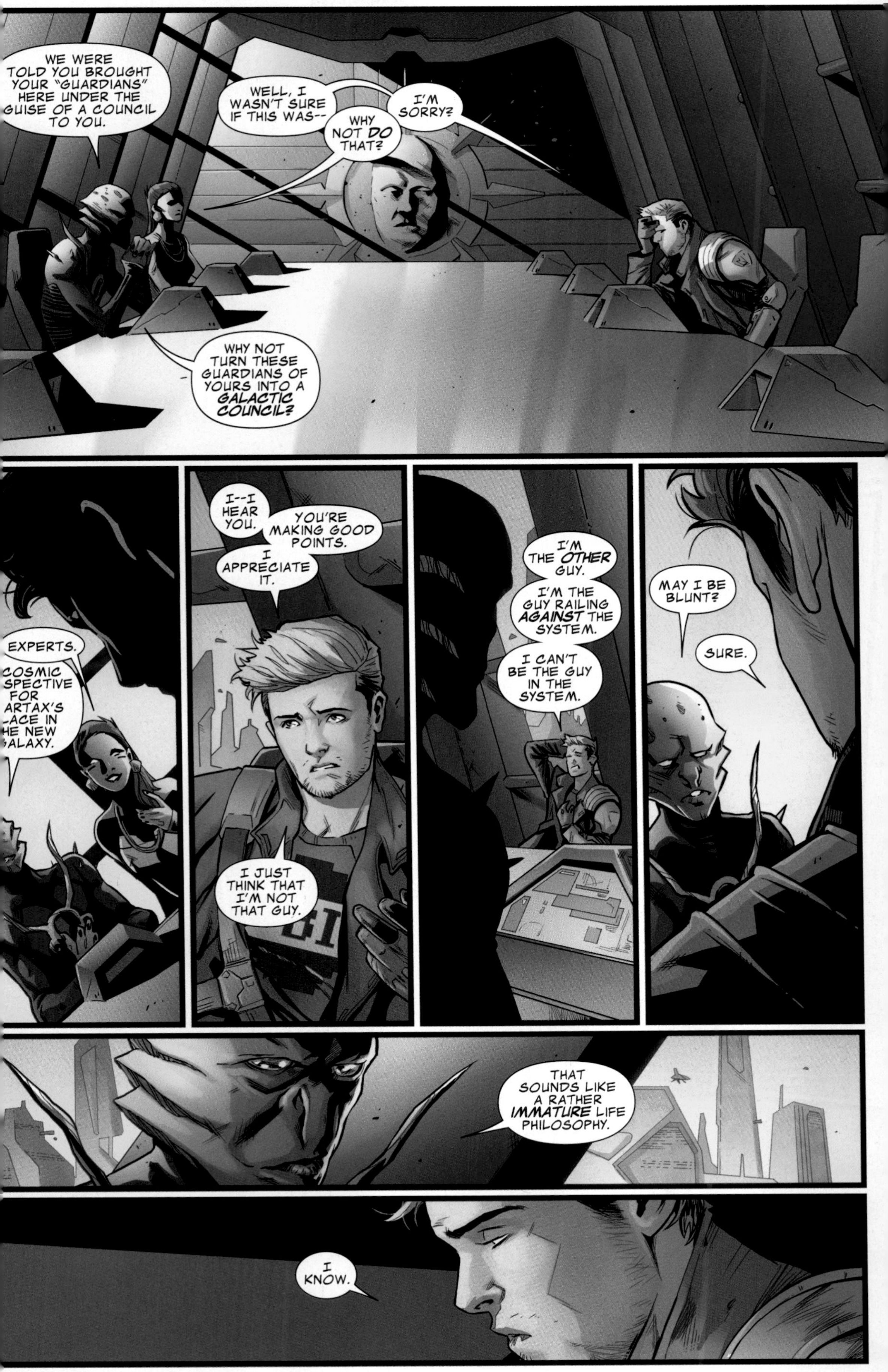
WE WERE TOLD YOU BROUGHT YOUR "GUARDIANS" HERE UNDER THE GUISE OF A COUNCIL TO YOU.
WELL, I WASN'T SURE IF THIS WAS--
I'M SORRY?
WHY NOT DO THAT?
WHY NOT TURN THESE GUARDIANS OF YOURS INTO A GALACTIC COUNCIL?
EXPERTS.
COSMIC SPECTIVE FOR ARTAX'S LACE IN HE NEW GALAXY.
I--I HEAR YOU.
YOU'RE MAKING GOOD POINTS.
I APPRECIATE IT.
I JUST THINK THAT I'M NOT THAT GUY.
I'M THE OTHER GUY.
I'M THE GUY RAILING AGAINST THE SYSTEM.
I CAN'T BE THE GUY IN THE SYSTEM.
MAY I BE BLUNT?
SURE.
THAT SOUNDS LIKE A RATHER IMMATURE LIFE PHILOSOPHY.
I KNOW.

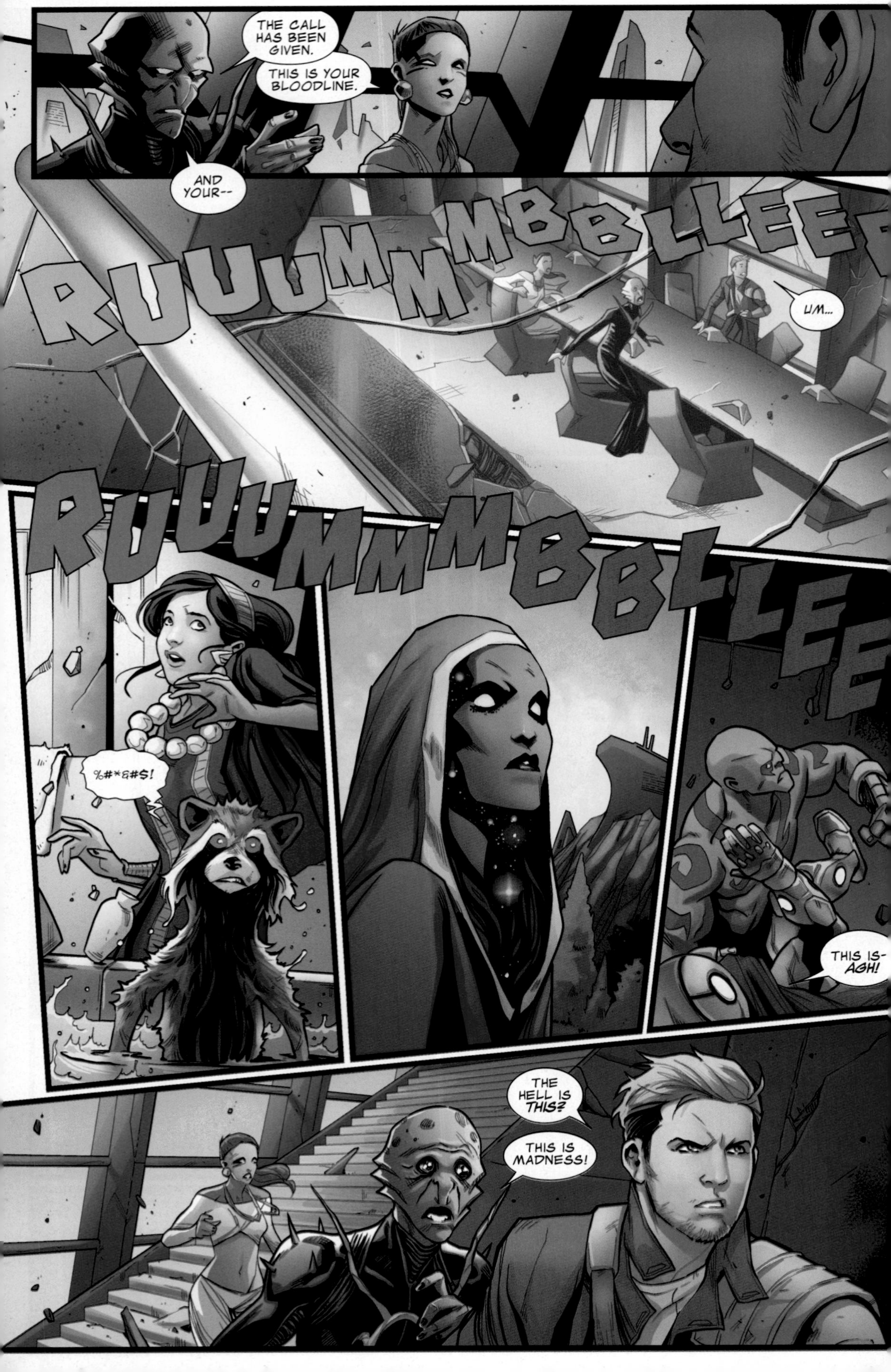
THE CALL HAS BEEN GIVEN.
THIS IS YOUR BLOODLINE.
AND YOUR--
RUUUMMMBBLLEEE
UM...
RUUUMMMBBLLEEE
%#*&#$!
THIS IS-- AGH!
THE HELL IS THIS?
THIS IS MADNESS!

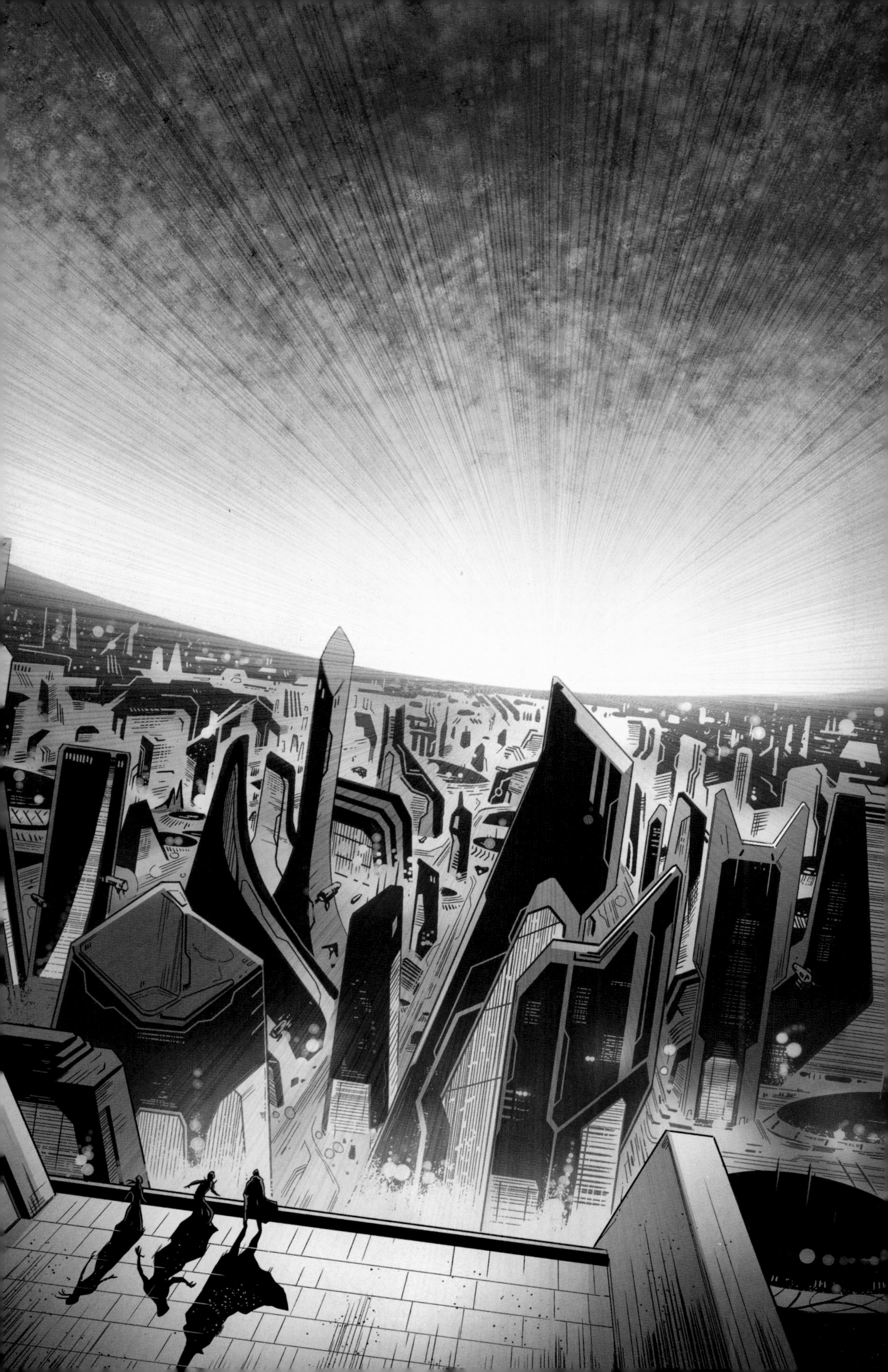

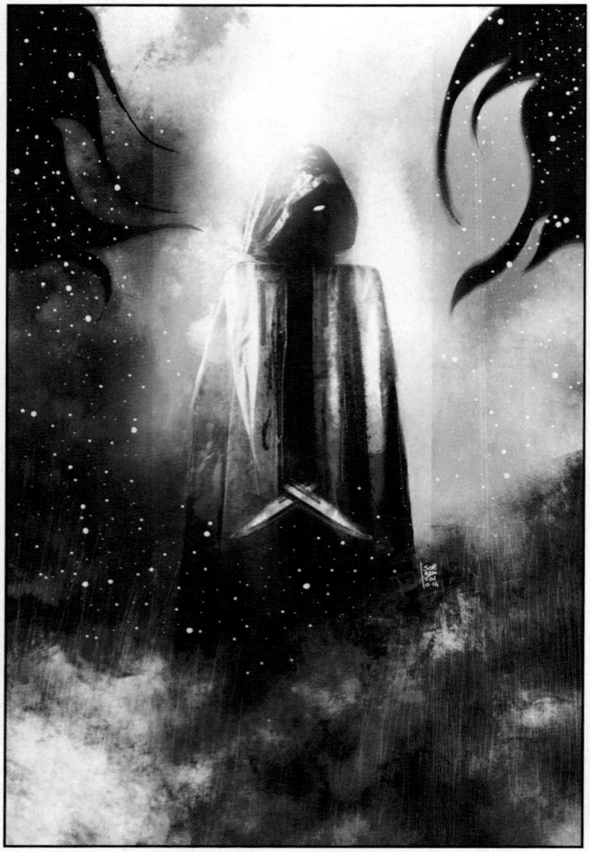

#24 COSMICALLY ENHANCED VARIANT
BY ANDREA SORRENTINO

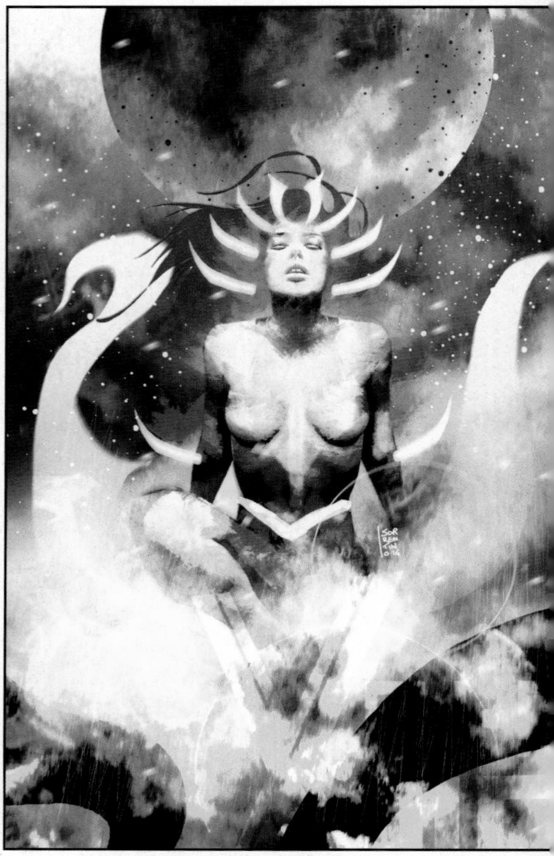

#25 COSMICALLY ENHANCED VARIANT
BY ANDREA SORRENTINO

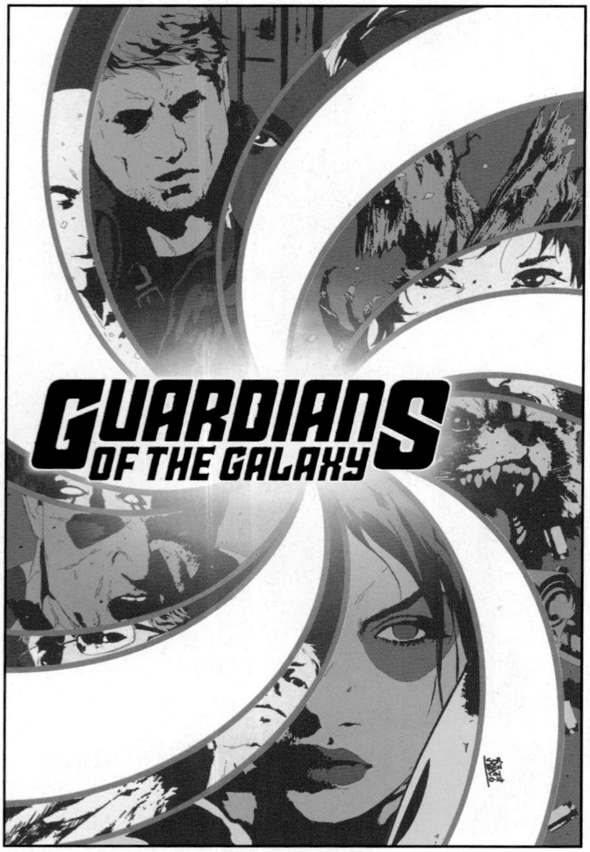
GUARDIANS
OF THE GALAXY

#25 VARIANT
BY ANDREA SORRENTINO

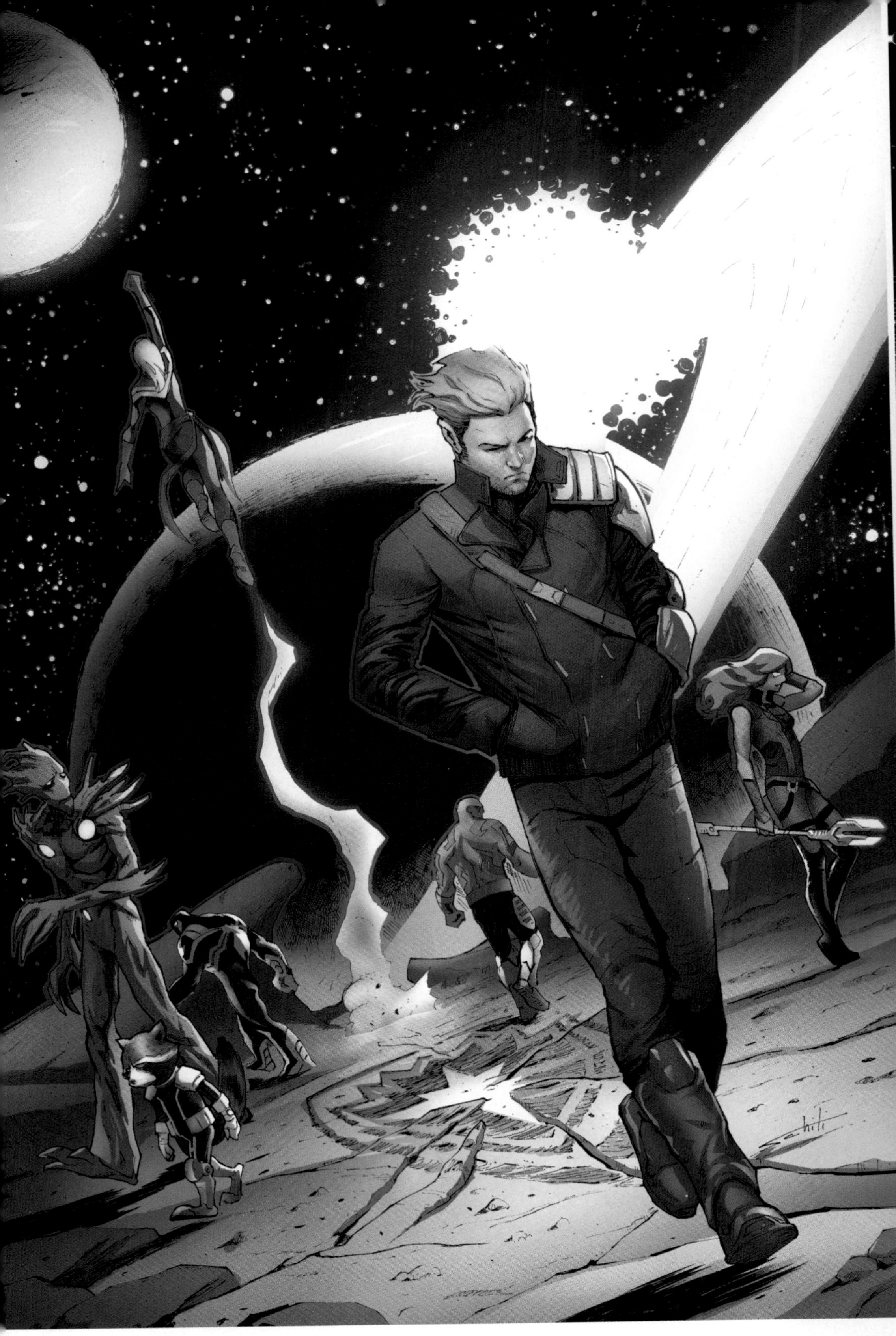

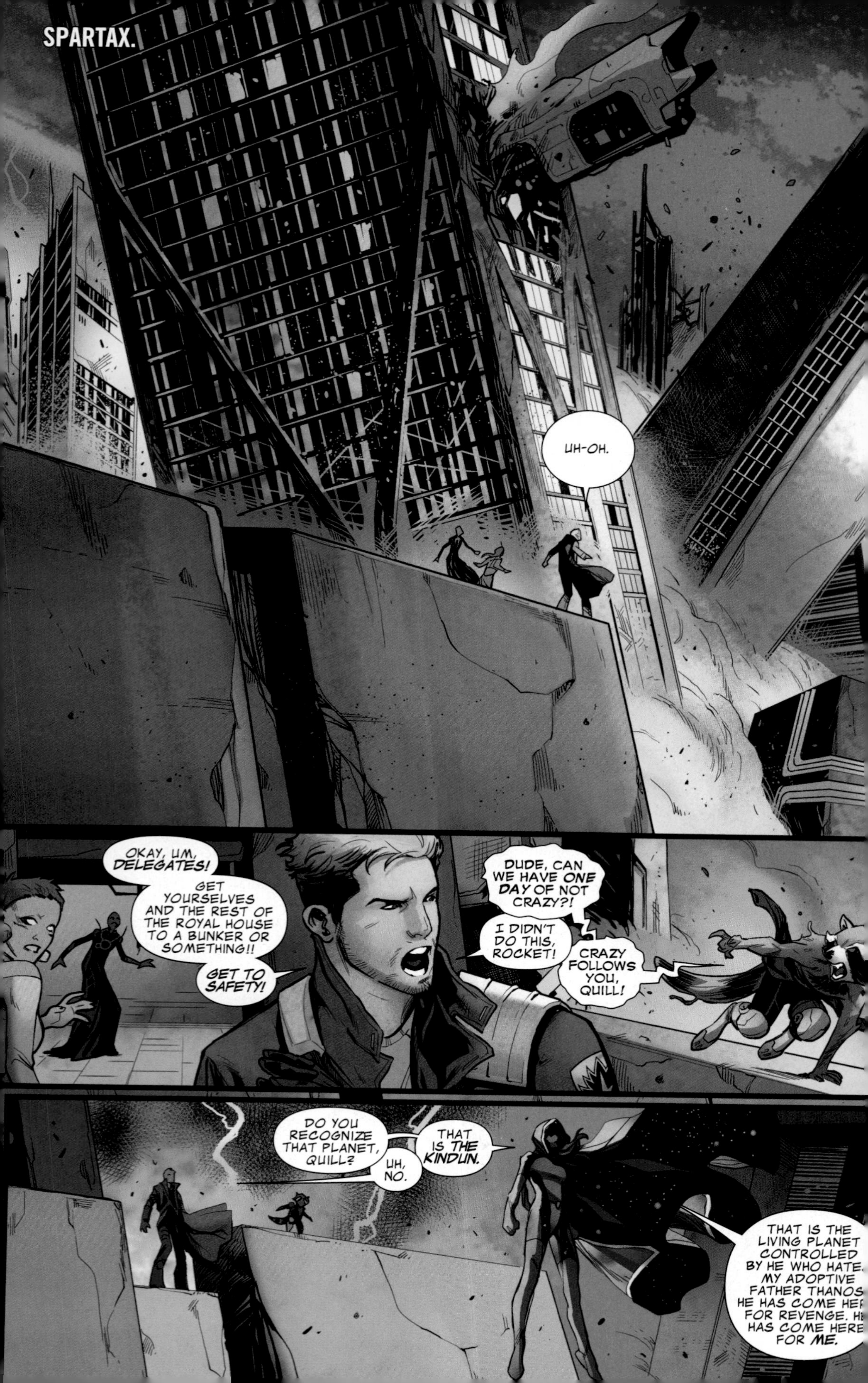
SPARTAX.
UH-OH.
OKAY, UM, DELEGATES! GET YOURSELVES AND THE REST OF THE ROYAL HOUSE TO A BUNKER OR SOMETHING!!
GET TO SAFETY!
DUDE, CAN WE HAVE ONE DAY OF NOT CRAZY?!
I DIDN'T DO THIS, ROCKET!
CRAZY FOLLOWS YOU, QUILL!
DO YOU RECOGNIZE THAT PLANET, QUILL?
UH, NO.
THAT IS THE KINDUN.
THAT IS THE LIVING PLANET CONTROLLED BY HE WHO HATE MY ADOPTIVE FATHER THANOS HE HAS COME HE FOR REVENGE. H HAS COME HERE FOR ME.

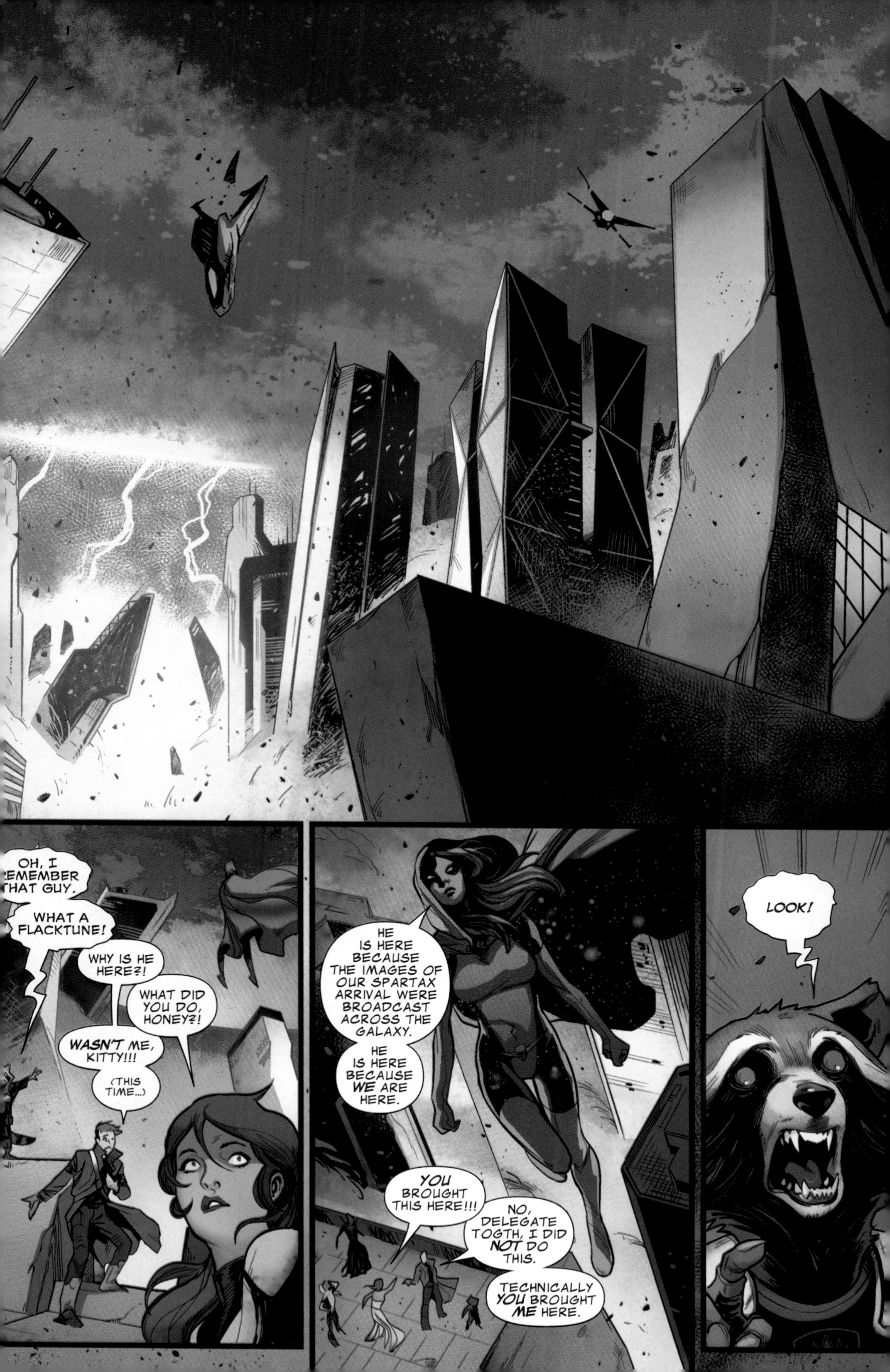
OH, I REMEMBER THAT GUY.
WHAT A FLACKTUNE!
WHY IS HE HERE?!
WHAT DID YOU DO, HONEY?!
WASN'T ME, KITTY!!!
(THIS TIME...)
HE IS HERE BECAUSE THE IMAGES OF OUR SPARTAX ARRIVAL WERE BROADCAST ACROSS THE GALAXY.
HE IS HERE BECAUSE WE ARE HERE.
YOU BROUGHT THIS HERE!!!
NO, DELEGATE TOGTH, I DID NOT DO THIS.
TECHNICALLY YOU BROUGHT ME HERE.
LOOK!

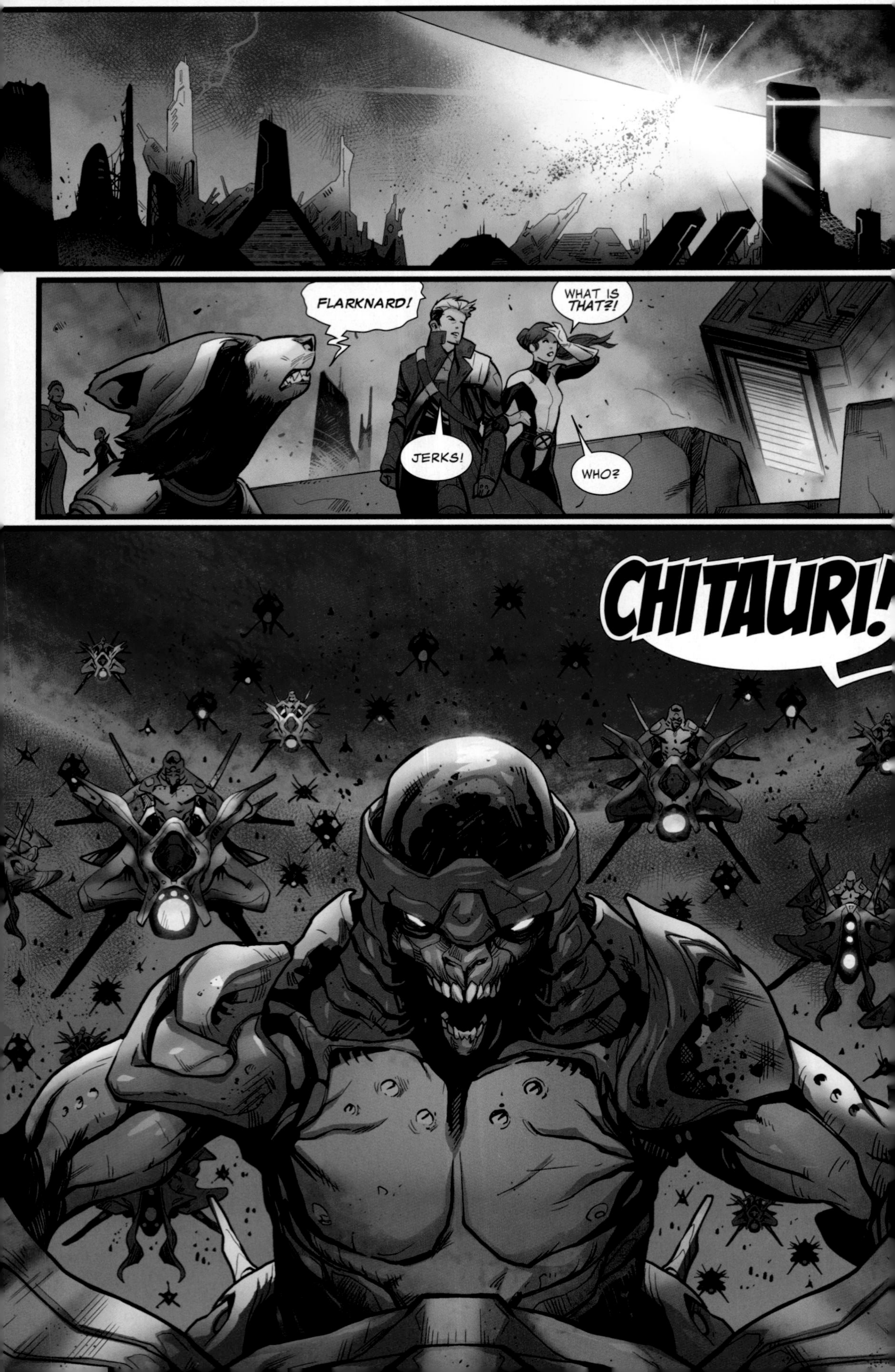
FLARKNARD!
WHAT IS THAT?!
JERKS!
WHO?
CHITAURI!

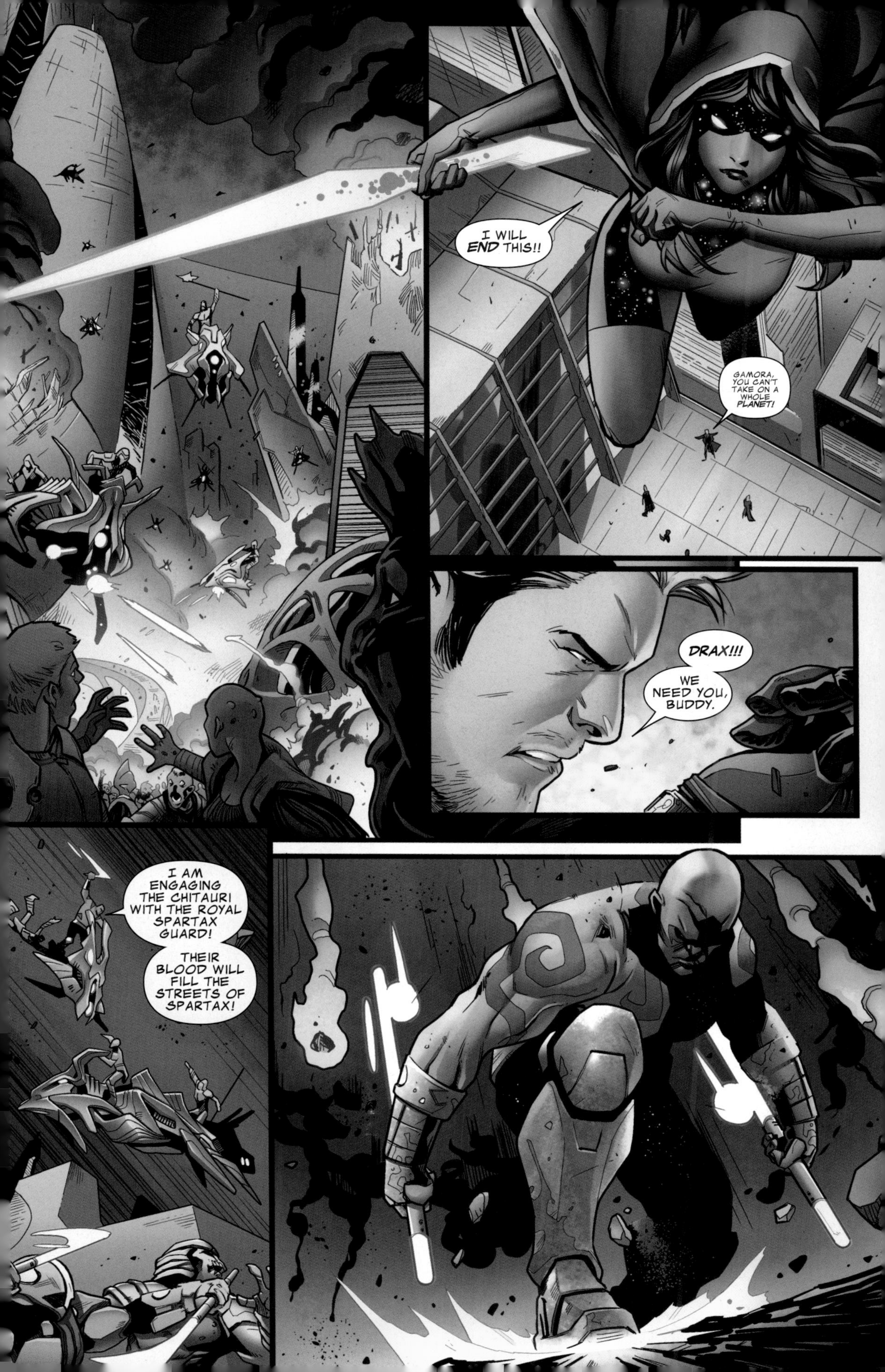
I WILL END THIS!!
GAMORA, YOU CAN'T TAKE ON A WHOLE PLANET!
DRAX!!!
WE NEED YOU, BUDDY.
I AM ENGAGING THE CHITAURI WITH THE ROYAL SPARTAX GUARD!
THEIR BLOOD WILL FILL THE STREETS OF SPARTAX!

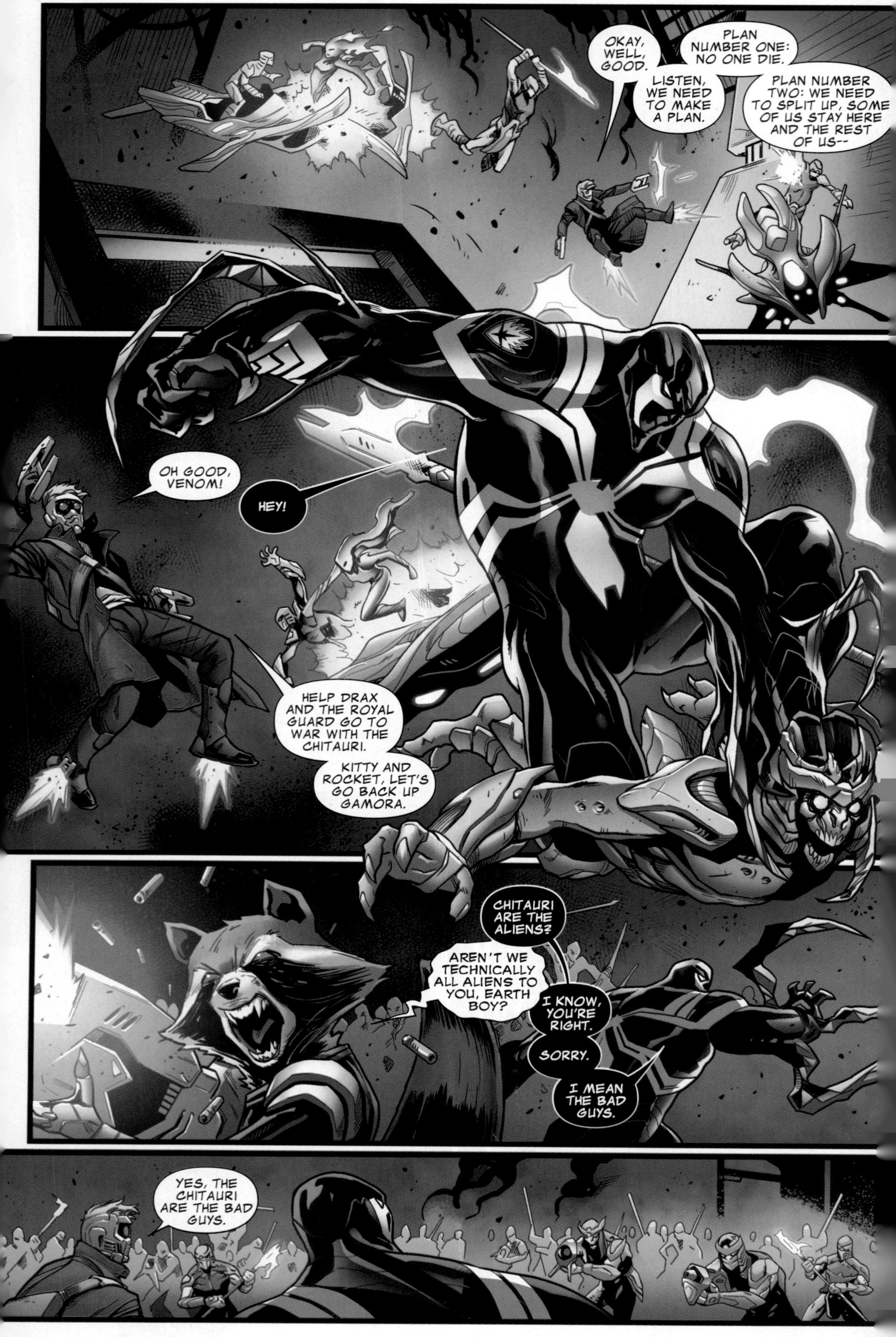
OKAY, WELL, GOOD.
PLAN NUMBER ONE: NO ONE DIE.
LISTEN, WE NEED TO MAKE A PLAN.
PLAN NUMBER TWO: WE NEED TO SPLIT UP, SOME OF US STAY HERE AND THE REST OF US--
OH GOOD, VENOM!
HEY!
HELP DRAX AND THE ROYAL GUARD GO TO WAR WITH THE CHITAURI.
KITTY AND ROCKET, LET'S GO BACK UP GAMORA.
CHITAURI ARE THE ALIENS?
AREN'T WE TECHNICALLY ALL ALIENS TO YOU, EARTH BOY?
I KNOW, YOU'RE RIGHT.
SORRY.
I MEAN THE BAD GUYS.
YES, THE CHITAURI ARE THE BAD GUYS.

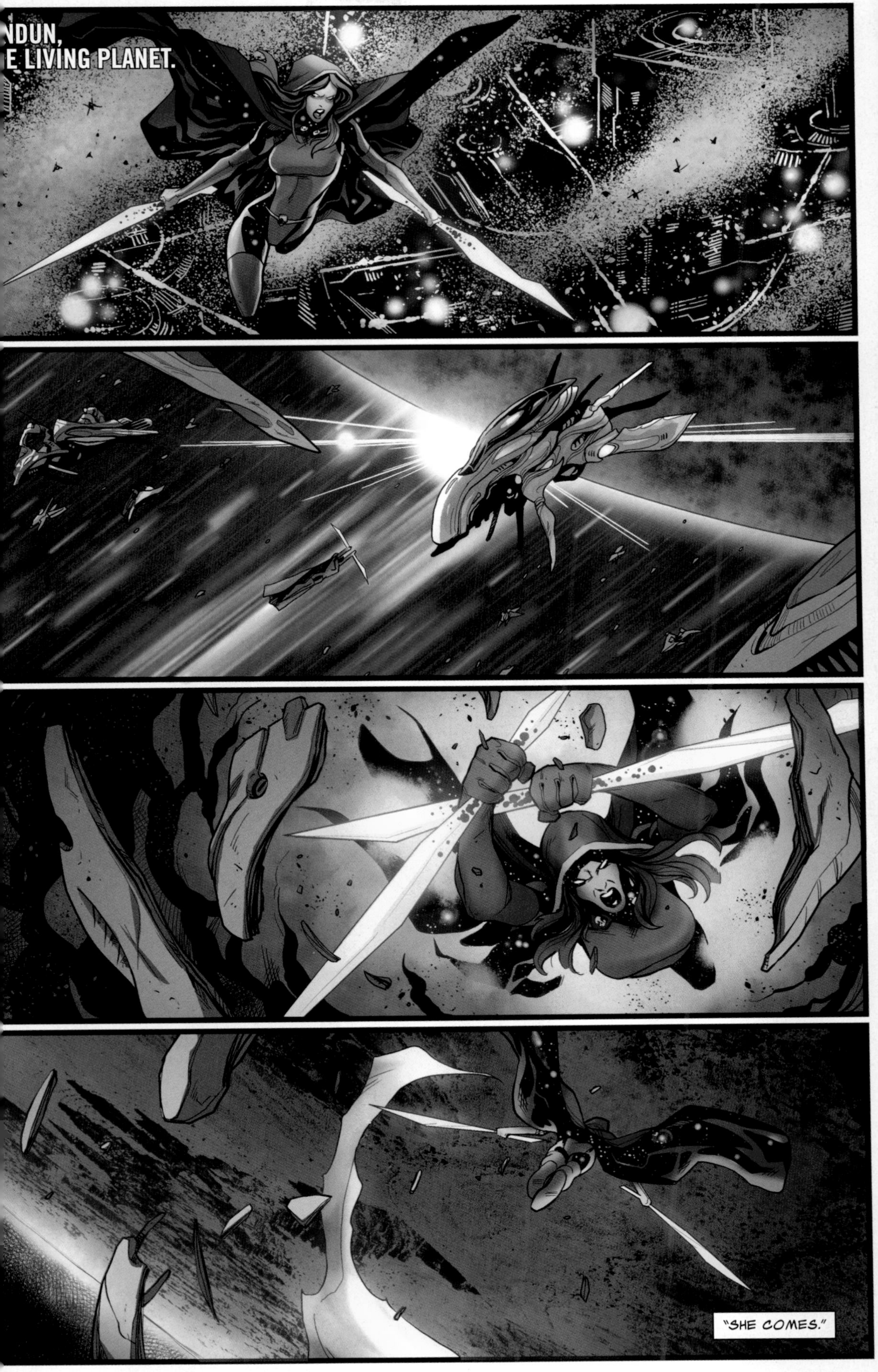
NDUN,
E LIVING PLANET.
"SHE COMES."

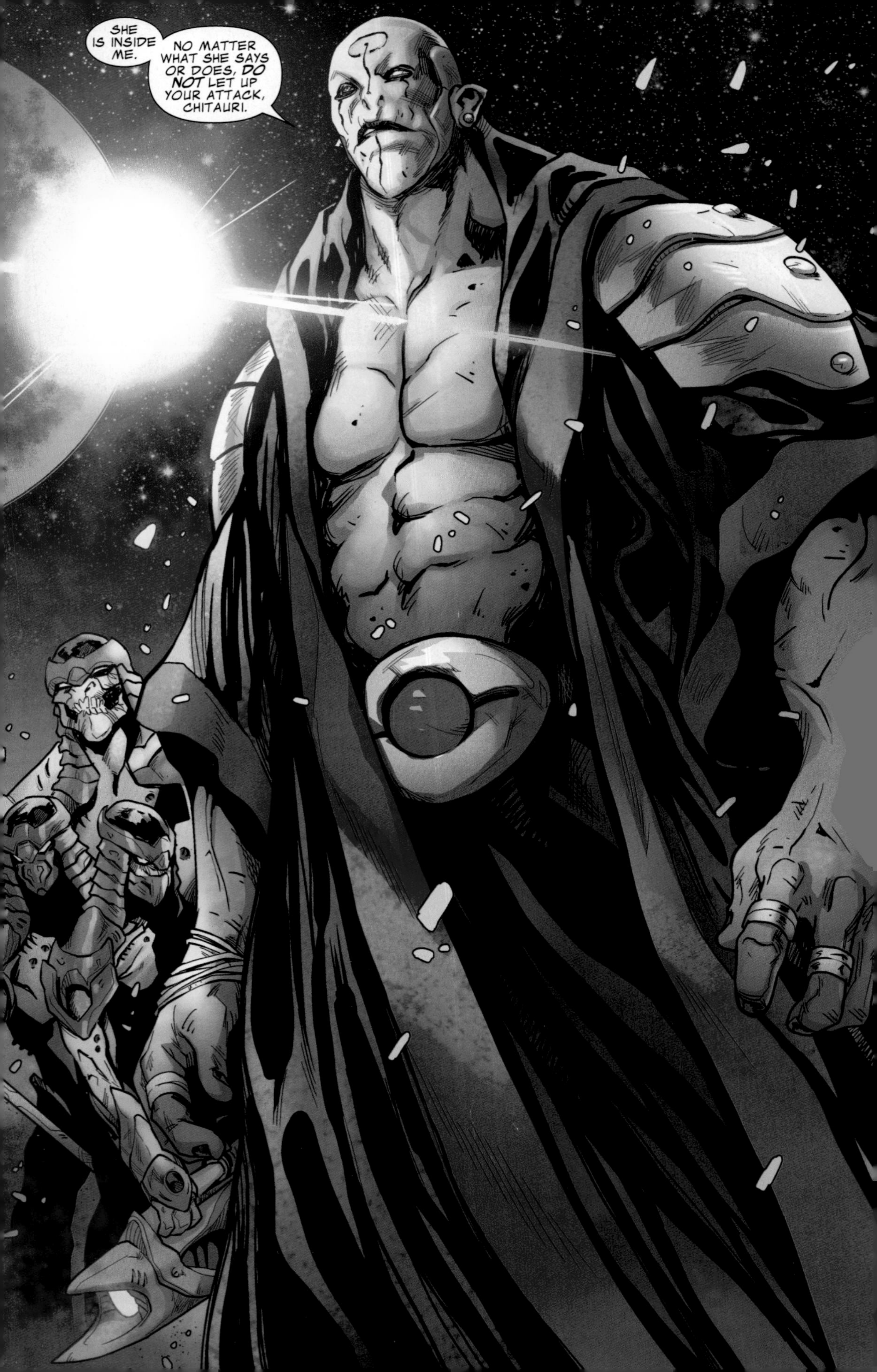
SHE IS INSIDE ME.
NO MATTER WHAT SHE SAYS OR DOES, DO NOT LET UP YOUR ATTACK, CHITAURI.

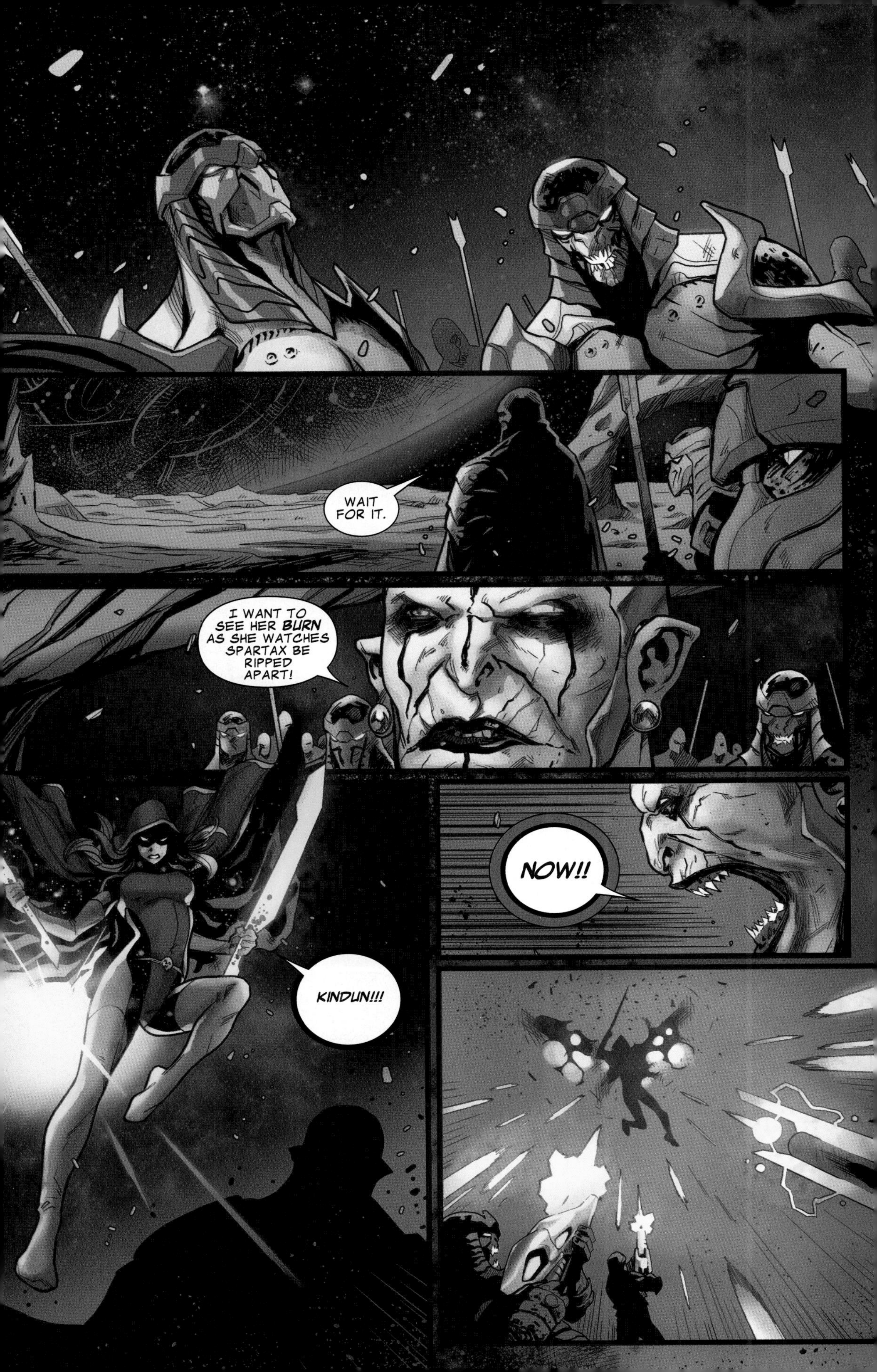
WAIT FOR IT.
I WANT TO SEE HER BURN AS SHE WATCHES SPARTAX BE RIPPED APART!
KINDUN!!!
NOW!!

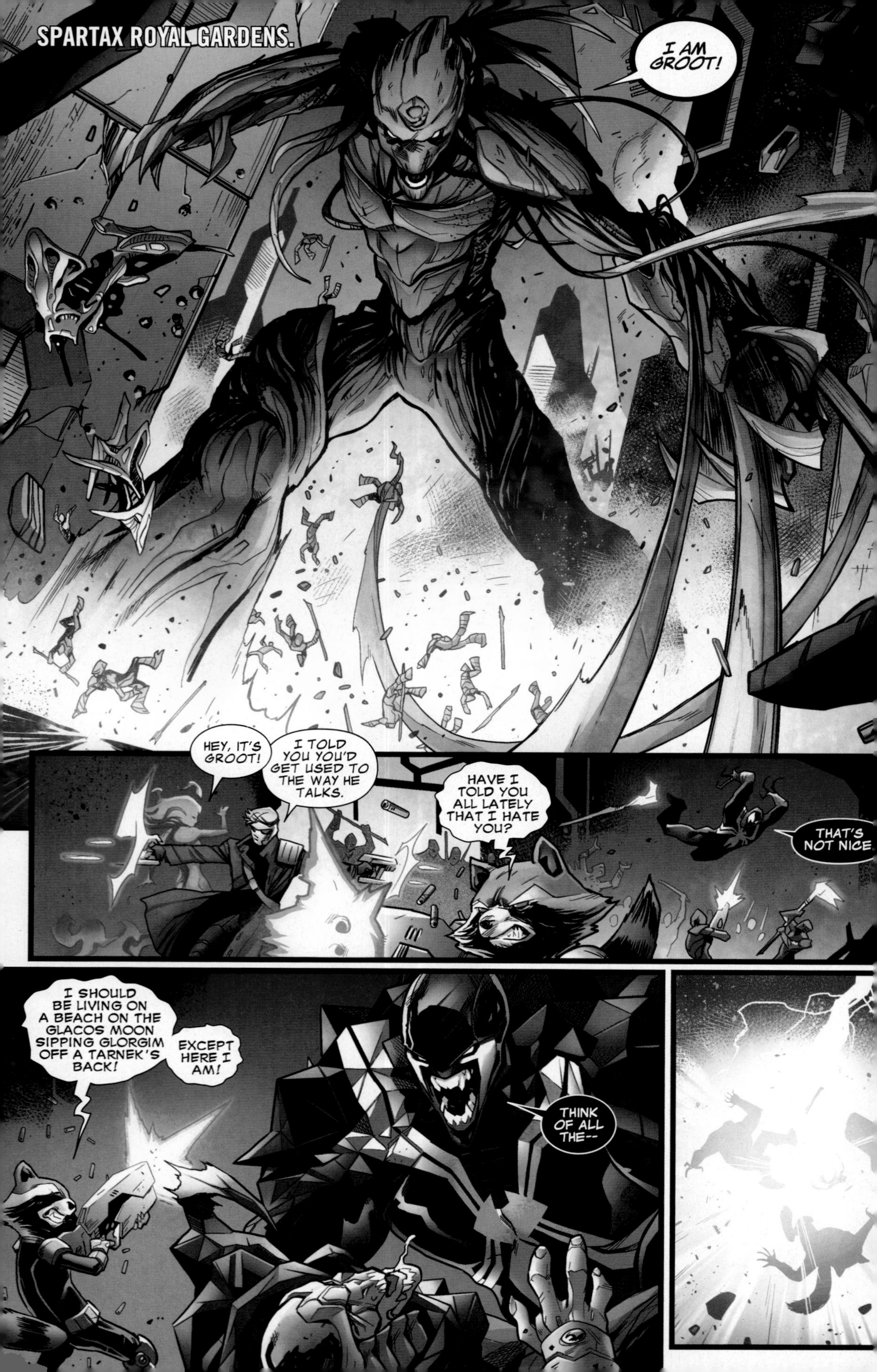
SPARTAX ROYAL GARDENS.
I AM GROOT!
HEY, IT'S GROOT!
I TOLD YOU YOU'D GET USED TO THE WAY HE TALKS.
HAVE I TOLD YOU ALL LATELY THAT I HATE YOU?
THAT'S NOT NICE
I SHOULD BE LIVING ON A BEACH ON THE GLACOS MOON SIPPING GLORGIM OFF A TARNEK'S BACK!
EXCEPT HERE I AM!
THINK OF ALL THE--

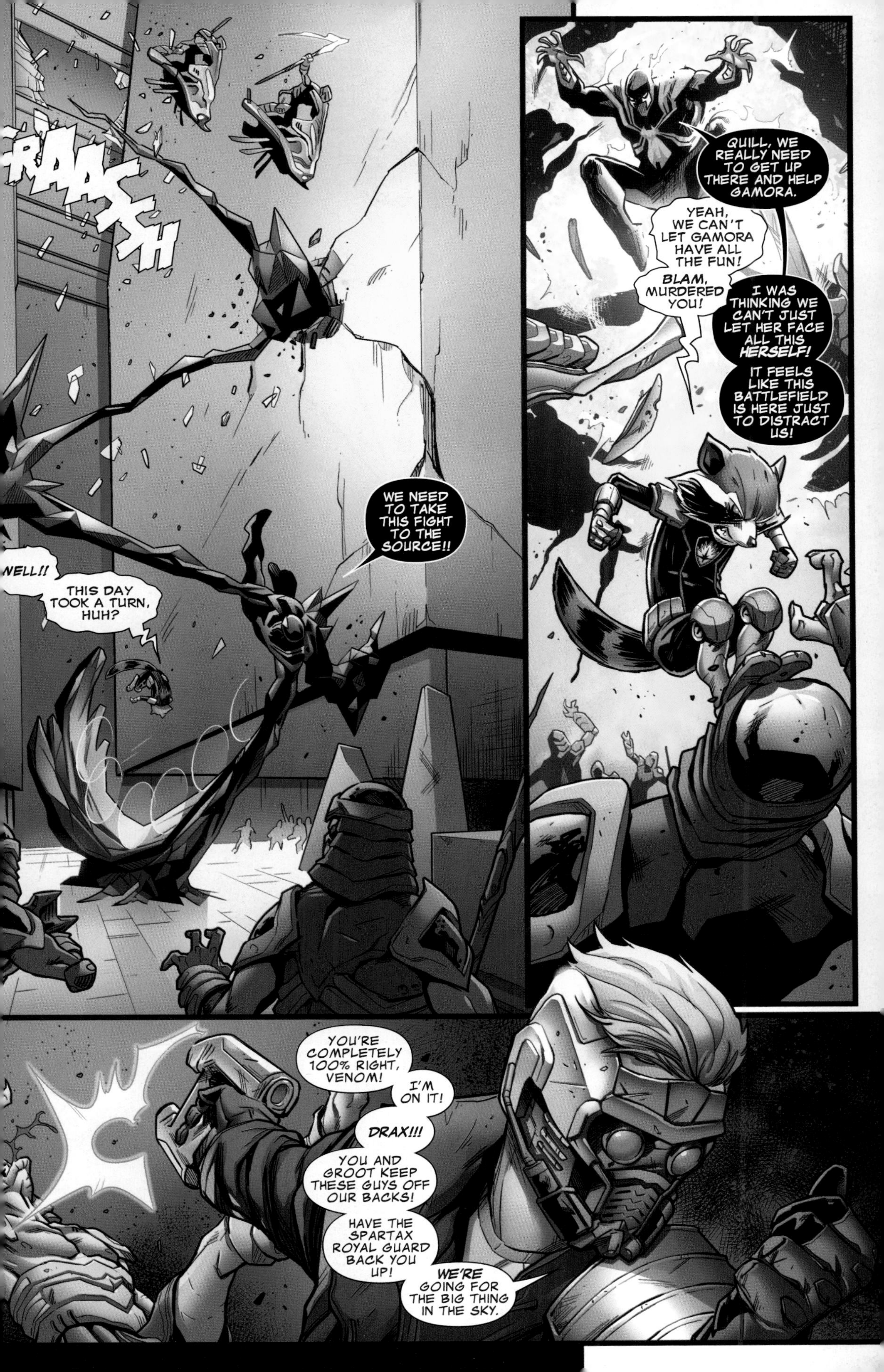
KRAASSH
WELL!!
THIS DAY TOOK A TURN, HUH?
WE NEED TO TAKE THIS FIGHT TO THE SOURCE!!
QUILL, WE REALLY NEED TO GET UP THERE AND HELP GAMORA.
YEAH, WE CAN'T LET GAMORA HAVE ALL THE FUN!
BLAM, MURDERED YOU!
I WAS THINKING WE CAN'T JUST LET HER FACE ALL THIS HERSELF!
IT FEELS LIKE THIS BATTLEFIELD IS HERE JUST TO DISTRACT US!
YOU'RE COMPLETELY 100% RIGHT, VENOM!
I'M ON IT!
DRAX!!!
YOU AND GROOT KEEP THESE GUYS OFF OUR BACKS!
HAVE THE SPARTAX ROYAL GUARD BACK YOU UP!
WE'RE GOING FOR THE BIG THING IN THE SKY.

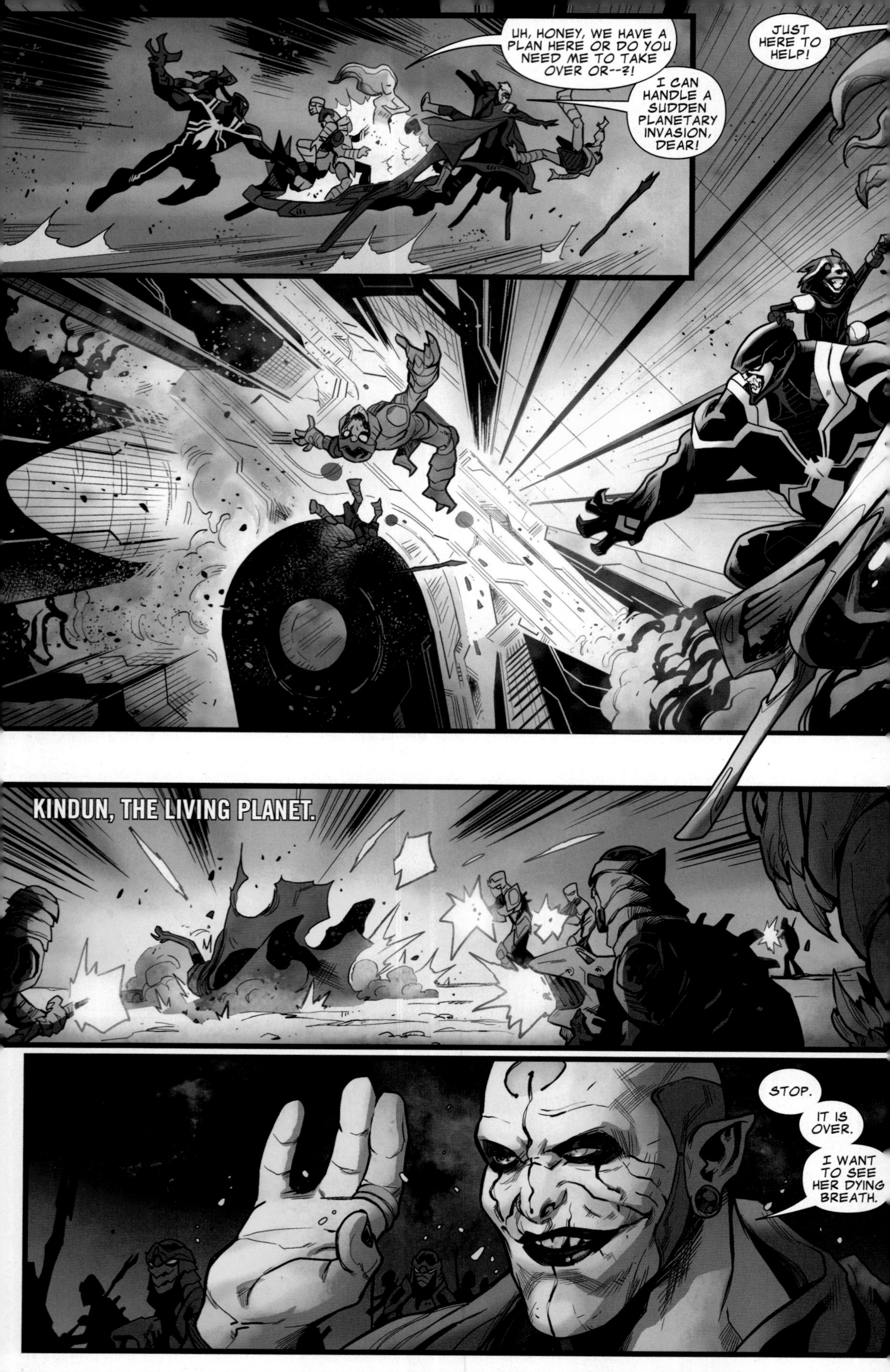
UH, HONEY, WE HAVE A PLAN HERE OR DO YOU NEED ME TO TAKE OVER OR--?!
JUST HERE TO HELP!
I CAN HANDLE A SUDDEN PLANETARY INVASION, DEAR!
KINDUN, THE LIVING PLANET.
STOP.
IT IS OVER.
I WANT TO SEE HER DYING BREATH.

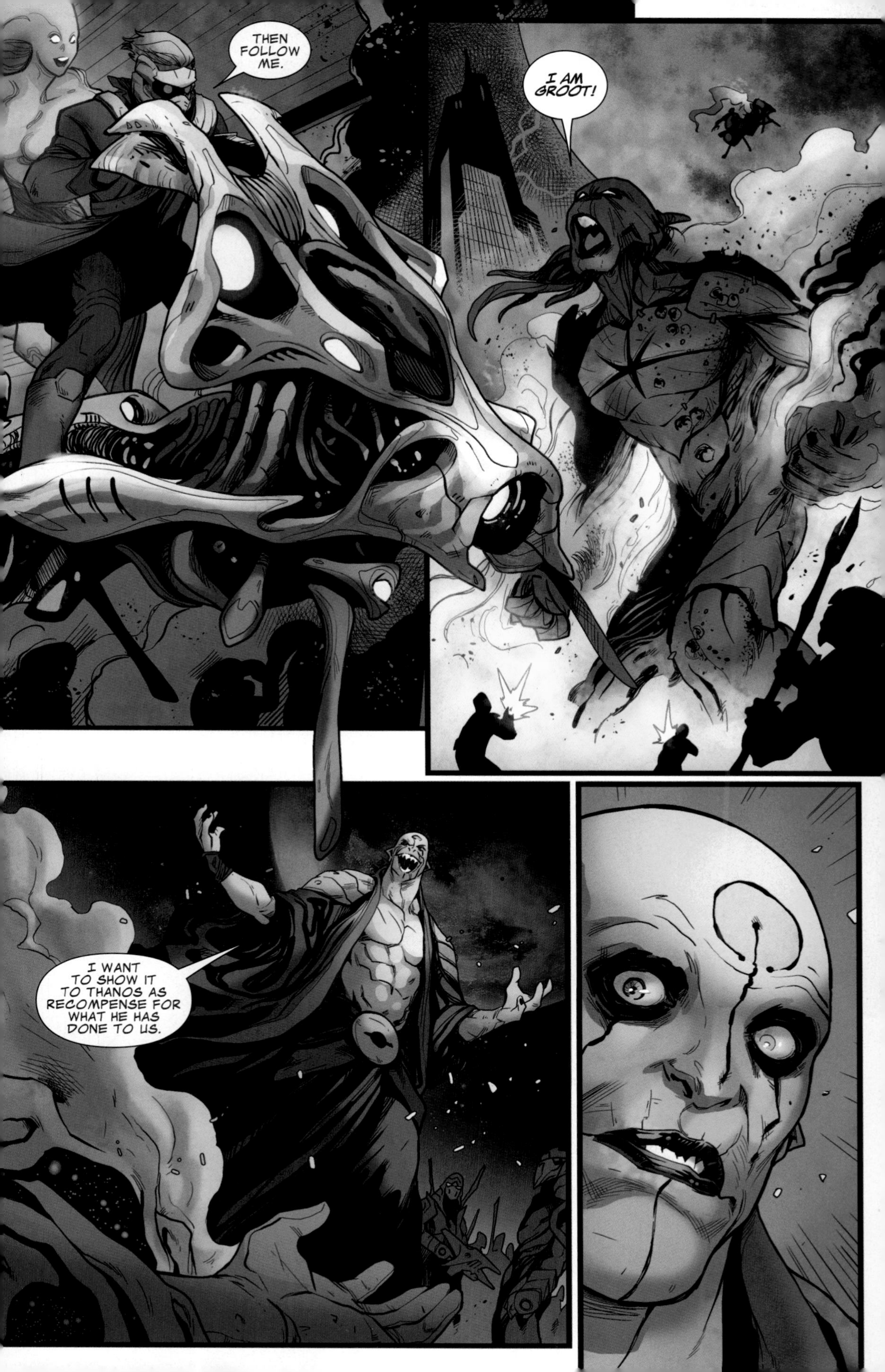
THEN FOLLOW ME.
I AM GROOT!
I WANT TO SHOW IT TO THANOS AS RECOMPENSE FOR WHAT HE HAS DONE TO US.

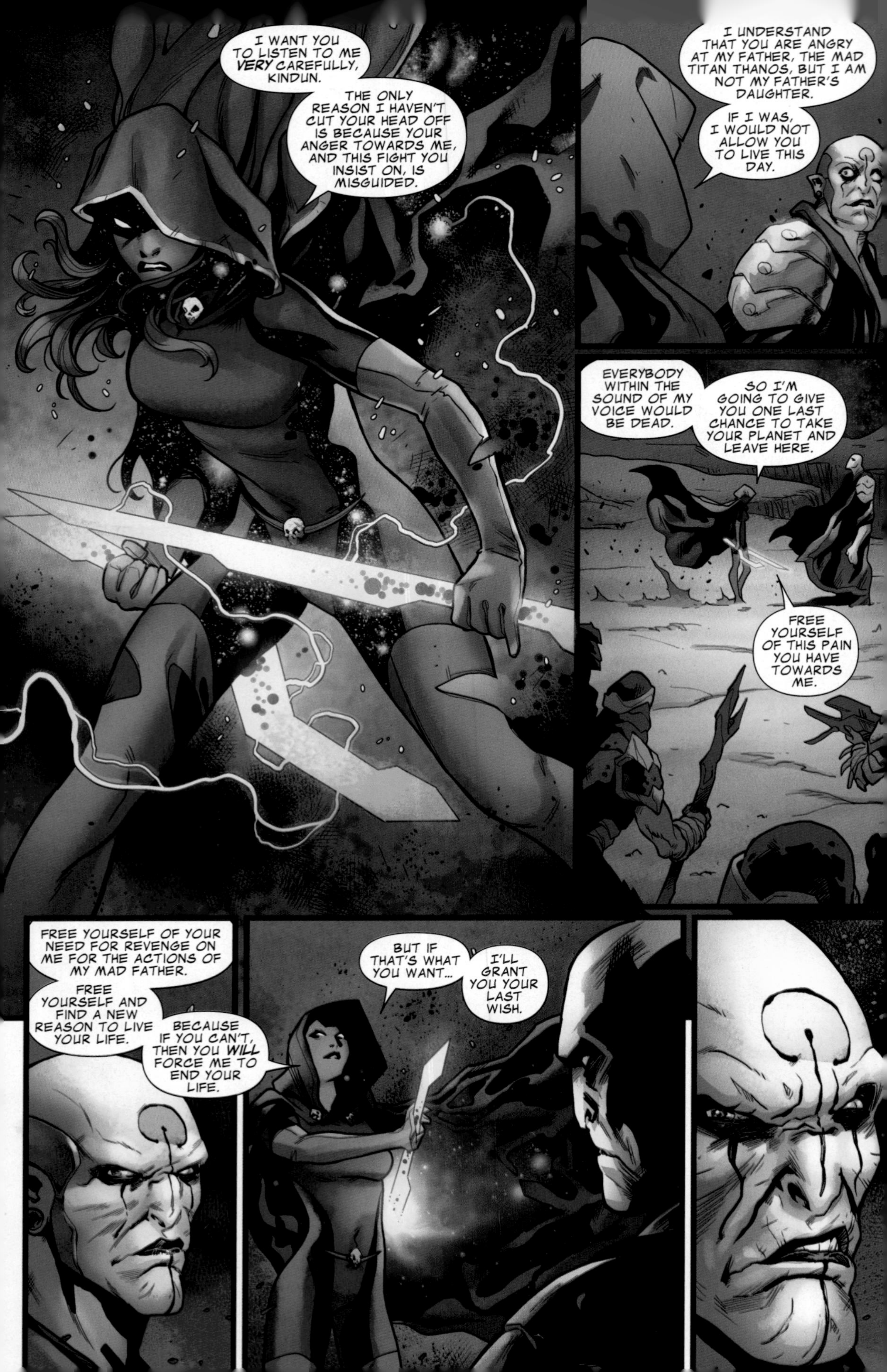
I WANT YOU TO LISTEN TO ME VERY CAREFULLY, KINDUN.
THE ONLY REASON I HAVEN'T CUT YOUR HEAD OFF IS BECAUSE YOUR ANGER TOWARDS ME, AND THIS FIGHT YOU INSIST ON, IS MISGUIDED.
I UNDERSTAND THAT YOU ARE ANGRY AT MY FATHER, THE MAD TITAN THANOS, BUT I AM NOT MY FATHER'S DAUGHTER.
IF I WAS, I WOULD NOT ALLOW YOU TO LIVE THIS DAY.
EVERYBODY WITHIN THE SOUND OF MY VOICE WOULD BE DEAD.
SO I'M GOING TO GIVE YOU ONE LAST CHANCE TO TAKE YOUR PLANET AND LEAVE HERE.
FREE YOURSELF OF THIS PAIN YOU HAVE TOWARDS ME.
FREE YOURSELF OF YOUR NEED FOR REVENGE ON ME FOR THE ACTIONS OF MY MAD FATHER.
FREE YOURSELF AND FIND A NEW REASON TO LIVE YOUR LIFE.
BECAUSE IF YOU CAN'T, THEN YOU WILL FORCE ME TO END YOUR LIFE.
BUT IF THAT'S WHAT YOU WANT...
I'LL GRANT YOU YOUR LAST WISH.

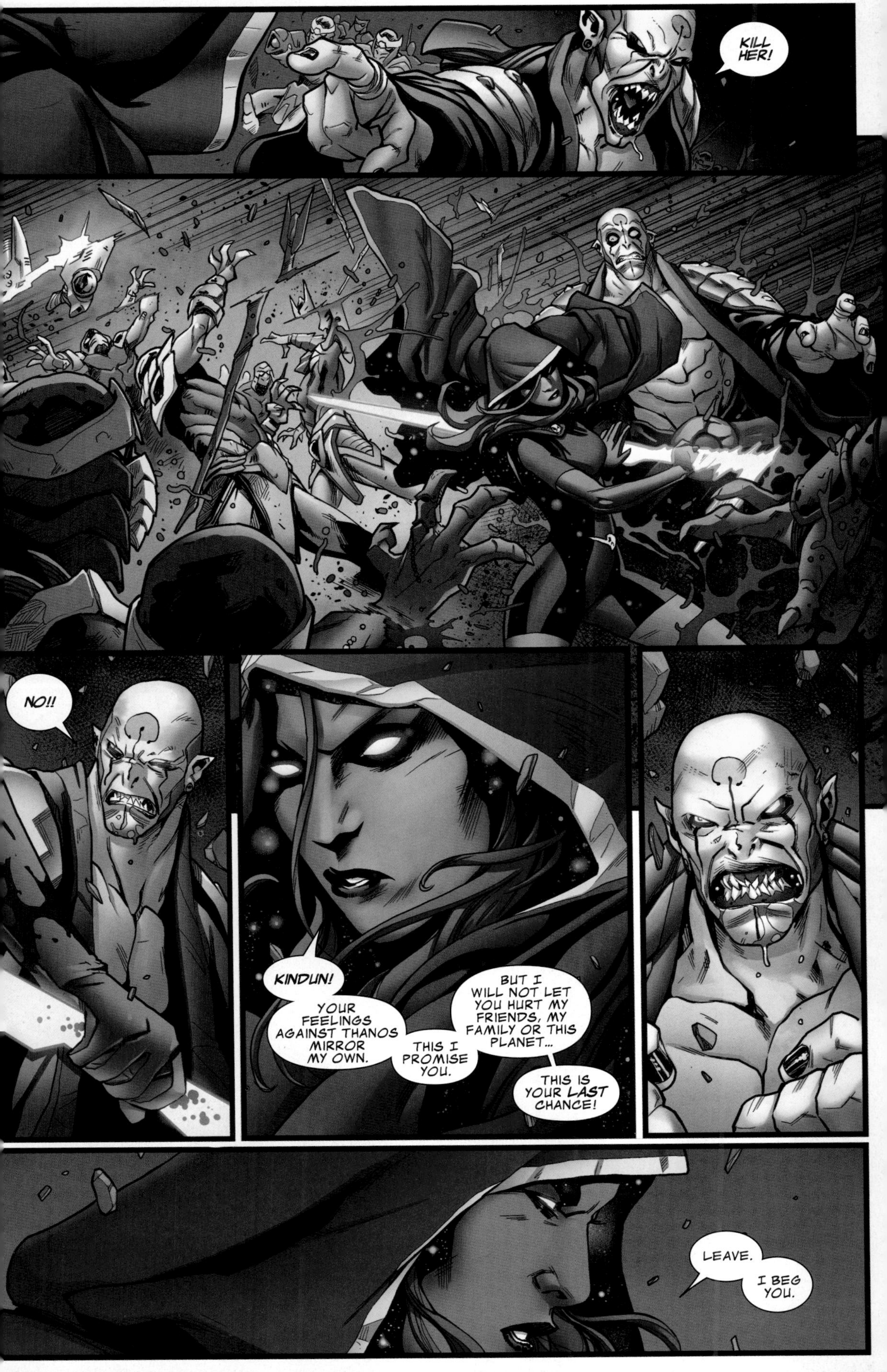
KILL HER!
NO!!
KINDUN!
YOUR FEELINGS AGAINST THANOS MIRROR MY OWN.
THIS I PROMISE YOU.
BUT I WILL NOT LET YOU HURT MY FRIENDS, MY FAMILY OR THIS PLANET...
THIS IS YOUR LAST CHANCE!
LEAVE.
I BEG YOU.

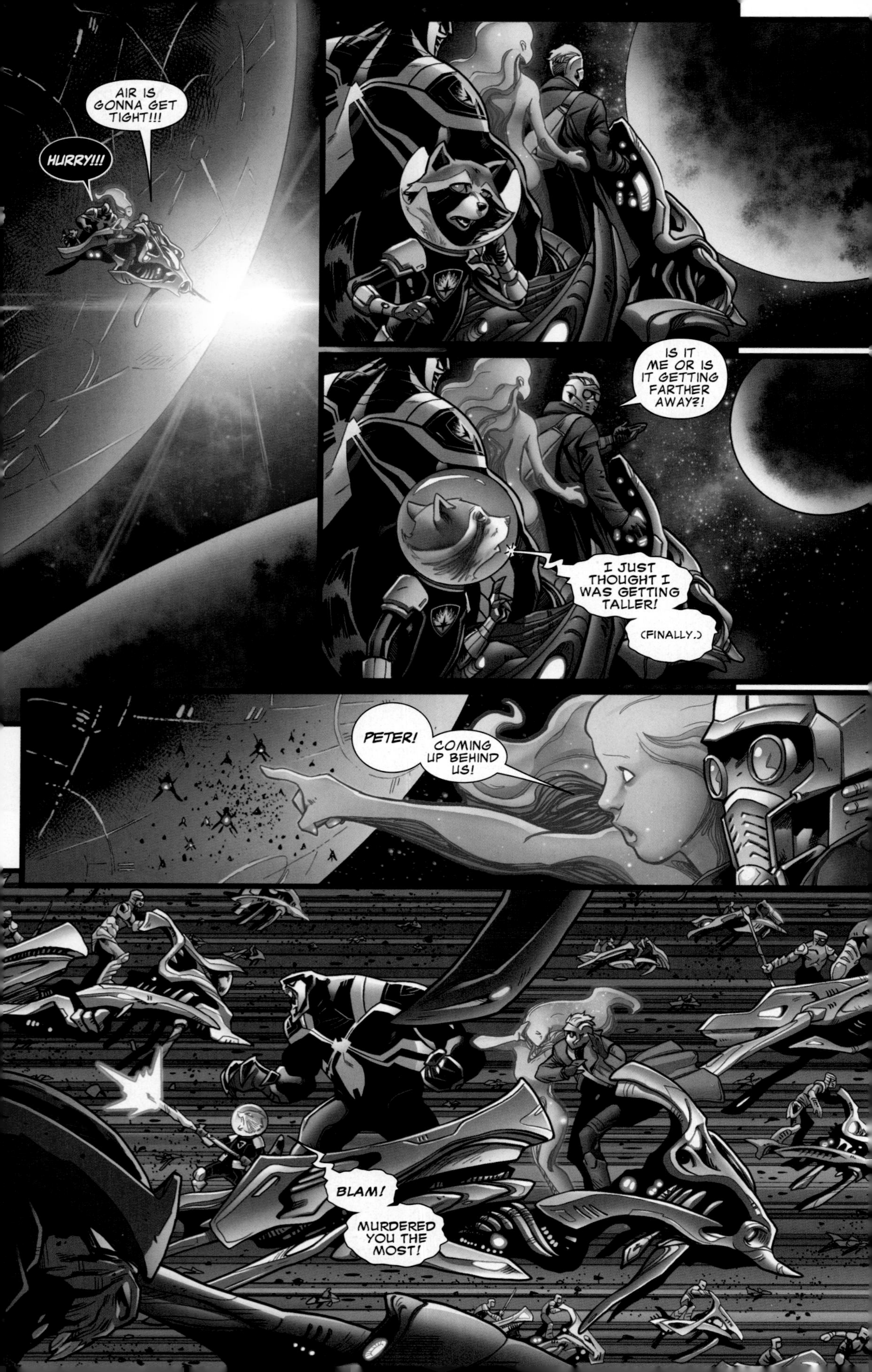
AIR IS GONNA GET TIGHT!!!
HURRY!!!
IS IT ME OR IS IT GETTING FARTHER AWAY?!
I JUST THOUGHT I WAS GETTING TALLER!
(FINALLY.)
PETER!
COMING UP BEHIND US!
BLAM!
MURDERED YOU THE MOST!

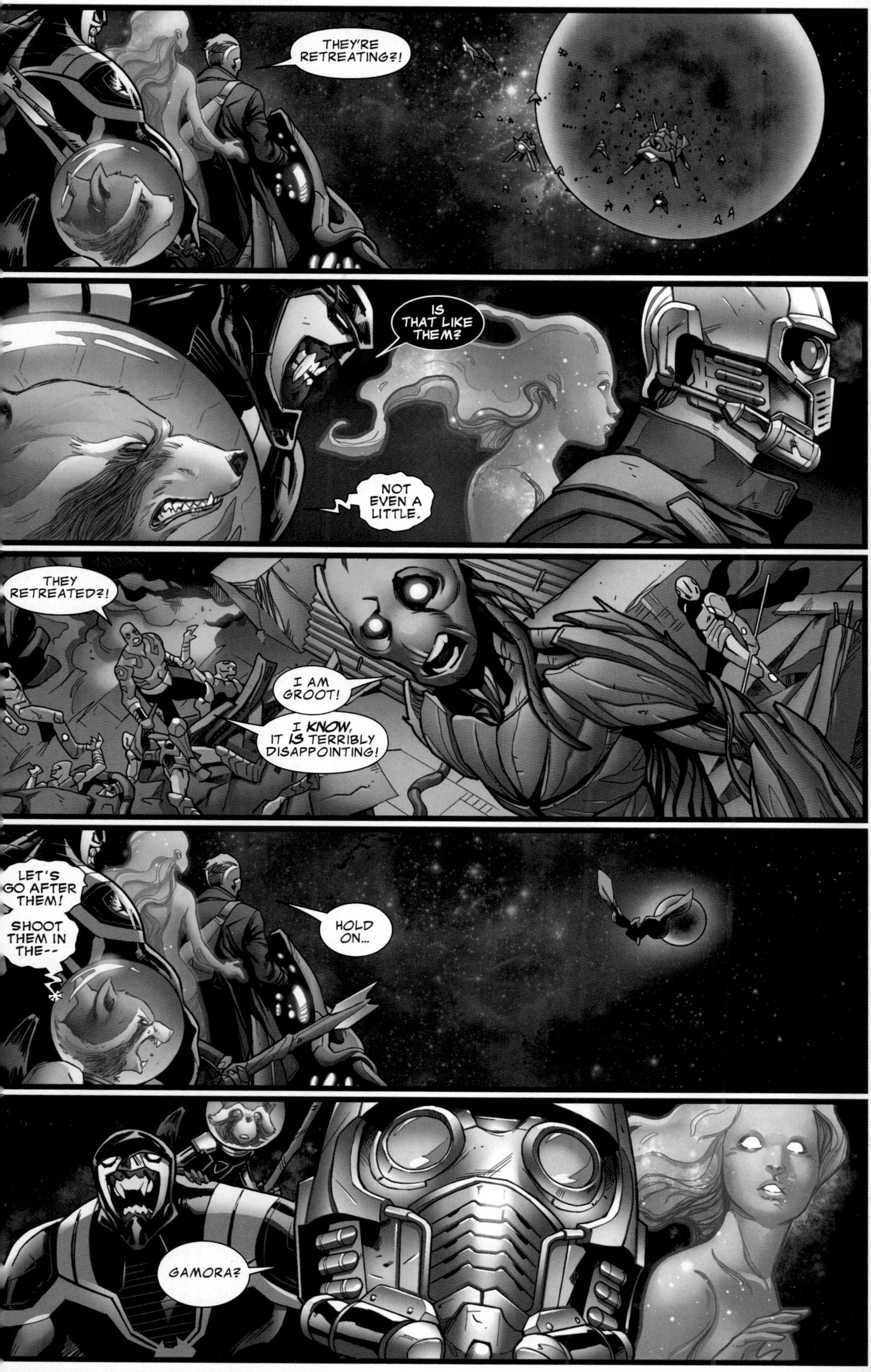
THEY'RE RETREATING?!
IS THAT LIKE THEM?
NOT EVEN A LITTLE.
THEY RETREATED?!
I AM GROOT!
I KNOW, IT IS TERRIBLY DISAPPOINTING!
LET'S GO AFTER THEM!
SHOOT THEM IN THE--
HOLD ON...
GAMORA?

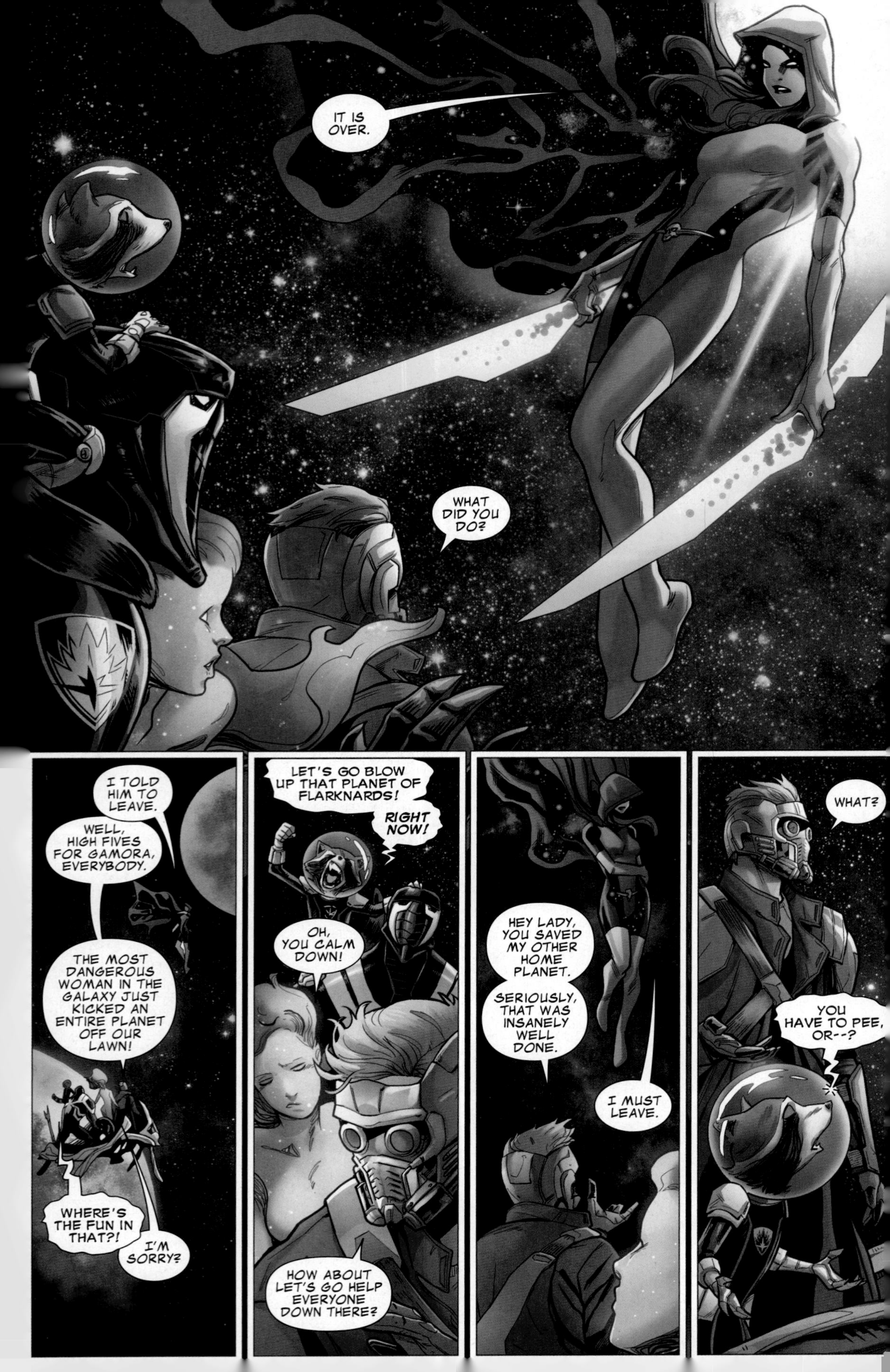
IT IS OVER.
WHAT DID YOU DO?
I TOLD HIM TO LEAVE.
WELL, HIGH FIVES FOR GAMORA, EVERYBODY.
THE MOST DANGEROUS WOMAN IN THE GALAXY JUST KICKED AN ENTIRE PLANET OFF OUR LAWN!
WHERE'S THE FUN IN THAT?!
I'M SORRY?
LET'S GO BLOW UP THAT PLANET OF FLARKNARDS!
RIGHT NOW!
OH, YOU CALM DOWN!
HOW ABOUT LET'S GO HELP EVERYONE DOWN THERE?
HEY LADY, YOU SAVED MY OTHER HOME PLANET.
SERIOUSLY, THAT WAS INSANELY WELL DONE.
I MUST LEAVE.
WHAT?
YOU HAVE TO PEE, OR--?

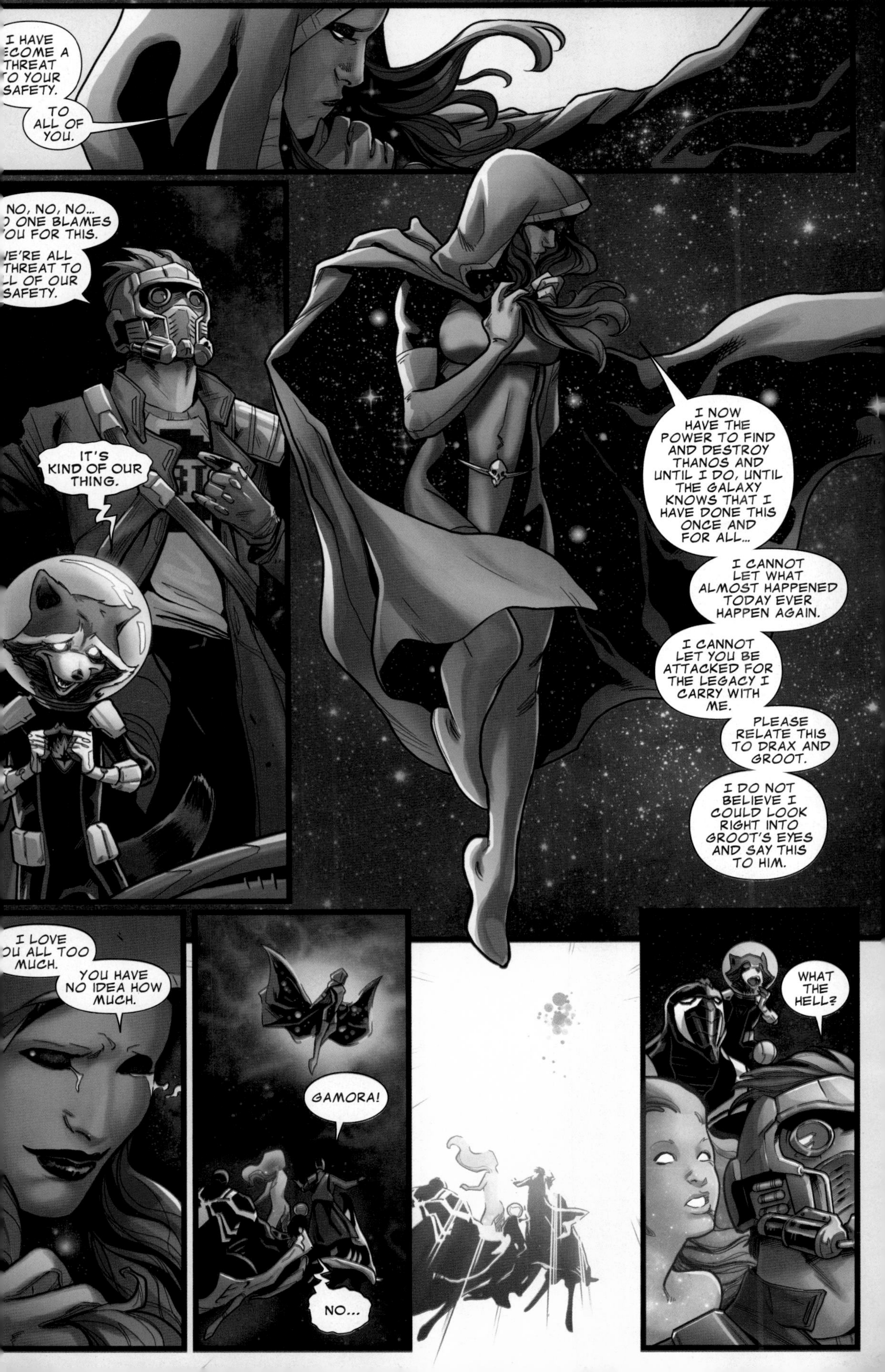
I HAVE
ECOME A
THREAT
O YOUR
SAFETY.
TO ALL OF YOU.
NO, NO, NO...
O ONE BLAMES
OU FOR THIS.
E'RE ALL
THREAT TO
LL OF OUR
SAFETY.
IT'S KIND OF OUR THING.
I NOW HAVE THE POWER TO FIND AND DESTROY THANOS AND UNTIL I DO, UNTIL THE GALAXY KNOWS THAT I HAVE DONE THIS ONCE AND FOR ALL...
I CANNOT LET WHAT ALMOST HAPPENED TODAY EVER HAPPEN AGAIN.
I CANNOT LET YOU BE ATTACKED FOR THE LEGACY I CARRY WITH ME.
PLEASE RELATE THIS TO DRAX AND GROOT.
I DO NOT BELIEVE I COULD LOOK RIGHT INTO GROOT'S EYES AND SAY THIS TO HIM.
I LOVE
OU ALL TOO
MUCH.
YOU HAVE NO IDEA HOW MUCH.
GAMORA!
NO...
WHAT THE HELL?

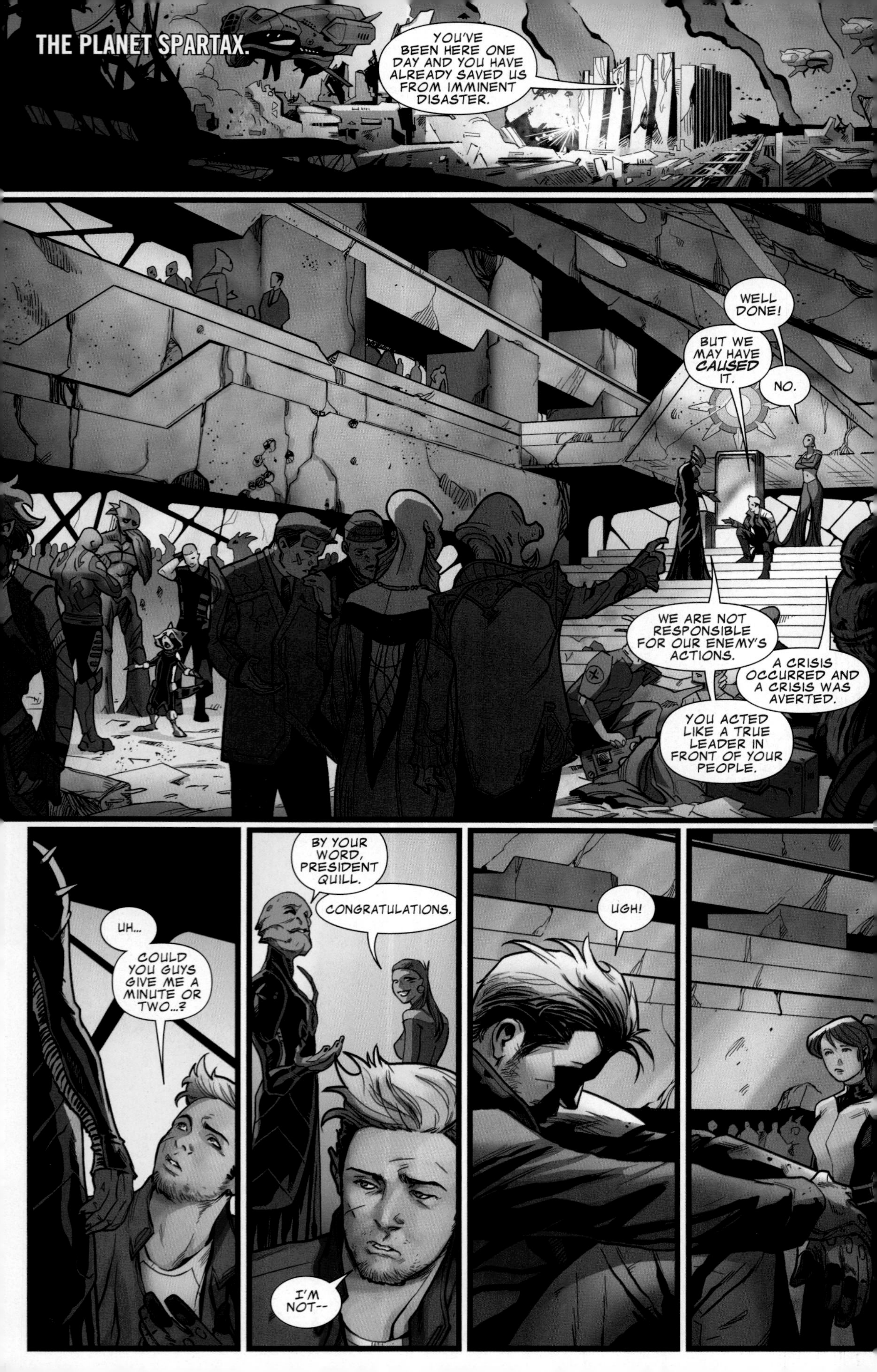
THE PLANET SPARTAX.
YOU'VE BEEN HERE ONE DAY AND YOU HAVE ALREADY SAVED US FROM IMMINENT DISASTER.
WELL DONE!
BUT WE MAY HAVE CAUSED IT.
NO.
WE ARE NOT RESPONSIBLE FOR OUR ENEMY'S ACTIONS.
A CRISIS OCCURRED AND A CRISIS WAS AVERTED.
YOU ACTED LIKE A TRUE LEADER IN FRONT OF YOUR PEOPLE.
UH...
COULD YOU GUYS GIVE ME A MINUTE OR TWO...?
BY YOUR WORD, PRESIDENT QUILL.
CONGRATULATIONS.
I'M NOT--
UGH!

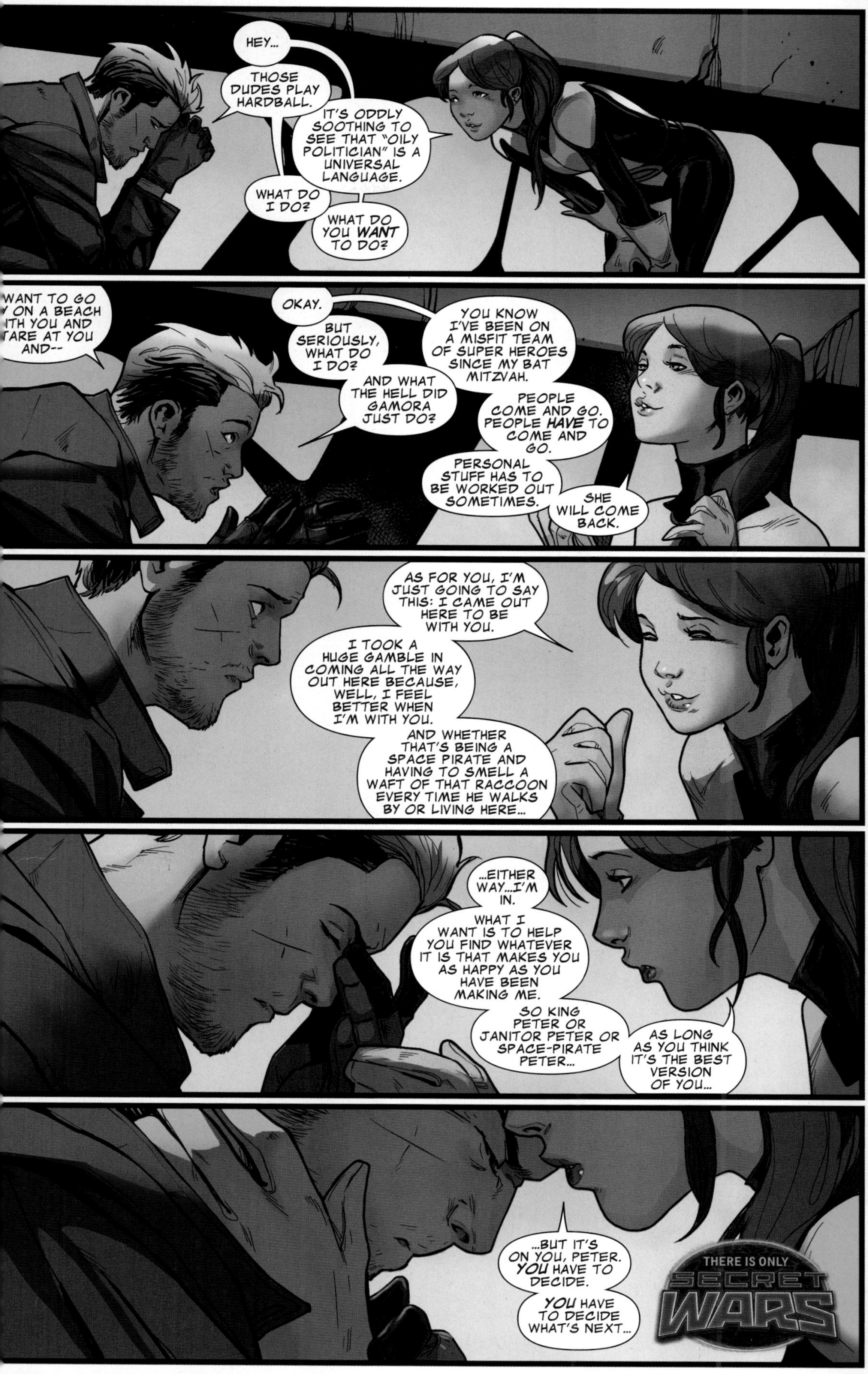

HEY...
THOSE DUDES PLAY HARDBALL.
IT'S ODDLY SOOTHING TO SEE THAT "OILY POLITICIAN" IS A UNIVERSAL LANGUAGE.
WHAT DO I DO?
WHAT DO YOU WANT TO DO?
WANT TO GO ON A BEACH ITH YOU AND TARE AT YOU AND--
OKAY.
BUT SERIOUSLY, WHAT DO I DO?
AND WHAT THE HELL DID GAMORA JUST DO?
YOU KNOW I'VE BEEN ON A MISFIT TEAM OF SUPER HEROES SINCE MY BAT MITZVAH.
PEOPLE COME AND GO. PEOPLE HAVE TO COME AND GO.
PERSONAL STUFF HAS TO BE WORKED OUT SOMETIMES.
SHE WILL COME BACK.
AS FOR YOU, I'M JUST GOING TO SAY THIS: I CAME OUT HERE TO BE WITH YOU.
I TOOK A HUGE GAMBLE IN COMING ALL THE WAY OUT HERE BECAUSE, WELL, I FEEL BETTER WHEN I'M WITH YOU.
AND WHETHER THAT'S BEING A SPACE PIRATE AND HAVING TO SMELL A WAFT OF THAT RACCOON EVERY TIME HE WALKS BY OR LIVING HERE...
...EITHER WAY...I'M IN.
WHAT I WANT IS TO HELP YOU FIND WHATEVER IT IS THAT MAKES YOU AS HAPPY AS YOU HAVE BEEN MAKING ME.
SO KING PETER OR JANITOR PETER OR SPACE-PIRATE PETER...
AS LONG AS YOU THINK IT'S THE BEST VERSION OF YOU...
...BUT IT'S ON YOU, PETER. YOU HAVE TO DECIDE.
YOU HAVE TO DECIDE WHAT'S NEXT...
THERE IS ONLY SECRET WARS

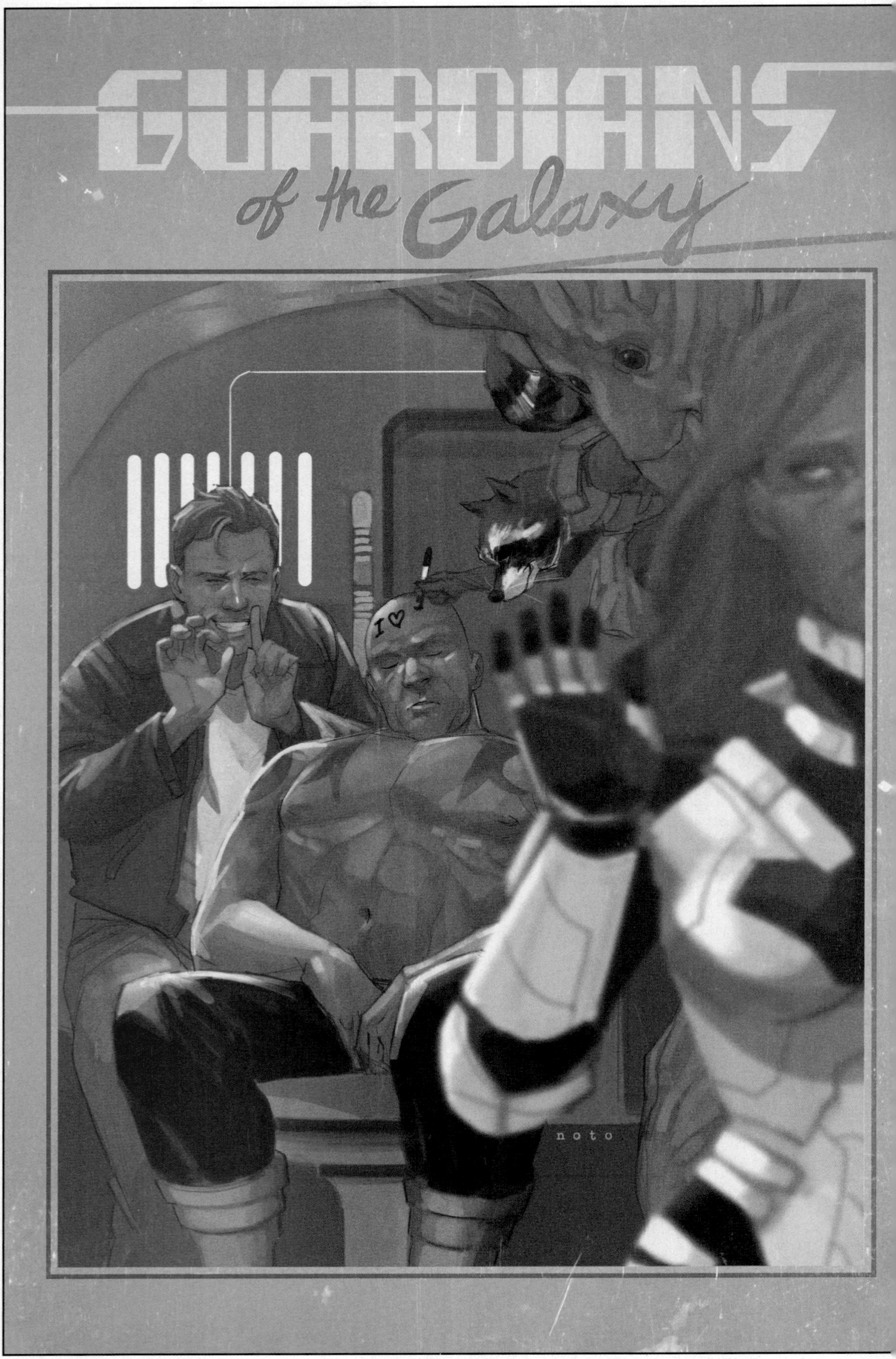
GUARDIANS
of the Galaxy
I ♡
noto

#24 VARIANT BY PHIL NOTO

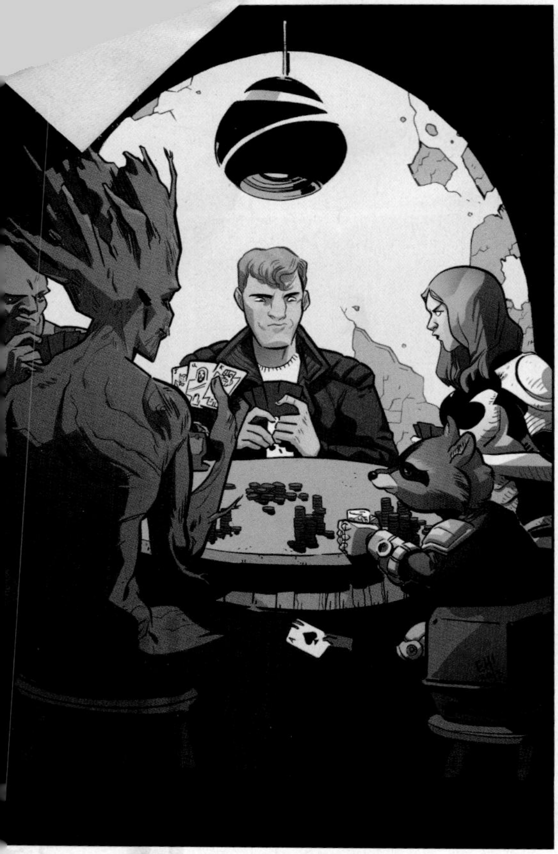

#25 WOMEN OF MARVEL VARIANT
BY ERICA HENDERSON

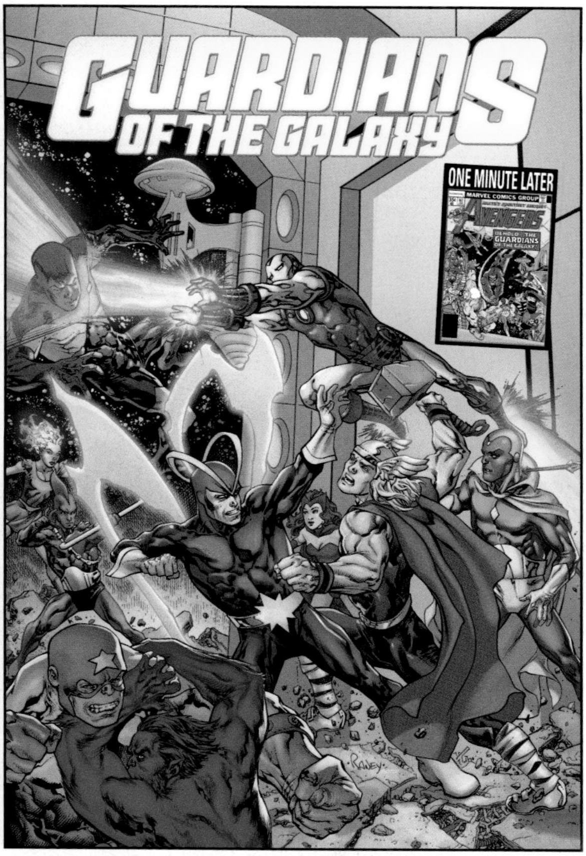
GUARDIANS OF THE GALAXY
ONE MINUTE LATER
MARVEL COMICS GROUP
AVENGERS
GUARDIANS
RANEY

#26 ONE MINUTE LATER VARIANT
BY TOM RANEY & CHRIS SOTOMAYOR

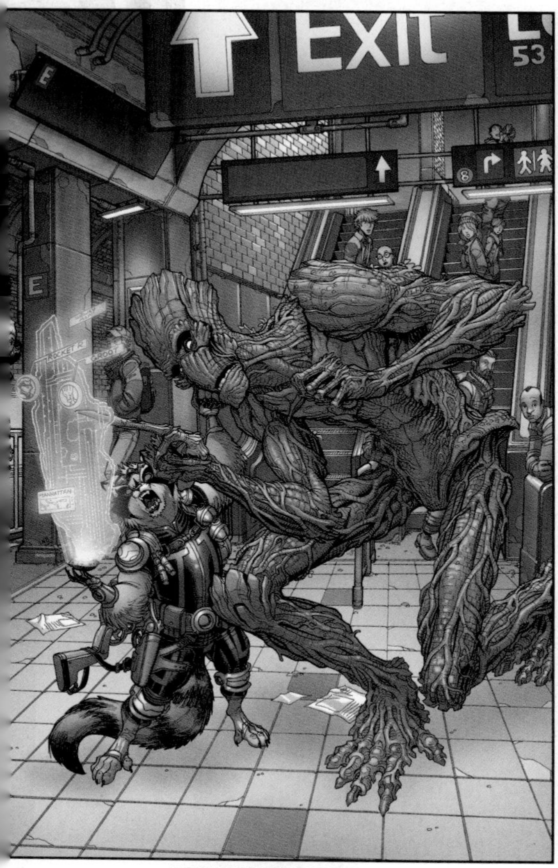
EXIT

#27 NYC VARIANT
BY NICK BRADSHAW & EDGAR DELGADO

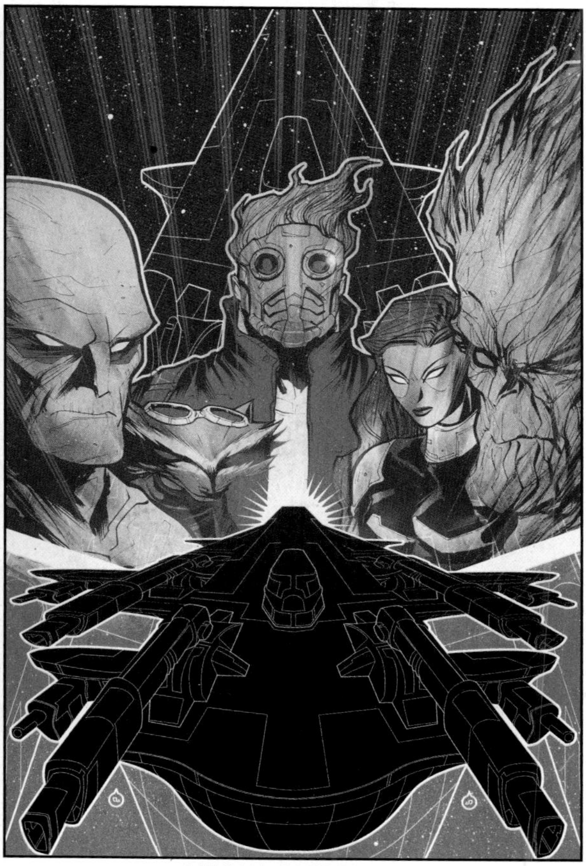

ANNUAL #1 VARIANT
BY JUAN DOE

"This is the place to start reading the X-books."
– IGN.com

"This is the place to start reading the X-books" — IGN.com
ALL-NEW X-MEN
YESTERDAY'S X-MEN
BENDIS
MARVEL NOW!
IMMONEN
AR

ALL-NEW X-MEN VOL. 1: YESTERDAY'S X-MEN PREMIERE HC

978-0-7851-6637-5 • OCT130757

"Beautiful and funny, heartfelt and intriguing."
– CBR.com

MARVEL NOW!

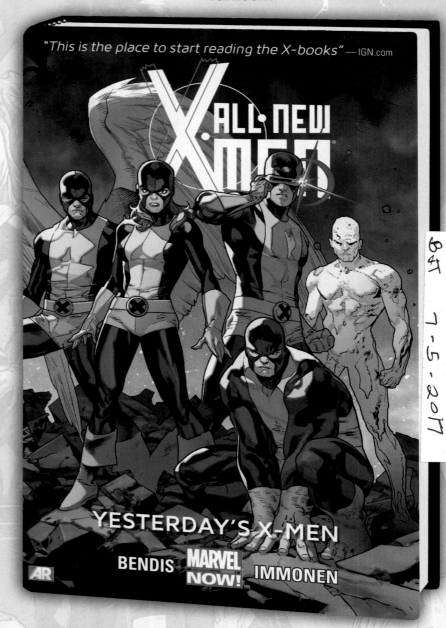

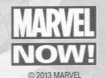